Anthropology of Contemporary Issues

A SERIES EDITED BY

ROGER SANJEK

A list of titles in the series appears at the end of the book

The Solitude of Collectivism:

ROMANIAN VILLAGERS TO THE REVOLUTION AND BEYOND

David A. Kideckel

Cornell University Press

Ithaca and London

First published 1993 by Cornell University Press.

International Standard Book Number 0-8014-2746-0 (cloth)
International Standard Book Number 0-8014-8025-6 (paper)
Library of Congress Catalog Card Number 92-31985
Printed in the United States of America
Librarians: Library of Congress cataloging information appears on the last page of the book.

⊗ The paper in this book meets the minimum requirements of the American National Standard for Information Sciences–Permanence of Paper for Printed Library Materials, ANSI Z39.48-1984.

To Judith
and to the memory of
Aurel Bălan

Contents

Illustrations, Maps, Figures

Illustrations

Maps

Figures

Tables

[xi]

Preface

With the collapse of the socialist system the contradictions that overwhelmed it have become the stuff of legend. Subject to hyperbole and innuendo during the Cold War, the faults and failures of Eastern European socialism are now readily analyzed and enumerated by legions of commentators eager to document their political astuteness. Much like the Cold War critics, however, these more recent observers generally ignore the realities of daily life in socialist societies. With all its problems, the Eastern Europe of the socialist years was, after all, a place where people lived their lives, raised their families, and aspired to many of the goals that motivated their Western counterparts. Thus if we are to understand the failures and even some of the successes of socialism, we must first consider the actual lives of the people who lived it, how they did so, and what their daily lives ultimately meant for the larger society.

The title of this book reflects one of the basic contradictions of life in many socialist communities: the socialist system, though ostensibly designed to create new persons motivated by the needs of groups and of society as a whole, in fact created people who were of necessity self-centered, distrustful, and apathetic to the very core of their beings. Though this book focuses on one region of Romania, the state of affairs I found there has been noted by many analysts of life in other Eastern European countries. One of the earliest and most elegant statements of this situation was provided by Czeslaw Milosz, who in *The Captive Mind* borrowed the Islamic concept of *ketman* to express the simultaneous public avowal and private rejection of belief and the essential cost of this forced hypocrisy on personality and social relations.

Milosz, too, saw socialist life as encumbered by constant personal compromises that maintained one's public persona at the cost of the private self. And though the collapse of socialism was expected to liberate people from these pernicious compromises—a view best summed up by the signs that sprouted throughout Prague toward the end of Czechoslovakia's "velvet revolution": "Now we can be nice to each other again"—the likelihood of this eventuality is still open to question.

This book considers the development of life in one region of socialist Romania in light of the personal struggles of its citizens to follow their particular choices. Though I focus on the daily lives of Olt Land villagers, I have tried to provide a sense of how local life was influenced by and in turn influenced the nature of life in the socialist state; in particular, how individual compromises reinforced political stagnation. Though Eastern Europe's politics and local life have changed dramatically since I first visited Romania, events there since 1989 reinforce the belief that the more things change, the more they stay the same. The difficulty of changing practices and outlooks established by forty-odd years of socialism not only forms the basis for the book's last chapter but is also the subtext that runs through it.

In Chapter 1 I introduce the Olt Landers and their region and explain the procedures by which I came to know them. Chapters 2, 3, and 4 outline the basic conditions for the emergence of Olt Land life. Chapter 2 considers the history of the Olt Land village and how its inhabitants, though differentiated economically, were unified by cultural practice and social relationships. Chapter 3 considers the development and nature of the Romanian socialist system, particularly during the Ceauşescu years. Chapter 4 examines the intersection of the conditions outlined in Chapters 2 and 3 in the implementation of socialism and the kinds of production and social relationships this process set in motion. Chapters 5, 6, and 7 comprise an ethnography of socialist village life. Chapter 5 views labor in socialist institutions and Olt Land households and its contribution to the atomization of local social relations. Chapter 6 considers how household life and interhousehold relations are influenced by such labor processes. Chapter 7 examines the diverse meanings and identities produced by this system. Finally, Chapter 8 considers the Romanian revolution and its aftermath in the Olt Land region. It suggests some likely transformations of Olt Land society in the postrevolutionary period and considers the significance of the Olt Land case for the anthropology of Eastern Europe. My conclusions, I'm afraid, are as ambiguous as Olt Land life. Though the revolution has revived the common sense of purpose lost in socialist labor, the atomization produced by socialist society has left little in the way of raw materials to work with. In the Olt Land, unfortunately, not only does practice not make perfect, but it has embellished imperfections ill deserved by these longsuffering people.

A large number of individuals and institutions assisted with this work in various ways and each deserves great thanks. Three separate periods of research in Romania (1975–76, 1979, and 1984) were sponsored mainly by the International Research and Exchanges Board (IREX), whose institutional relations were indispensable for social science activities in Eastern and Central Europe. In addition, various research stints were funded by the University of Massachusetts European Studies program (1974), the U.S. Department of Education Fulbright-Hays program (1975–76), and a research grant from the American Association of University Professors, administered by Central Connecticut State University (1000). Special thanks are due George Clarke and Richard Pattenaude at CCSU for their help and encouragement. I am also indebted to the *American Ethnologist* for permission to use material published in that journal in 1982.

Perhaps the most significant group of people involved in this research were the five other members of the erstwhile "Romanian Research Group" at the University of Massachusetts at Amherst. Many of the basic ideas for this book were generated and tried out in discussions within our group both in Romania and at Amherst in the mid-1970s. The group context was a definite plus for a variety of reasons, not least because it coincided with the way Eastern European scholars organized their research. Thus our activities and interests were intelligible to host communities and individuals. Our members, at work in separate communities, often disagreed about the nature and meaning of Romanian events and processes. Nonetheless, the general support we gave each other and the creature comforts we provided, as well as the assistance with information and around the bureaucratic maze, contributed to a successful, even joyful research experience. Exchanges at our monthly meetings at the Hotel Carpaţi in Braşov or "around the white tables" at South College were among the most intellectually stimulating (and personally disruptive) of my life. Though the bulk of the research for this book was carried out after the group members went our separate ways, the experience was one I heartily recommend for other anthropological endeavors.

Each of the group's members deserves special mention. I owe John W. Cole a tremendous debt. He brought me into academia, originally piqued my interest in Romania, and has been an intellectual guide, close friend, and colleague for over twenty years. Marilyn McArthur and Steven Randall were also important to this project, not least for the contrasting information about Saxon Germans and uncollectivized mountain communities they provided. Special thanks are owed Steven Sampson and Sam Beck, who have offered advice and ideas from start to finish. Their encouragement, knowledge, friendship, and collaboration will always be remembered, as will the many incidents that enlivened our Romanian experience over a decade and a half.

Romanians also greatly contributed to my project. Thanks are owed first to my professional colleagues. Michael Cernea (now at the World Bank, then with the University of Bucharest's sociology faculty) offered insights about collectivization and its relation to village households. Romulus Vulcănescu helped me through the maze of the Romanian academic community, secured permissions for me, and exposed himself to threat and political abuse to assist our project and my research in particular. Mihai Pop was ever ready with sage advice and good brandy. Nicolae Gheorghe never ceased to amaze me with the depth of his insight and the pace of his life. Nor will I forget the kindness of Trăian Herseni, who, though seriously ill, met with me regularly at his home and shared his personal and scholarly understandings of Olt Land life and history. Alexandru Bărbat and Cornel Irimie also gave timely advice. Maria, Andrei, and Nadia Derevenco were staunch friends, as were Feri and Alice Josza, whose humor and wisdom the world needs. I also thank Petru Iluţ, Marin Popescu, and Maria Cobianu-Băcanu for their help both in Romania and in Massachusetts. The scholars and staff at the University of Bucharest's Sociology Research Center, ably directed by Ioan Drăgan, provided much-needed help in both intellectual and practical matters.

It would be easy to list hundreds of Olt Landers who shared their lives with me and helped with this research. Such a list, however, could never do justice to the kindness, help, forbearance, and companionship I received. Still, special mention must be made of Aurel Bălan, without whose patience and deep humanity this work would have been impossible. He is truly missed. Cornel and Stela Teulea,

Florentin and Maria Olteanu, and Ilie and Maria Judele also shared their unique visions of Olt Land life with me and I remain forever in their debt (and they in mine, after their skill at poker). Valeriu, Cornelia, Lucia, and Ioan David first made me at home in Hîrseni and Gheorghe and Olimpia Judele also opened their lives to me, often at much cost to themselves. Other friends include Victoria Bălan, Gabriela and Sorin Miloiu, Marcela and Ioan Mesaroş, Nicolae and Maria Grancea, Ioan Pică, Viorel and Raveca Dragotă, Gheorghe and Viorica Lie, Viorel Judele, Eugen Ovesea, Doină Mogă, Iosif Stoichiţu, Ioan and Maria Rînea, Trăian Cînduleţi, Ioan and Maria Boşcă, and Iosif Kreiner (wherever he may be). To all I send a hearty "Se trăiască şi la mulţi ani!" (Long life!).

Though my analysis often looks askance at many features of Olt Land life under socialism and beyond, I in no way intend any disrespect for the decisions and practices of my friends and informants. Their lives were critically dependent on those decisions, and the social system in which they lived gave them little leisure to temporize over them. Too often anthropologists take false pride in "living just like the people" they are studying. Living in the socialist Olt Land forced me to realize how disingenuous this notion is. I was constantly aware that, unlike my friends in the mobilization state, I could leave when I wanted and participate essentially when and where I wanted. Thus, though I may evaluate their lives, I make no claim to judge their choices, and would have found it hard to do other than they did. It has been said that all peoples get the ethnographers they deserve. If that is the case, then the Olt Landers' strength, wisdom, and ability to deal with the pressure in their lives stand me in good stead.

Many other colleagues also assisted my research and writing. Joel M. Halpern was a constant source of encouragement and a knowledgeable voice about the Eastern European *longue durée*. Oriol Pi-Sunyer offered timely comparative perspectives. I also thank Katherine Verdery, Gail Kligman, Jack Lucas, Mitchell Ratner, Chris Hann, H. Martin Wobst, Robert Rotenberg, and Andrew Lass. Readers at Cornell University Press offered many helpful comments. Special thanks to Peter Agree, to Barbara Salazar for her exceptionally detailed editorial work, and particularly to Roger Sanjek, who helped free the Connecticut One.

Finally, my family's assistance, encouragement, and patience with things Romanian enabled me to complete this project. This area was my choice, and my family's role in it speaks highly of their love and commitment. It hasn't been easy, as Romanian events and people regularly and to this day engage our lives. My parents, Ben and Ida Kideckel, though skeptical of my involvement, were always encouraging. Judith lived much of it with me, provided an important and necessary perspective on it all, and still never fails to chide me for rationalizing the Ceauşescus in the mid-1970s. Zachary was made in Transylvania, and his personal interest clearly shows despite his aversion to *sărmale* (stuffed cabbage) and *mămăligă* (corn-meal mush). And Caitlin's few years also have been regularly taken up with "'Mania," Gypsy friends, and a distracted father. Mimi, too, was involved in many ways, not least by bearing up during my absence.

Given the pace of change in Eastern Europe, no doubt many of the details I describe will not long be recognizable. I hope this prediction applies especially to the solitude of Olt Land lives and the personal compromises it has entailed.

DAVID A. KIDECKEL

Town Hill, Maine

A Note on Romanian Names and Pronunciation

The usual terms of address in Romania are *Domnul* (Mr., abbreviated *Dml.*), *Doamnă* (Mrs., abbreviated *Dma.*), and *Domnişoară* (Miss, *Dra.*). All names of villagers used in this book are pseudonyms, though the names of communities are not. Many Transylvanian community names have Romanian, Hungarian, and German variants. Thus Braşov is known also as Brassó (Hungarian) and Kronstadt (German). Because of the potential for confusion, I use Romanian names throughout this book except when I indicate otherwise.

Romanian is pronounced like Italian, with the stress usually on the penultimate syllable of words ending in vowels and on the final syllable of words ending in consonants. As in Italian, front vowels soften *c* and *g* to *č* (as in *chew*) and *dj* (as in *gem*). Hard *c* and *g* (as in *cat* and *ghost*) are indicated by *c* or *ch* and *g* or *gh*. *H* is guttural, like the Russian *kh* and the Scottish *ch*, and final *i* is silent. Other Romanian phonemes are *ă* (as in *about*), *â* and *î* (both like the *i* in *static*), *ş* (*sh*, as in *show*), and *ţ* (*ts*, as in *cats*). The Hungarian *ö* is pronounced like the *o* in *dome*.

An *a* at the end of a place name is pronounced like *ă* but the accent is omitted. The place names that appear most frequently in this book are Făgăraş (Fuh-guh-*rahsh*), Hîrseni (Hir-*sehn*), Drăguş (Druh-*goosh*), Cîrţişoara (Kir-tsee-*shwah*-ruh), Braşov (Brah-*shov*), and Sibiu (See-*byoo*). The name of the late Romanian dictator, Nicolae Ceauşescu, is pronounced Nee-ko-*lah*-yeh Chow-*sheh*-skoo.

The Solitude of Collectivism

[1]

Labor, Culture, and
the Long Romanian Night

Workers of the world, unite!
　　Karl Marx and Friedrich Engels, *The Communist Manifesto*

The essence of our internal situation is precisely expressed in the
way that the working class has no other cadres and no other
organization than that by which it is dominated.
　　Rudolf Bahro, *The Alternative in Eastern Europe*

Today everyone looks after their own pocket first. There is really
no appetite for friends or kin when you have to survive.
　　Olt Land worker, 1984

　　The events in Eastern Europe in 1989 marked a turning point in
world history. The historic compromise between Solidarity and the
state in Poland after forty years of struggle spilled over into full-scale
reform in Hungary, hastened the mass migration that led to the fall of
the Berlin Wall, catalyzed the "velvet revolution" of Czechoslovak
students, poets, and playwrights, and ultimately spawned the bloody
Romanian Christmas. The magnitude and pace of these events have
generated reams of commentary and hundreds of conferences, each
seeking to capture their essence. For me, the collapse of the Cold War
order seems more like news footage of the demolition of a crumbling
building than the proverbial chain reaction of dominoes. At one moment the edifice stands tall in faded glory. Then, in a staccato se-
quence of dynamite flashes, the walls fall in, the floors give way, and
the building crashes. In the final frame bystanders cheer as they gaze
at the smoldering rubble, apparently with little thought of the reconstruction yet to come. That, of course, is the key question.

Prediction is truly a fool's game in East-Central Europe, and daily changes—the breakup of Yugoslavia, the dissolution of Solidarity, German unification—keep the ground unstable. Still, the region's transformation has raised significant questions about life and culture in modern Europe and has brought to light as many problems as it resolved. As one picks through the rubble of the old regimes, it is easy to recognize the shakiness of the foundations on which they rested. Yet the rusted beams of long-ineffective social and economic policy and the dry-rotted timbers of Communist politics force us first to understand the factors that enabled these systems to persist as long as they did, the forces that pushed them to collapse in revolution, and the kinds of societies that are likely to emerge from the wreckage of socialism.

Though I focus on changes in a single Romanian region—the industrialized Olt Land zone of south-central Transylvania, almost in the geographic center of the country—the questions raised and the conclusions drawn echo across the contemporary Eastern European landscape and inform the general debate on acquiescence and resistance in state societies as well (cf. Rebel 1989).

A growing literature in political anthropology focuses on the question of state domination of local life. Such approaches, however, either emphasize the heroism and resistance in local communities (Nash 1979, Scott 1984, Turton 1984) or, more rarely, their cooptation by state power and ideology (Taussig 1980, Willis 1981). The Olt Land case, however, as well as forty-odd years of socialism in East-Central Europe, suggests that the relationship of state and people is not so easily dichotomized. All of these cases, in fact, suggest a paradox: that the practice of daily life and the reproduction of social institutions in local socialist communities facilitated the state's domination even as it created the conditions and consciousness that hastened its demise.

The critical element in this paradox is labor, its social relationships and cultural meanings. Both the socialist Romanian state with its cult of labor (see, e.g., Georgescu 1984) and Olt Land villagers with their self-definition as hardworking and practical elevated labor to a key symbol and relationship. In their attempts to control the terms, nature, meaning, and outcomes of their labor, the Olt Landers were both dominated and revolutionized. They were revolutionized as political control and absorption of resources by the political center created the conditions for the emergence of an angry peasant-worker class. They were dominated as their social and ideological responses to this system turned life inward, eroded local social relations, and limited identities and organization for concerted action. In Marx's terms, Olt Land labor produced a class *in* itself—that is, a structured and dominated social group—but prevented the emergence of a class *for* itself, one able to organize for purposes of collective resistance.

These ambiguities—a society that was fragmented and unified, quiescent and revolutionary, self-absorbed and politically conscious—constantly confronted me in Olt Land communities. Though the socioeconomic structure of Olt Land villages was fairly homogeneous, for example, the villagers' behavior indicated increased differentiation. Olt Landers expressed well-formed political sentiments in one voice and denied them furiously in another. People perceptively joked that collective farming is done by *şapte cu mapă şi una cu sapă* (seven with briefcases and one with a hoe) and evoked membership in a solidary group, *noi* (us), conceptually opposed to the state and its agents, *ei* (them).[1] This unity, however, was neither permanent nor a goad to action. Even as collective farm members complained loudly and in unison of increased labor demands and unfair pay, they accused each other of theft and laziness. Though they divided the world into "us" and "them," they sought relationships with "them" and avoided requests for economic assistance or reciprocal labor from "us." The ruinous circumstances of the late years of Romania's socialist state, which rationed such necessities as heat, light, milk, and eggs, reinstituted forced labor and delivery of produce, and even forced the production of children (Cole & Nydon 1990), provoked only smatterings of dissent—until the edifice crumbled. Such was the solitude of collectivism.

Olt Land Ambiguities: Labor, Ethnography, and Explanation

Few journalistic accounts of 1989 or texts on Soviet-style societies devote much consideration to daily life and labor as sources of acquiescence or resistance to the state (see Fukuyama 1989, Gati 1990, Gwertzmann & Kaufman 1990). The rise, persistence, and fall of socialism are explained mainly by reference to state-level practices

---

1. Us/them distinctions were rife throughout socialist East Europe. See Teresa Toranska's *They* (1986) for a series of interviews with the Polish "them."

alone: the machinations of dictators, bureaucracies, and secret police. When individuals are considered, they are often viewed as homogenized masses struggling to break free of unnatural socialist constraints and reassert their universal (capitalist) human nature. The minutiae of local life under socialism are avoided, as they aren't particularly sexy from a marketing standpoint. John Doe-escu's timeclock is less compelling than the Ceauşescus' multitiered House of the Republic, the depredations of the Securitate, or the domination of state and party by the Ceauşescus' relatives—what one observer cleverly termed "socialism in one family" (de Flers 1984). More to the point, macro-level analyses of East-Central European societies have been shaped by the leading role of the disciplines of economics and political science in Soviet and Eastern European studies and by Cold War pressures to mythologize those societies and the power of the socialist state (Sampson & Kideckel 1989).

Now, there is no question that conditions at the state level contributed to the reproduction and overthrow of socialist domination. By themselves, however, they explain neither that domination, the revolution, nor the subsequent development of East-Central European societies. Consider the lightning-like collapse of those regimes when their populations had had enough. In Romania, the marchers of Timişoara, the students of Bucharest, and coalitions of workers and peasants throughout the country caused Ceauşescu's house of cards to fall within a matter of days. We must consider also, unfortunately, the attempts to perpetuate much of the system by numerous social groups that found collective agriculture, state-owned industry, and centralized planning in their interest (Cojocaru 1990, Pop 1990).

The importance of the Eastern European case for history, social science, and world geopolitics demands alternatives to macro-level analysis. Such explanations must especially consider the interaction of large-scale systems and local phenomena observed by on-site, in-depth, long-term ethnographic analysis. Only in this way will we uncover the sources of political action or inaction and the future of the East-Central European peoples.

Ethnographic data are necessary complements to East-Central European social analysis for three reasons. First, though local life in socialist states was greatly influenced by national policies, those policies rarely determined the bulk of local events and processes. State policies were invariably reinterpreted and transformed by the diverse groups at whom they were directed. Second, macro-level analysis

[4]

cannot discern the differential impact that particular state policies had on diverse populations, regions, and communities or document variations in the meanings of the actions taken by various groups as they devised their own strategies for political and economic survival (Cole 1980:12–13). Third, though socialist governments attempted to organize and control society by pervasive corporate organizations—the fabled socialist bureaucracy (Chirot 1978, Hirszowicz 1980)—in fact such organizations were thoroughly interpenetrated by personal social relations that often determined their character (Sampson 1987).

Objections to ethnographic analysis often focus on the unrepresentative nature of villages and regions. Some anthropologists counter this criticism by claiming that the communities where they work are more typical than others (e.g., Hann 1985). Perhaps they are; but all localities have random, idiosyncratic features that derive from their unique qualities and histories. Since every community is unique, even widespread local conditions cannot be assumed to represent a microcosm of the state. The issue of local representativeness needs to be reformulated. In fact, community uniqueness is not problematic but in itself has explanatory power. Each case is a specific instance of the interaction of national practice and local life and thus provides broad understanding of the possibilities of life in a particular national system (see Freeman 1970). Though we cannot understand communities by considering national-level data exclusively, we can understand the character of states only by considering their impact on real people.

Building Socialism, Tearing It Down: Fieldwork and Reflexivity

I conducted fieldwork in the Olt Land region for three years, mostly between 1974 and 1984 and briefly in 1990, after the revolution. My research thus encompassed three distinct periods in Romanian society: economic and political promise in the early 1970s; the crisis of the 1980s; and the revolution and its aftermath. Though I focus mainly on the continuities of life in these periods, the times differed enough to influence the way I perceived and evaluated Romanian life. As Romanian society changed over these years, my mild optimism about its government turned to wholehearted antagonism toward it and my enthusiasm about the possibilities of local life disappeared. Ethnographic fieldwork, after all, involves more than detached observation of life as it swirls about the observer. It is an interactive process

[5]

between fieldworker and field, subjects and researchers, political and historical entities whose understanding and interaction are shaped by culture, class, and related self-interest.[2] My perceptions of Olt Land life and Romanian socialism were also influenced by the group of anthropologists of which I was a part during my early fieldwork and the historical moment at which we began our research.

In the early 1970s the war in Vietnam raged, Watergate was daily in the news, and socialism was an evolving system whose prevailing rationale was national development and egalitarian human relations. In some ways Romania and Ceauşescu were beacons in this international movement. Ceauşescu's denunciation of the Warsaw Pact's invasion of Czechoslovakia in 1968 and what appeared to be his liberal social policy in the late 1960s contributed to a sense of promise for Romania and our willingness to rationalize discomforting events and institutions (see, for example, Romanian Research Group 1977). Furthermore, our group entered Romania on the heels of a developing friendship with the United States, symbolized by President Nixon's visit there in 1969 and the United States' granting of "most favored nation" trading status to Romania. Our permission to live in Romanian homes and research Romanian life was another way to cement the bond between the two countries.

Many laws impeded easy communication between Romanians and foreigners,[3] but these bureaucratic obstacles were swept away for us and we were given carte blanche in many areas. We were allowed to live with Romanian families. We traveled where we wanted and spoke with whom we wanted without need for prior approval. And a wide variety of local documents and statistics were made available to us. I will never forget the absurdity of the days I spent microfilming maps and five-year plans, provided me by the staff of the Braşov County planning office, which had *Secret de Servici* (or "Secret, for planning office personnel only") stamped on them. Every time the office door opened I was certain I'd be arrested. When a prominent Communist Party official walked in and saw what I was doing, I stammered and fumbled with my camera. He smiled and then held open the page of

2. My treatment of these issues here is necessarily brief. Steven Sampson and I discuss the political nature of fieldwork in Romania and socialist society in greater detail in two articles: Kideckel & Sampson 1984, Sampson & Kideckel 1989.

3. In 1973 it became illegal for unrelated foreigners to stay overnight in private Romanian homes, and the Official Secrets Act demanded that all conversations between Romanians and foreigners be reported in writing to the police within twenty-four hours.

the planning book so I could get a better picture. Clearly the Cold War verities on which I had been raised demanded revision.

The Cold War, in fact, was background to much of what our group thought and wrote about Romania in the 1970s and 1980s. We were determined to understand Romanian society in its own terms and not fall prey to the politicocentrist verdict mentality and the automatic suspicion of things socialist that this international struggle implied (Sampson & Kideckel 1989:163–64; see also Kideckel & Sampson 1984:86–92). True to our cultural-relativistic bent, context was everything, and here the context was a country attempting to undo centuries of dependency—perhaps too rapidly and with too much emphasis on ethnic exclusivity, but surely its heart was in the right place.

Thus, intent on poking holes in Western notions of totalitarianism and the complete dominance of local life by state and party, I approached agricultural collectivization by considering how local communities adapt and change national policy according to their own needs and organizational principles (Kideckel 1979, 1982). As Romania changed, however, so did my research interests. Though I had documented the ability of local communities to revise or circumvent national policy, it became clear that such circumvention was for the short-term benefit of households and of little relevance for long-term social change. As the revolutionary potential of the Olt Land village (Kideckel 1983) dissolved in a haze of compromise and status pretensions (Kideckel 1985), I began to ask what factors contribute to the atomization of local populations.

The Cold War also figured implicitly in the daily activities and relationships of the field. At first people couldn't believe that an American could be interested in Romanian village life for any but political reasons. After I managed to put down rumors of my espionage, however, people then saw me as a possible agent of the Romanian state—though not for long, fortunately. Still, everywhere I went, administrators used my presence for social control. They openly admonished people to be on their best behavior so that the American would have a proper impression of the country. At one particularly raucous collective farm assembly, the president on the dais demanded order by saying, "Is this what you want Americans to know about how we run our affairs?" At the same time, I had to be wary lest I interpret critical behavior or speech intended for my benefit as truly indicative of opposition to the state.

Over the course of my fieldwork the practical difficulties of research

[7]

in Olt Land communities paled next to the deterioration of village life and the malaise of late socialism. True, life was difficult in the 1970s, but there was a sense that things were improving. This optimism was even reflected in an informal opinion survey I ran in 1979: nearly all respondents replied positively to the statement: "Life for my children and grandchildren will be better than mine." In the 1980s, however, Romania's international debt mounted, Ceauşescu sought to pay it off through forced labor and deprivation of the population, and political controls tightened. Then village research became difficult indeed, but more because of the anguish and suffering of those who by now had become friends and "family" than because of the practicalities of life in a grim society.

Especially difficult was the knowledge that people with whom I came in contact were subject to interrogation and punishment for the mere fact of that contact. One former host lost 10 percent of his salary for three months because he provided me a place to sleep in the village—at the request of local party officials! Whereas earlier I could go almost anywhere in the region (but was periodically—and legitimately—checked up on), I was now followed openly by uniformed police almost everywhere I went, even along the village streets. Still, some people were in such dire economic and physical straits that they ignored the potential political costs and sought me out for an audience and occasionally for assistance. Olt Landers were never very reticent about their complaints, especially physical ones. By the mid-1980s some older people now literally cried about their declining health and standard of living, and everyone I spoke with requested medicines.

After I returned home I found it difficult and sometimes embarrassing to be a Romanian specialist. Except for an occasional Christmas card, my active correspondence with academics and villagers dried up. Romanian colleagues no longer showed up at conferences where they were expected, or if they did, they were accompanied by security officials who closely supervised them. Some American colleagues questioned how I could have been so accepting of a system so rotten. And any reflection at all on village friends and informants was depressing. This book was even delayed by the circumstances of life in Ceauşescu's Romania. Concerns for some informants who could have been identified by my descriptions prevented me from discussing certain aspects of local life and twice caused me to scrap the project entirely, until news of the Romanian revolt came in December 1989.

The years since then have been a heady time for students of Eastern

European and Romanian affairs. Though it's difficult to keep up with changes in the region (and next to impossible to find appropriate texts to help one consider such changes anthropologically), it's also exhilarating and enervating—exhilarating for the possibilities of real change, enervating for the continuing and pernicious socioeconomic problems. Thus the sense of unbounded optimism that Olt Landers had during the Easter season of 1990, when I returned to the region, has again given way to letters that speak of a difficult and contentious present and an uncertain future; of conflict over land and the massive out-migration of intellectuals, educators, and the economically ambitious. It's easy to trace these problems to conditions at the national level—persistent ethnic tensions, a violent political process, underdevelopment. But the only way to begin to overcome such problems is to accept responsibility for one's own life and band together with one's neighbors to recreate a lost local corporatism. The obstacles in the way are daunting; I hope they are not insuperable.

Olt Land Region, Village, and People

The Olt Land region is the perfect place to view the ambiguities of socialist and postsocialist life, for it, too, is rife with contradiction. With a mainly Romanian and Gypsy population, the region (Map 1) is separated from Ţara Româneasca (the provinces of Muntenia and Oltenia) by the Carpathian Alps, here at their highest elevation in Romania (Mount Moldoveanu reaches 2,543 meters). Physically part of Transylvania (the Romanians call it Ardeal, the Hungarians Erdely), the Olt land is separated from the rest of it by the Olt River on the north and west. North across the Olt are the viniferous hills of pe Ardeal/de pe Tîrnave, with its Saxon, Gypsy, Magyar, and Romanian population. To the west are the Saxon lands around the city of Sibiu. On the east, the low Perşani Mountains (rising 500–1,500 meters) separate the Olt Land from the fertile Bîrsa Plain, the region around Braşov, populated by Saxons, Gypsies, Magyars, Szeklers, and Romanians. Unlike Transylvania, the region is a low plain (the "Făgăraş Depression") that ascends gradually from the Olt to the Carpathians across an alluvial floodplain, a mixed zone of arable rolling hills and rocky meadow and pasture before reaching the abrupt Carpathian wall.

Standing on the Olt hills over Făgăraş, one can often make out each

[9]

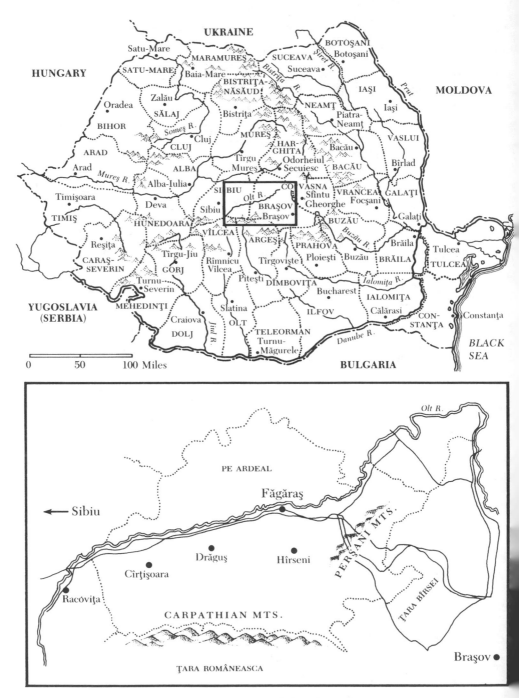

Map 1. Romania and the Olt Land

zone and the snow-covered distant peaks. From Hîrseni, 12 kilometers south of Făgăraş, the mountains' beauty is both awesome and forebidding; once I stood with villagers on the plains and watched an unseasonal storm destroy much of the commune's flock. The Carpathians thus cast a long and ambiguous shadow over Olt Land life. Haven for bandits, runaway serfs, military conscripts, and anticommunist guerrillas,[4] they connote both freedom and struggle. People looked longingly at *munţii noştrii* (our mountains) and spoke of fishing, eating, and drinking with friends in free spaces; yet in the same breath they invoked them to explain the past poverty and hard labor of Olt Land life. Beyond them, it was said, the lazier southerners got bounteous harvests merely by spitting on the soil, and in Ardeal grapes grew of their own accord. But Olt Landers are condemned by the mountains to lives of toil tempered by their moral superiority.

In a sense, this simple environmental determinism is not far from the truth. Economically, the Carpathians are both burden and boon. The weather patterns they promote make agriculture an unpromising livelihood. High rates of annual rainfall (691 mm. on the plain and 1,000 in the mountains) and poor, hard-to-drain soils contribute to frequent flooding. Cold temperatures (8.2°C annual median) and frosts from early September until mid-May shorten the growing season appreciably. Still, upland forests and meadows offer pasture, wood, and stone for craft industries and domestic needs.

In this region circumscribed by the mountains and the Olt River, the prevailing middle-peasant agriculture produced a settlement pattern characterized by large numbers of physically and demographically small villages, often arranged as *sus-jos* (upland-lowland) twins along the rivulets and streams flowing from the mountains to the Olt (Irimie 1948:43). Village socioeconomic profiles differed mainly according to location. Closer to the Olt River towns of Făgăraş and Avrig, villages had more fertile soils, easier access to markets, and mixed agricultural/commercial profiles. Villages in the middle region were agropastoral with marginal commerce. And those closest to the mountains were oriented to forest, pasture, herding, and woodworking, supplemented by an underproductive agriculture.

Given their environment, relative ethnic homogeneity, and common history, the Romanians of the sixty-five or so Olt Land villages

---

4. For a time after the 1989 revolution, people were afraid that remnants of Ceauşescu security forces would also take refuge there.

have developed a high degree of regional identity. They call themselves *Făgărașeni*, after the region's largest city, or *Olteni*,[5] after the river, and see themselves as unlike the dimwitted *Ardeleni* (Transylvanian Romanians) and the lazier and more dishonest *Regateni* (Romanians from Țara Românească), whose name derives from Regat, the old Romanian kingdom.

Driving south from Făgăraș, passing the sulfurous smokestacks of the Chemical Combine on the right and the stunted, yellowed wheat and rye, certainly the result of factory emissions, one traverses Ileni village, whose main street parallels and then crosses the Sebeș River. At the end of Ileni we pass a *troiță* (a roadside shrine) and the village cemetery, and at once the red-tiled roofs of Hîrseni come into view. As we approach Hîrseni commune (Map 2) in the spring, the villages seem just this side of paradise, though to get to them we have to pass under crackling power lines, which Olt Landers blame for all manner of ailments. The sunlit red tiles of the house roofs and spires of the two churches in Hîrseni village highlight the white of apple blossoms. The air is thick with the smell of manure. Animal sounds are everywhere. Entering Hîrseni, we pass a sign welcoming visitors to the commune and another extolling the local bakery's bread. Here we see the only clue that anything is amiss. In the current economic crisis little flour but the unpopular rye is available, and someone has impaled one of the infamous loaves on the sign with a graffito reading: "Come and get it!"

As we travel through one Olt Land village after another, they all seem pretty much of a piece. Except when the buses stop to take on or let off commuting workers or during intense agricultural activity, village streets are largely empty. Village centers (Map 3) have small commercial zones with a general store, a bar and café, a bakery, and an occasional barbershop or other commercial establishment. The collective farm office, the school, the post office, and the town hall are also generally located in the center, occasionally in the former home of a wealthy villager who left or was forcibly exiled during the first years of socialism and whose home was deeded to the state. Over time these buildings have steadily been replaced by structures built specifically for their particular purposes. Other nondomestic buildings and institutions near the village center include medical offices, a children's

5. This term is the same as that used by others in Romania for people from Oltenia, a province in southwest Romania.

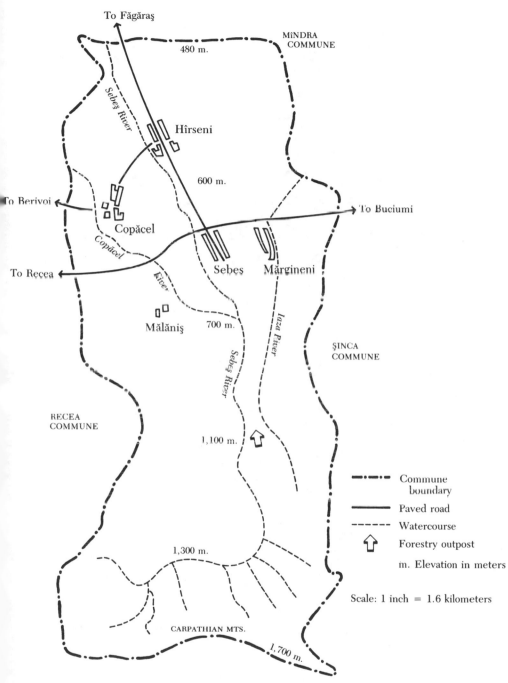

To Făgăraş

MÎNDRA COMMUNE

480 m.

Sebeş River

Hîrseni

600 m.

To Berivoi

To Buciumi

Copăcel

Copăcel

To Recea

Sebeş   Mărgineni

Iaza River

ŞINCA COMMUNE

Mălăniş   700 m.

River

Sebeş River

RECEA COMMUNE

1,100 m.

— · — · — Commune boundary

———— Paved road

-------- Watercourse

⇧ Forestry outpost

m. Elevation in meters

1,300 m.

Scale: 1 inch = 1.6 kilometers

CARPATHIAN MTS.

1,700 m.

Map 2. Hîrseni commune

[13]

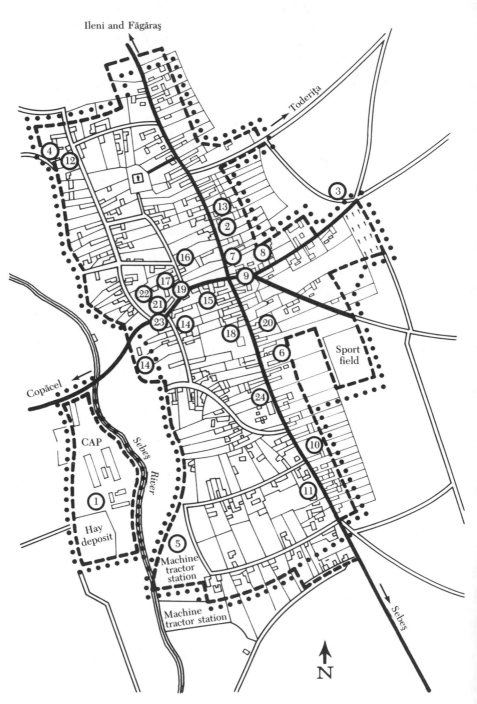

Map 3. Hîrseni village

nursery, a meeting hall, and churches and rectories. A tractor park and garage, barns for collective farm animals, and an occasional soccer field or school play area are located on the periphery. As testimony to the wisdom of the state planners, people in Hîrseni bemoan the location of the animal barns upwind of the village.

The main streets of Olt Land villages today are paved, though side streets turn into morasses of mud and manure in winter and spring. A drainage ditch runs along each side of the street, next to a narrow walkway that is seldom used; most people prefer to walk in the street. No plot of grass separates a house from the walkway. All houses are set hard by the street to make use of every bit of land, a practice Olt Landers say contrasts with the practice elsewhere in Romania and Transylvania. Houses are built around a courtyard, faced by a wood, brick, or plaster wall with a high wood or metal gate and tightly shuttered windows. Unless the house is quite new, a small wooden bench where one can sit and talk with neighbors is fixed next to the door that leads to the courtyard. The facade of the house varies in accordance with the year it was built and the attitudes of the residents. Most houses built or remodeled in the 1960s and 1970s are ornately decorated with multicolored geometric designs in plaster, small bits of mirror, and columns. Some recent homes are much simpler, faced with gray plaster; others are remarkable for their size and ostentation. Every village has a few houses of raw brick in the process of construction or renovation.

---

1. Collective farm animal barns
2. Collective farm headquarters
3. Scales
4. Brandy distillery
5. Tractor park garage
6. Veterinary dispensary
7. Commercial complex (restaurant, bar, general store)
8. Bakery
9. Bread stand, barbershop
10. Tailor
11. Blacksmith
12. Knitwear
13. Bootmaker
14. Welder
15. Town hall/library
16. Police

17. Volunteer fire brigade
18. Post office
19. Kindergarten
20. Grade school
21. In-patient clinic
22. Clinic mess hall
23. Medical dispensary
24. Meeting hall

● ● ●   Village boundary
↑↑↑↑↑   Communal cemetery
[↑]   Church
▬▬▬   Unpaved street
═══   Paved street
═══   Watercourse
[▭]   Household courtyards, homes, outbuildings, gardens

[15]

With few exceptions, central courtyards are smaller near the village center than at the margins. The number of rooms in the house and their decorative style depend on the affluence of the household (Figures 1 and 2). All houses, even those of officials, have at least one or two icons or pictures of religious scenes and a Romanian Orthodox calendar on the walls. Some people even have a few painted glass icons, for which Olt Land artists are renowned. All households also stencil designs on their walls, and some wealthier households layer multiple stencils with metallic paint, so that the walls appear to shimmer. Wealthier households set aside one room to be used only on ritual occasions, such as a wake or a wedding reception. Most households had a separate outbuilding used as a summer kitchen, to keep the main house cool in summer. Though most families now have stoves fueled by bottled gas, the wood stove in the summer kitchen is still used extensively. Other outbuildings include animal sheds, chicken coops, and barns. Houses built in the 1970s lack accommodations for stock animals, since agriculture was waning as a subsistence practice then, but this trend has since been reversed.

Most villagers, even the wealthy, still show signs of their past frugality. Kitchen tables are covered by a locally made tablecloth, which is covered by a large plastic cloth, which itself is covered by a thinner plastic sheet. In the winter, at least in homes where the residents still consider themselves to be a household, people congregate in one or two rooms to conserve firewood. (Until just a few years ago, central heating was as unheard of as indoor toilets.) When people receive guests, though, they spare no expense. Even in difficult times it is considered shameful not to offer a variety of foods and drinks, no matter the time of day. Plates are piled high; small shotglasses are filled to overflowing with *rachiu* (a brandy made of mixed fruits) and are refilled even before they are empty. The only acceptable excuse for refusing either food, drink, or cigarettes is a doctor's orders, and even that justification is closely questioned—less because the hosts doubt the guest's word than because they find ailments fascinating. Hosts recite one proverb after another to persuade a guest to eat and drink more: "Vin după bere face o plăcere; bere după vin face un chin" (Wine after beer is pleasurable; beer after wine is torture); "Două băuturi strică; doua mîncări nu strică" (Mixing drinks will make you sick; mixing foods never will). It would be impolite of them even to hint that a guest ought to leave. I learned this the hard way. At three in the morning after an all-night game of poker, which my friends

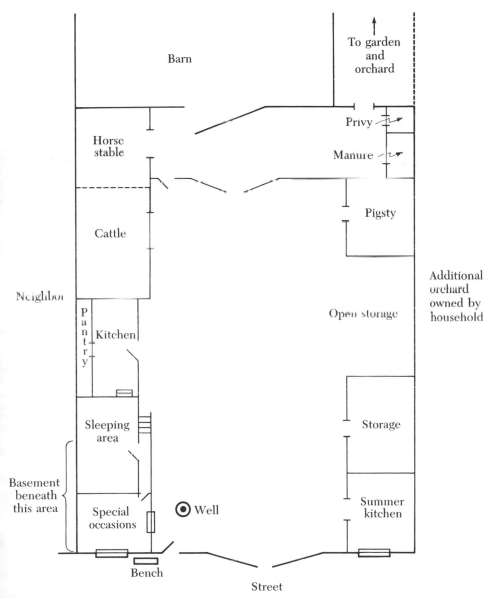

Figure 1. Upper-middle peasant house

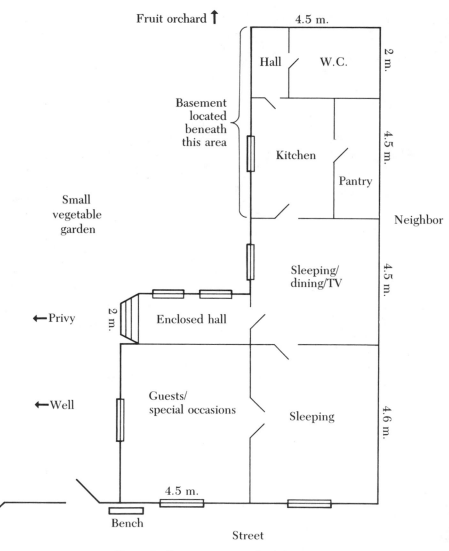

Figure 2. Contemporary worker's house

demanded I teach them, I asked them to leave, as I had a long workday planned and needed a bit of sleep. Though they were mildly surprised, they left in good humor. Later I never stopped hearing about how rude Americans are, though the story was always told in kindness and with much laughter.

Most people, elders in particular, are conservative in their manner and dress. With the advent of socialism, most people in the region stopped wearing traditional dress, except on ritual occasions, and many never do so at all. *Drăguşeni,* however, are an exception; in Drăguş it is not unusual to see men in the traditional tight woolen pants, white tunic, wide leather belt, embroidered vest, and felt hat. Women in Drăguş wear the national dress less often. Work dress is standard across the region. Unless a woman is young and works in town, she habitually wears an apron and kerchief; if she is doing farmwork, she wears one kerchief tied tightly around her hair and another thrown loosely over that. In the village she wears thick woolen stockings in all seasons. Many men who work at the factory wear a business suit and a worker's cap, and carry a briefcase to hold their lunch of bread, onion, and fatback. In the winter a man wears a lambswool hat and vest. The vast majority of men smoke and drink. All women will take a drink on occasion, but only young women who work in town and Gypsy women smoke cigarettes, the former at home and the latter in public too.

The Olt Land extends over parts of both Braşov and Sibiu counties, but most of my research was carried out in the four constituent villages of Hîrseni commune, in Braşov County.[6] Eighty-one households in Hîrseni village, the commune center, formed the core group. For comparative purposes I also collected data in Drăguş village, Braşov County;[7] Cîrţişoara, in Sibiu County; and the city of Făgăraş. My methodology developed out of my initial research on collective farming and its relation to village social structure and cultural practice. My concern for collectivization early on led me to survey a random sample of Hîrseni households regarding their participation in collective farm-

6. A commune, generally comprising more than one village and administered from a commune center (*reşedinţă comunei*), is the basic administrative unit in contemporary Romania. Hîrseni commune, with a total 1984 population of approximately 3,500, comprised the villages of Hîrseni (the center), Copăcel, Sebeş, Mărgineni, and the Gypsy hamlet Mălăniş.

7. Drăguş was extensively studied in the interwar years by the Romanian Sociological School, headed by Dimitrie Gusti. A restudy is in the works and is to be published soon.

ing over its twenty years of operation, the amount and type of land the collective farm allotted them for their own use, offices held, and attitudes toward farm labor and administration. I conducted the surveys as I talked with villagers while they worked in the fields, and then followed up with at least one interview in their houses. These initial interviews, along with civil and economic statistics collected at the offices of the People's Council, or town hall, and minutes and observations recorded at past and present farm assemblies then served to identify and categorize household types. I then interviewed a few members of selected households in greater depth on several occasions. I also surveyed schoolchildren as to their ideal careers and spent a lot of time talking to people about their work and its meaning to them.

Unfortunately, until my last bit of fieldwork after the revolution, I recorded none of my interviews after my first informant demanded that I destroy the tape. (I was also asked to destroy the first genealogy I wrote down.) My informants' obvious concern about the ultimate use to which a tape might be put compelled me to stop the practice. Direct quotations of informants' remarks, however, represent their words and intentions as accurately as possible. Photography presented a different sort of problem. All of my informants were so eager to have their pictures taken—they gladly stopped any activity to pose and competed with each other for copies of photographs—that I finally limited my use of this technique, too.

I spent considerable time as a participant observer in labor and social activities to evaluate the quality of local social relations. I took most meals with tractor drivers and administrators at the collective farm's mess hall, served as the driver for the farm president and head agronomist for a time, harvested potatoes with various households, participated in autumn all-nighters distilling *rachiu,* and regularly attended meetings of collective farm members, work teams, boards, and commissions. Despite repeated attempts, during the 1970s and 1980s I was never allowed inside the region's large chemical or machinery plant. Discussion of labor there is based largely on interviews. After the revolution, however, I did have a series of tours and meetings at the Făgăraş machinery works. During most of my fieldwork, I also visited small-scale dairy processing plants, construction sites, and various offices. All of these activities helped to clarify the interrelation of labor, society, and values.

Labor, Culture, and Political Practice

Whereas work is simply the application of physical energy to a goal-directed task, labor is a *social* process carried out by individuals or organized groups to transform nature for human use. Though it was only one factor in the evolution of Olt Land communities, it was a critical one, as it ultimately touched on and influenced every other aspect of community life, from the demographic structure and internal organization of households to conceptions of the self and others that unified or divided people in political action. Furthermore, the Romanian socialist state focused on the transformation of labor as the key to social change, and Olt Landers themselves were preoccupied with the terms, conditions, and qualities of their labor, which they understood as the essence of their lives and culture. Their preponderant concern must therefore be our own.

Labor was an arena of conflict between the socialist state and the village household. This contest over the control of time, human energy, and resources shaped local social and political relations and the villagers' attitudes toward the state, property, and socialism itself. This basic notion loosely follows and ties together arguments about socialist society that have grown from Milovan Djilas's "New Class" thesis and from related works (Bahro 1978, Campeanu 1986, Djilas 1955, Konrád & Szelényi 1979, Rév 1987), Marxist anthropological ideas about the relations of labor and culture (Roseberry 1989, Wessman 1981, Wolf 1982, Worsley 1984), and anthropological ideas about the effects of interpretations of meaning on practice (e.g., Bourdieu 1977, Marcus & Fischer 1986, Ortner 1982).

In accord with Marxist ideas about class relationships, I assume that the quality and nature of labor and the culture and practice of laborers are influenced first by the ownership, control, and use of the productive resources on which society depends. In all state societies, and especially in Eastern European socialist ones, where the dominant role of the Communist Party hierarchy was sanctioned by law, control over productive resources was held disproportionately by a dominant class that directed resources to serve its own ends. Such control not only gave these groups the lion's share of the society's resources but legally reinforced the principles on which their dominance rested and enabled them to work under the most pleasant conditions.

In state societies the control of labor and resources is inextricably related to cultural meaning. Through this control and the political power it confers, the dominant seek to perpetuate their position in society, in part by determining the nature of other social groups and institutions in which individuals take part, such as family, community, school, and kin group. By controlling meaning and culture, the dominant manage to "represent [their] interests as the universal interests of 'the people,' the whole society" (Turton 1984:44). This control of meaning further limits the working population's ability to conceive of other ideological and social possibilities even as it qualifies them to participate in the division of labor elaborated by and in the interest of the dominant (Therborn 1980).

Thus, though local social institutions may seem far removed from the labor process, in truth they are often the chief factor that links dominant groups to local communities and on which their dominance ultimately depends. Local institutions are bent to the purposes of dominant social groups as much by ideological means as by overt political and economic force. The dominant groups disseminate their ideology through schools and the media, by secular ritual, and by any other means they can devise to shape workers' consciousness and perception of work and society, such as the "traditions" of industrialism and collectivism manufactured in Eastern Europe (Hobsbawm & Ranger 1983, Kideckel 1988).

The dominant groups' control over laborers' institutions and culture is never perfect and always subject to contest and change. The social and cultural institutions and practices of the dominated, though generally less well organized and lacking in resources, nonetheless can retain a measure of vigor and alternative meanings for several reasons, even though these alternatives are circumscribed by the formal political and legal systems. People are aware of other societies and ideas and so can conceptualize alternatives. Some people were enculturated in other times and respond favorably to other values. In some instances, the dominant allow or even encourage local social and cultural practices and institutions so as to limit the resistance of local communities or because the costs of replacing such institutions with new ones are too high. In any case, a variety of local practices and meanings are available to dominated populations, and their continued existence provides diverse social relationships, meanings, and organizational possibilities that the dominated can use to contest the power of the dominant, if only surreptitiously.

Each local social institution, relationship, or expression of cultural meaning exhibits some aspect of the dominant group's political or cultural goals. As local and state institutions struggled over culture and labor in socialist Romania, however, both local practices and those of the state were invariably transformed in ways that no one had foreseen. It was these practices that most captured my interest. Anthropologists and others oriented to local life and small-scale communities often define political practice within dominated communities as a challenge to domination (Ortner 1982, Scott 1984). But this is not the only possible outcome. Difficult times and illiberal political regimes can also produce mean-spirited and self-indulgent practices as people try to strike the best possible bargain with those in control. Such practices challenge the dominant as certainly as revolutionary rhetoric, passive aggression, and moral (that is, reciprocal) economic exchange.

The Village Household

Of all social institutions, the household provides the primary context for the clash of state and individual, mediates the relationship between culture and labor, and influences the political ideology and practice of the dominated, particularly in peasant or peasant-worker societies. In the recent past, rural households in Romania were the chief units of economic production and the main sources of individual affect, identity, and political support; until the revolution they were also the critical units in collective farms and in other state production institutions.

A universally applicable definition of the household is difficult to come by, as household structures and functions vary from culture to culture (Bender 1967; Smith, Wallerstein, & Evers 1984; Wilk & Netting 1984:4; Yanagisako 1979:162–66). One point of general agreement is that a household differs from both a family and a domestic group. Members of a household are not necessarily related, and people who share a residence do not necessarily form a household, nor is separate residence necessarily indicative of separate household status (Netting, Wilk, & Arnould 1984:xxvi). Most attempts to understand the general nature of households thus shift the definition "away from structure (How do we place limits around a group?)" to focus on activity (Wilk & Netting 1984:4) and on prevailing power relations in society (Medick 1976).

[23]

Life in the socialist Olt Land, then, produced a variety of household types. Households varied first in accordance with their external relations with people in positions of political power and with wider social networks in the village community, and second in their resulting ability to control their labor and the economic goals to which it was directed. Members of all households, however, pooled their income (see Seddon 1976) and considered themselves to form a single unit. Though production took place largely outside the household, on collective farms and in factories, the household was still critical in the culture-labor relationship, for two reasons. First, it was the context for socialization to both labor and the world in which labor was carried out (cf. Therborn 1980) and thus influenced individual goals within the socialist division of labor and attitudes toward the labor process itself. Second, since some individuals defined themselves as members of a household even though they were not residing with the other members at the moment, they acted as part of an economic and political unit and consciously employed their labor, resources, reproductive and educational potentials, and wider networks of kin and other social relationships to further the survival and well-being of the other members. When we understand the particular development and structures of Olt Land households and the practices of the individuals who formed them, we more clearly see the intersection of labor and culture and the production of resistance and domination in the socialist state.

Olt Land household and community lives derive from the presocialist past, when sociability was expected to ameliorate the effects of economic underdevelopment (Verdery 1983 discusses an analogous case), upward social mobility was admired, and wealth, entrepreneurial behavior, and technological innovation were respected. Olt Land households retained much of this cultural orientation as the socialist system, with its unwieldy production apparatus, its obsolete technology, and its lack of resources, continued to rely on household production for much of its population's subsistence. A society centered on the household was also encouraged by the particular way socialism was implemented in the region. All of these conditions, then, encouraged the persistence of the relations and forces of presocialist life, albeit reworked for socialist conditions.

Under the conditions of socialist labor, the persistence of the household as the chief social and economic unit in the Olt Land community encouraged competition, social differentiation, and the alienation of producers from one another. Though a range of rural presocialist social

[24]

groups and relationships were maintained, relations within and between them came to be based on calculation, instrumentality, and feigned sociability (cf. Wolf 1966). Common class position and joint political action were deemphasized in favor of differentiation strategies formed in the labor process and expressed in changing household organization, social relations, identity, and ideology.

[2]

The Origins of Olt Land Culture,
Class, and Consciousness

O Olt Land, corona of fire, accursed region of bitter rye bread.

Beloved Olt Land,
As many crucifixes as meadows,
A constant joy to return to;
But in Transylvania
As many pitchforks as meadows.
Its ugliness repels!

Interwar regional folk sayings

The ambiguities of the socialist village can be traced to the nature of community processes long before the socialist state sought to transform them. Presocialist Olt Land communities, in fact, provided a poor environment for the realization of the socialists' plans. They were riven by economic competition and political uncertainty and thus were potentially fertile areas for class conflict. Efforts to promote such struggles, however, were checked by a variety of economic leveling mechanisms, corporate social institutions, and norms of behavior developed over five hundred years of peasant life.

Olt Land middle peasants respected thrift, hard work, and land. Neither rich enough to hire others nor so poor as to have to sell their labor, they projected an illusion of calm and progress that created as many problems as it smoothed over. Their way of life forced emigration of surplus population, produced endemic petty commercial competition, encouraged a consuming hunger for land, and generated constant economic conflict. Their social networks readily expanded and contracted in response to local conditions or to larger political and economic realities. By its flexibility, local social life buffered regional

[26]

change. Though regional contradictions were muted, however, they never disappeared. This was the soft underbelly of village life which made it vulnerable to the socialists' attack.[1]

Feudalism and Regional Origins

The origins of the Olt Land middle peasantry can be traced to the tenth century, when feudal-like social and economic relations spread throughout Transylvania (Chirot 1976, Stahl 1979, Verdery 1983). In Transylvania proper, the feudal social hierarchy was dominated mainly by the Hungarian aristocracy; then came Magyar-speaking Szekler and German free peasants, with Romanian serfs at the bottom.[2] From 1366 to 1464, however, Olt Land feudal society was dominated by a Romanian aristocracy that originated across the Carpathians in Muntenia, the eastern zone of Wallachia (Literat & Ionașcu 1943:8–10, Meteș 1935:ix, Szadeczky 1892:2). During their century of domination these Muntenian dukes laid the basis for the region's staunch Romanian nationalism as they settled a free Romanian peasantry and, more significant, imported a native Romanian landowning nobility (*boierimeă*) into the region (Pușcariu 1892). Thus, though Olt Land serfs and nobles were distinguished by degrees of privilege and status, they were from the first joined by similarities in language and culture. Additionally Olt Land Romanian feudalism was moderated by curbs placed on the nobles' power by the Muntenian dukes, the division of nobles' estates through inheritance, and the indiscriminate bestowing of titles, which produced many villages inhabited entirely by nobles.

Romanian ethnicity and nationalism were further engendered by the spread of Magyar latifundia and political power and Saxon German commercial domination as Transylvania and the Olt Land fell under Habsburg rule in the fifteenth century (Map 4). Romanian serf and noble alike were confronted with alien linguistic and cultural groups even as the region felt the full weight of economic domination by these outsiders. The expansion of Magyar estates and the cessation of land

1. My analysis of presocialist Olt Land life has benefited from discussions with three Olt Landers who became leading members of their disciplines in Romania: the sociologist Traian Herseni, the economist Alexandru Bărbat, and the ethnographer Cornel Irimie.

2. I am oversimplifying somewhat. Katherine Verdery (1983), for example, suggests that Transylvanian feudal classes comprised individuals of all ethnic groups, though the various ethnic groups did tend to be concentrated in particular classes.

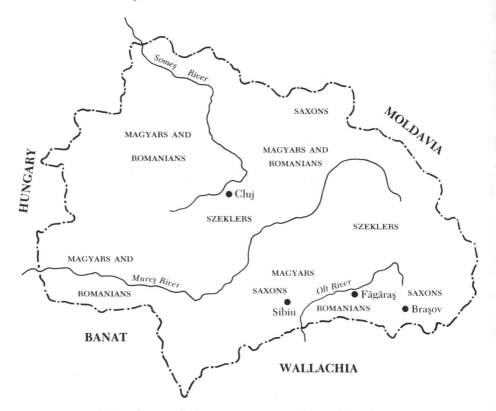

Map 4. Distribution of ethnic groups in Transylvania, fifteenth century

grants to Romanians largely relegated Romanian nobles to an impoverished subsistence agriculture, while export agriculture was carried out on Magyar latifundia run by Saxon rentiers and coerced serf labor (Puşcariu 1907:81). The Olt Land thus became a feudal backwater and transit zone for trade between the great Saxon cities of Braşov and Sibiu.

The Romanian feudal experience was bitter indeed, and five hundred years later older and middle-aged informants still speak of it often. Romanian serfs were required by law to work as many as 104 days a year on nobles' estates but were coerced into working twice as many (Kovacs 1973:10, Meteş 1921:283). Serfs could own up to 20 *jugar* of land (about 11.5 hectares), but two-thirds of a serf's property was appropriated by the lord at the serf's death. A noble also expected gifts in kind and in cash at major religious holidays both from serf households and from the village as a whole. Feudal labor and political restrictions caused considerable instability in the region's Romanian population, which fluctuated from 32,050 in 1733 to 23,898 in 1750 as serfs regularly fled over the Carpathians into the Romanian lands (Meteş 1935:xiii). Inroads made by Saxon rentiers and Hungarian nobility further pressured the native Romanian nobility, whose lands were alienated with the aid of Austro-Hungarian legal processes.[3]

The social and economic circumstances of Olt Land Romanian villagers were thus leveled under Magyar domination. Undercapitalized nobles sold land to Saxons and titles to other Romanians who had grown rich by herding. Some serfs were granted titles for service in wars against the Turks. Olt Land communities became a pastiche of nobles with deeds and titles dating to the Muntenian dukes, déclassé nobles, recently titled former serfs, and freemen and serfs of diverse circumstances (see Prodan 1976, Stahl 1979). Families whose titles could be traced back through many generations had great prestige, but Magyar power prevented them from using their status to increase their wealth and power. To protect themselves against Magyar power, Romanian Olt Landers began to develop the many-stranded social ties and widespread cooperative networks that characterized life on the eve of the socialist transformation.

Feudal Politics, Religion, and Olt Land Identity

The Olt Land Romanians first became socially differentiated as a result of Habsburg policies developed to clam an increasingly unstable Transylvania. By the late seventeenth and early eighteenth centuries the Transylvanian Magyar nobility had gained thorough control of the province, and their stringent policies had prompted increasing violence by the serfs. In an effort to check this instability, the Habsburgs created the Uniate church in 1690, linking Roman Catholic affiliation with the Orthodox liturgy to encourage the Romanians to identify with Catholicism and thus with the crown. Somewhat later the Austrians recruited Romanians into a border guard to close the Transylvanian–Romanian frontier and police the increasingly restive Romanians.

3. The Supreme Făgăraş Judiciary on March 3, 1657, restricted the rights of nobles who rented land, eased the crown's ability to confiscate land for nonpayment of tax, and "freed" nobles to sell their estates at will (Meteş 1935:xv).

Through the eighteenth century religious conversions produced a sizable Uniate population in nearly every Olt Land village (Manuila 1931), and the economic benefits offered to converts created a significant socioeconomic division in the Romanian population. Priests were given noble status and, along with other converts, tax reductions and favorable sharecropping arrangements on Uniate church lands. Noble families, especially descendants of early settlers in the region, converted much more readily than serfs and newly emancipated freemen (Meteş 1930:16), and the tax concessions and access to church lands put them several steps ahead of their Orthodox cousins. The results of Olt Land Uniatism thus diverged from the Habsburgs' goals, as it provoked religious conflict and political instability among the Romanians. In the villages the schism was expressed in religious endogamy, a separate trading network for each sect, and skirmishes between village youths.

The formation of the border regiments also contributed to social differentiation. The regiments, founded by the empress Maria Theresa in 1761 and billeted in Olt Land border villages, consisted mainly of Uniate villagers, the only group the Austrian administrators considered trustworthy. Even as the border guards suppressed Orthodox political expression, they subsisted on food collected from Orthodox peasants (Beck 1979, Verdery 1983:154). The regiments thus contributed to the increasing tension in the political environment and encouraged nationalist animosities.

As the Magyar nobles chafed under Austrian rule, they became increasingly nationalistic. Here, too, the Habsburgs' purposes were crossed, for Romanian national consciousness was often fomented by Uniate clergy who had gained knowledge of Romanian history during their studies in Rome and Vienna (Hitchens 1969, 1979). Olt Landers, evoking images of the Muntenian dukes and free Romanian peasantry in the region's heroic past, were particularly active in this movement. These diverse nationalist movements came to a head in the revolutionary mid-nineteenth century. The Magyar Transylvanian nobility was reined in as Transylvania officially became part of Hungary. Romanian serfdom was dissolved but the largely Romanian-populated Olt Land was left as an economic backwater. Though serfdom's end set in motion processes that contributed to the emergence of the regional middle-peasant way of life, the feudal legacy left the region segmented by class and religious differences that would have their parts to play in the socialist transformation.

The Olt Land Political Economy, 1848–1945

The Olt Land was under a variety of political regimes from 1848 to 1945. Like all of Transylvania, it was subject to Hungarian rule until the end of World War I, first under the direct control of the Habsburgs and after 1867 under Hungary alone (Map 5). After the war it became part of Greater Romania (Map 6). The nationality of the region's ruler, however, was of less significance to its society than economic underdevelopment, overpopulation, agricultural underproduction, competition for land, lack of credit, and the peasants' indebtedness. These problems had paradoxical effects on the villages. On one hand, class divisions widened with increased agricultural competition, expanded commerce, massive emigration, and an influx of capital from villagers who had emigrated. On the other hand, class differences were moderated (and thus maintained) by cooperative community social relations and practices, themselves crafted from institutions inherited from the feudal past.

The Austro-Hungarian Compromise of 1867, incorporating Transylvania into Hungary, was a major socioeconomic blow to Olt Land Romanians. Social privileges enjoyed by non-Magyar nationalities were eliminated and new laws restricted the use of non-Magyar languages in the schools and in public life (MacCartney 1937:24–31, Rusu-Şirianu 1904). More important, the Compromise made Transylvanian and Olt Land industry dependent on Magyar capital, oriented it to markets outside the province, and encouraged extractive industry instead of labor-intensive agricultural processing that might have benefited the region's peasantry (Verdery 1983:202–6). In fact, the loss of nearby markets and industrial restrictions continued to affect the region even after its unification with Romania. Greater Romania's industrial investment focused on zones that were already industrialized. Other areas fell further behind (Roberts 1951).

Thus the Olt Land's industry and commerce remained underdeveloped under both Magyar and Romanian regimes. Between 1870 and 1910, for example, only four new enterprises were located in Făgăraş, and they may well have been owned by non-Romanians.[4] By 1935 Făgăraş still had only twenty-six factories (nineteen Romanian-

---

4. Even as late as 1935, after thirteen years of Romanian control and Magyar outmigration, commerce in Făgăraş was still controlled primarily by non-Romanians. Of a total of 367 owners of firms and services that year, only 153 or about 42% were Romanian (Bărbat 1938:170).

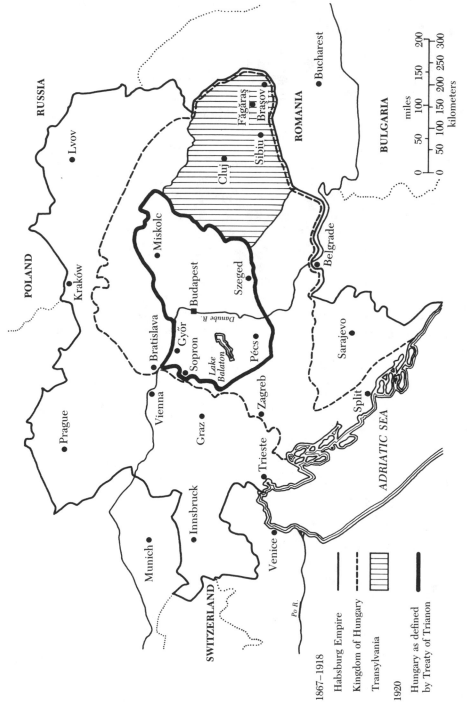

Map 5. Habsburg Empire, Kingdom of Hungary, and Transylvania, 1867–1920

RUSSIA

POLAND

• Lvov

• Kraków

• Prague

SWITZERLAND

• Munich

• Innsbruck

• Graz

Vienna •

• Bratislava

Sopron
• Győr

• Miskolc

Budapest

Danube R.

Lake Balaton

• Pécs

Szeged •

• Cluj

Făgăraș
Sibiu • Brașov

• Bucharest

ROMANIA

Belgrade •

• Sarajevo

Zagreb •

Split •

Trieste •

• Venice

Po R.

ADRIATIC SEA

BULGARIA

miles
0   50   100   150   200
0   50 100 150 200 250 300
kilometers

1867–1918
—————— Habsburg Empire
‑ ‑ ‑ ‑ ‑ Kingdom of Hungary
▦▦▦ Transylvania

1920
━━━━ Hungary as defined
      by Treaty of Trianon

Map 6. Greater Romania after World War I

owned) that employed more than ten workers, many either founded or expanded after World War I. Eleven additional factories founded after World War I went bankrupt by the end of the 1920s (Bărbat 1938:77, 180, 186–87). Of these new industries the Nitramonia Chemical Works, founded in 1926 as part of the Făgăraş Explosive Works (itself established in 1921), is particularly significant. It would later become the cornerstone of socialist industry, the region's chief employer, and a major influence on social change in Olt Land communities. In 1928, however, the first year for which statistics are available, it employed only 147 people, 127 workers and 20 supervisory or administrative personnel (Herseni et al. 1972:76).

[33]

Most of the region's industry was based on peasant households that processed local products for local markets. These cottage industries proliferated after Romanian unification with the rupture of the coerced trade links with Hungary, rapid increases in population, and a massive infusion of capital from returning emigrants.[5] Despite its growth, however, the Olt Land's industry was unable to absorb its surplus agricultural population, though it generated considerable competition and increased socioeconomic differentiation in the villages. An old Hîrseni blacksmith summed up the situation this way: "It was a time of great competition when everyone tried to have a little something extra in order to live . . . and because everyone had a trade no one really earned much. I competed with one, sometimes two other smiths in Hîrseni, and some people even went to Sebeş or Copăcel if they had relatives there."

The role played by village commerce and industry in regional class relations can be seen in the career of Ioan Cioră, who became rich by investing in a number of such ventures. Cioră, from a poor Hîrseni family, quit school after the third grade to work as a low-status herd boy. Always ambitious, while herding he carved wooden spoons to sell at the market in Făgăraş. In his late teens he left for Bucharest, learned auto mechanics, and with a small loan from a brother and his own savings bought a truck and returned to Hîrseni as a teamster for hire. By the outbreak of World War II this investment had grown into a small commercial empire that included a general store, a buzz saw, a restaurant, a threshing machine, a brandy distillery, and sizable orchards and hay lots.

Local views of Cioră's success say much about socioeconomic relations in the Olt Land. Though small-scale commerce and cottage industry were common, they were somewhat disdained; to Olt Landers, land was the only appropriate source of wealth. Commercial success was particularly suspect because of its association with urban Jews and Saxons (Cotaru 1938:322). Cioră, despite his wealth, was thus something of a village outcast until he became a substantial landowner. His land-poor origins even caused potential marriage partners to shun him, and he finally married a woman from another village.

5. For example, the 2,009 emigrants to the United States who returned after World War I brought with them 467 million lei (Bărbat 1938:278–80).

Olt Land Agriculture

Agriculture sat at the base of the rural economic system and had the greatest influence on local social relations. As elsewhere in postfeudal Eastern Europe (see Seton-Watson 1945:75–122), limited industrial development forced overdependence on agriculture, which was perpetually in crisis until World War II. The difficulty was exacerbated by rural overpopulation and peasant inheritance practices, and was reflected in land hunger and the equation of landownership with pro priety and prestige (Kideckel 1988; Verdery 1975, 1983). Despite the demand for land, however, conflicts over it were tempered in the postfeudal era by fairly equitable land distribution, cultivation practices that ensured subsistence for all, communal ownership of some resources, and a wide variety of socioeconomic leveling mechanisms.

Demand for land was first satisfied by the use of every bit of land possible. Thus Olt Land houses were built within a meter of village streets and cultivation expanded into zones of decreasing fertility. Between 1722 and 1910 the region's arable increased from roughly 16,000 to 50,000 hectares. And though much of the increase coincided with the introduction of maize and potato cultivation in the early eighteenth century, the process continued unabated in the nineteenth and twentieth centuries (Bărbat 1938:38, 69; Meteş 1935: lxx). In Drăguş the amount of arable increased by 15 percent between 1874 and 1938, while hay lands fell by 21.4 percent (Bărbat 1941:33), and in Hîrseni in the late nineteenth century the rocky, arid terrain between the Iazu and Teişu streams, an hour's walk from the village, began to be farmed.

Land distribution was relatively equalized by partible inheritance, insufficient markets to encourage large-scale cultivation, and the dense settlement pattern of the Făgăraş Depression. Thus in 1910 only 5 percent of the region's arable was in properties of 60 hectares or more, and the median size of an estate was about 7.3 hectares (Bărbat 1938:70, Moricz 1934:185). This situation was further modified by the national land reforms of 1921–1922, though they had less impact in the Olt Land than elsewhere in Transylvania, given its more equitable tenure situation (Bărbat 1938:106, Mitrany 1930:214, Moricz 1934:185–201). Not a single person's land was expropriated in Drăguş (Bărbat 1941:16), for example, and in Hîrseni only the churches lost property and three households received land. After the reforms only

1.3 percent of Olt Land estates were larger than 24 hectares and about 60 percent were between 2 and 9 hectares (Tables 1 and 2).

The parceling of land had more to do with the Olt Land rural crisis than unequal tenure. This problem became serious after feudalism ended in 1848 as a result of partible inheritance and high birth rates (see Beck 1979:128–31). As Olt Land estates, not large to start with, were divided and redivided, plots became too small to work efficiently, and more land was converted to unproductive boundaries and paths. In Hîrseni village in 1936, for example, fewer than 1,400 hectares of land were arrayed in 6,000 parcels. The largest landowner owned 24.18 hectares in 56 parcels, the largest a 2.3-hectare hay lot.

To alleviate the effects of parcelization, poor soil, and unequal land distribution, Olt Land villages generally adopted a three-field crop-rotation pattern through the nineteenth century. Community lands were divided into three *hotare* (areas), and households had to produce similar crops on two *hotare* while the third lay fallow. This arrangement forced smallholder and wealthy peasant alike into the same production schedule but gave smallholders with dispersed parcels access to all available cultigens. For the system to work, all households had to coordinate crop rotation; anyone who broke the pattern was ostracized and could be fined by the village council as well.

Changes in stockkeeping mirrored those in agriculture. As cultivation expanded from 1870 to 1910, the numbers of all kinds of livestock in the region grew enormously in response to the needs of emancipated peasant households and increased market demands. At feudalism's end the horse became the draft animal of choice in pasture-poor villages near the Olt, while extensive pasture in the rest of the region permitted a rapid increase in cattle. The numbers of water

Table 1. Landownership in Olt Land, 1922, by number of hectares

Hectares	Number	Percent
0.0–0.6	1,246	8.3%
0.6–1.8	2,116	14.1
1.9–9.0	9,252	62.0
9.0–24.0	2,117	14.1
24.0 +	194	1.3
Unknown	62	0.004
Total	14,987	99.8%

Source: After Bărbat 1938:107.

[36]

Table 2. Landownership in Drăguş, 1938, by number of hectares

Hectares	Number	Percent
Less than 1.2	7	2.3%
1.2–4.2	29	9.4
4.2–8.4	156	50.7
8.4–12.6	86	27.9
12.6 +	30	9.7
Total	308	100.0%

Source: Bărbat 1941:16.

buffalo increased nearly tenfold, from 5,577 head in 1870 to 50,971 in 1910 (Bărbat 1938:72). Bovines, in fact, were critical for Olt Land agriculture because, according to the local wisdom, their manure turned the "cold" soil "warm," and every hectare of land needed the manure of one bovine. Villagers cleaned animal stalls at least twice daily, carefully stored manure on raised and protected platforms, and spread it thickly on each *hotar*. Those with enough bovines manured hay parcels, and those with few animals followed the herds through the village to glean their leavings.[6]

As the key to successful agriculture, animals had great symbolic value to Olt Landers. A team of horses was the ultimate status symbol, and older Hîrsenites still tell with awe of the heads that turned as Iosif Oltean drove his white stallions through the village. Though horses signified prestige, water buffaloes were more suited to the region's ecology, and their qualities mirrored the way Olt Landers saw themselves. Mild and longsuffering, they worked slowly but purposefully, could be nourished on a minimal diet of corn cobs, and still gave milk with one-third more butter fat than cows' milk. Such qualities made them the region's animal of choice, and sour buffalo milk mixed with corn-meal mush was a dietary staple.

The communal control of pasture also permitted expanded stock-keeping and encouraged sociability in the postfeudal era. From 1848 until the early twentieth century most pasture was controlled by *composesoratele* (cooperative groups) of coreligionists in mixed villages or by groups formed on the basis of previous feudal status in religiously homogeneous villages. All households inherited essentially equal

6. Olt Landers' concern for manure was unabated in the socialist state, and its poor treatment by collective farms was blamed for their poor production.

[37]

rights to pasture and forest, which reverted to the village if a house-holder died without heirs (Caramelea 1944:9–10). By the early 1900s, however, the *composesoratele* began to be reconstituted into forest and pasture associations with membership determined by the purchase of shares, and the use of pasture or of a particular stand of trees was determined by a lottery influenced by wealthy villagers.

Because land tenure was relatively equitable and the emigration rate was high, peasants experienced less difficulty in the Olt Land than elsewhere in Romania. Still, the region did not completely escape the crisis that beset Romania before World War II, when all rural regions suffered from government policies to promote industrialization (Jowitt, ed., 1978): high import tariffs, steep price hikes on Romanian-made goods, a shift of investment from agriculture to industry (Mitrany 1930:425, Roberts 1951:177). Agricultural prices fell as high export taxes caused foodstuffs to flood internal markets, and agricultural credit dried up. The Romanian peasantry was caught in a classic price scissors. Debts mounted, many rural households were dissolved, and more and more cultivators joined the landless or land-poor proletariat.

Olt Landers responded to the crisis in a variety of ways. Speculation in land increased the power of the rich and promoted changes in village crop rotation. Wealthy householders with land in all *hotare* spearheaded drives to limit the fallow, and opposition to the system quickly became generalized. Most villages abandoned the practice by the 1930s. Cîrțișoara, with its considerable meadow and pasture, did so in 1930, Drăguș not until 1939 (Bărbat 1941:43). Pasture-poor Hîrseni compromised by converting to four-field rotation.[7] Other Olt Landers took to calling the Hîrsenites *ogoreni* (fallowers), and older Hîrsenites were still proud of the name in the 1970s. State policy also decreased the profitability of stockkeeping, and the numbers of animals declined precipitously. Only horses, suited mainly for traction, transport, and display, proliferated through 1938.

Despite increased proletarization and competition for land, Olt Land villagers retained their sociability by demographic practices that eliminated surplus population. The number of births per family during the interwar period fell to between two and three from a pre–

---

7. At one time the dearth of suitable pasture here had led to a forty-year legal battle by which Hîrseni hoped to secure access to pasture controlled by Sebeș, to the south. The case was finally settled in 1919, when Hîrseni was granted an additional 60 hectares (Irimie 1948:86).

An Olt Land village street at the turn of the century

World War I average of over five. Exogamous marriages, especially of young men unable to support a household, increased in frequency. And the migration of young people to America, the cities of Țara Româncasca, and nearby Saxon villages had major economic and cultural consequences.

Emigration

The emigration experience of young Olt Landers depended mainly on the future they perceived in the region itself (Beck 1979:129). Those with little hope of inheritance left for permanent residence in Țara Româneasca or to the United States. In fact, between 1880 and 1910, 11,021 men and 3,867 women left the villages of Făgăraș County for the United States, at a rate three times that of the rest of Transylvania. Men and women with better prospects became temporary migrants and sought industrial or other urban employment to finance a later return to village life. Of the 15,000 Olt Land emigrants to the United States, slightly over 2,000 returned (Bărbat 1938:96–97, 278–

80). When U.S. law restricted immigration after World War I, emigration to Ţara Românesca and to nearby Saxon villages grew precipitously. Young people emigrated from all Olt Land villages; only the wealthiest households retained all their members. Nearly all migrants to Saxon villages were unmarried men. So many of them emigrated that, according to Drăguş informants, in summer it was hard to find a young man in the village to help with farmwork.

Emigration had ambiguous effects. The money that migrants sent home and brought with them when they returned intensified competition. The first thing the cash-laden returnees did was to establish themselves on peasant estates, so land prices shot up. They then invested in petty commercial ventures or in one of the many new regional banks and credit associations, and thus also spurred economic differentiation. Still, even as emigration provoked competition, it limited unrest by removing frustrated young people before they could challenge the conditions that drove them away, and thus preserved the fictional calm of middle-peasant life and ideology for the villagers who stayed. Not incidentally, it also established a network of Olt Landers in the United States.

Though emigration furthered economic differentiation, it also enculturated young Olt Land migrants to take a positive view of these differences. At work as factory hands in America, as household workers in Bucharest, or as fieldhands in Saxon villages, Olt Landers identified with their employers, were grateful for the opportunities they provided, and thus supported the class system that forced their departure from their own communities. Though they certainly noticed the contrasts between their own lot and the lives of their bourgeois employers, the values of hard work and independence were reinforced as these young men and women saved their money toward the day when they could return to the village and establish themselves as independent householders. Many fieldhands on Saxon farms developed a close patron-client relationship with their employers and returned to the same family year after year. Though Saxons generally held these men in disregard (McArthur 1976), Romanians were of a different mind. Out from the tutelage of their fathers, they were exposed to advanced Saxon agricultural practices and business acumen, and fondly recalled their experiences four and five decades later.

The biographies of many Olt Landers born in the first two decades of the twentieth century especially weave together tales of the poverty of underdevelopment and the optimism of mobility; of working together with others in order to surpass them. The struggle to resolve these contradictions and the ubiquity of these experiences had profound effects on Olt Land life. Work outside the village was never its own reward but only a means to an end—a return to the village and respected middle peasantry.

Simion and Eufrosina Teulea were two such emigrants. Simion's father was a poor boy who came to Hîrseni as a *ziler* (day laborer) for the Orthodox priest. A hard worker, he had a good reputation, married a poor young local woman, had three sons, and built a respectable five-hectare estate. It was not large enough to support a family of five in the crisis economy of the 1920s and 1930s, though, so Simion and his brothers left the village in succession for seasonal employment.

Born in 1909, Simion finished fourth grade and worked as an occasional *ziler* in a neighboring village. He left Hîrseni at 15 and spent five years as a seasonal and then a permanent farmhand in the Saxon village of Cristian, near Braşov. When he reached adulthood, Simion wanted to find a wife near home, so he returned to Făgăraş, boarded in town, and worked at a distillery for seven months. He returned to Hîrseni to help his parents with planting, haying, and harvesting and by his labor to stake a claim on the family patrimony. As was customary, after serving a short stint in the military in 1931, he returned to Hîrseni to marry.

Eufrosina, the eldest of seven children of a poor household, married Simion when she was 17. As they were too poor to set up on their own, they emigrated to Bucharest and went to work in the home of a Jewish merchant. Eufrosina soon became pregnant and went to stay with her in-laws. After the birth of their child, a girl, Eufrosina returned to Bucharest but left the baby with Simion's parents—that is, in the household where they sent money and which they stood to inherit.

In Bucharest a co-worker's cousin got Simion a job at a radio station, and he worked there for six years, until World War II broke out and he was drafted into the army. Eufrosina returned to the village to care for her child and ailing in-laws. After the war Simion worked at the radio station for a time but soon left to return to the village for good. With their savings from twenty years of itinerant labor and their small inheritance, Simion and Eufrosina managed to accumulate an estate of slightly more than six hectares, which they farmed until the local collective farm was established in 1962.

Social Life in the Olt Land Village

Emerging corporate community structures and social relations both reflected and moderated the deepening crisis in Olt Land villages, and the contradictory pulls of competition and cooperation were most striking in the peasant household. Household relations between men and women were particularly affected by one hundred years of encroaching capitalism. Olt Landers had a clear ideological preference for male inheritance, and a household's prestige depended largely on the qualities of its male head. Socioeconomic reality, however, deemphasized patriarchy and the traditional sex roles. Women influenced far more than domestic life. The legalization of partible inheritance gave them a separate resource base. The emigration of men encouraged uxorilocality and female village endogamy, and made women indispensable for creating and maintaining links among households.[8] Women who emigrated also contributed significantly to their households' economic success. Despite ideology, most household economic decisions were made jointly by the household head and his wife, and with the exception of plowing (for which women were thought to be too weak), nearly all labor was shared by men and women equitably.

Relations were less peaceable between brothers and sisters and between men and women of different generations (see Beck 1979:212–14). Though siblings were potential allies in labor and village affairs, they competed for the basic resources needed by an independent household. The shortage of land, partible inheritance, the large size of pre–World War I families, and the deteriorating interwar economy all promoted conflict between siblings in the presocialist community. The land question also confounded intergenerational relations. As a new household could be formed only by a couple with sufficient land, a shortage of land forestalled marriage. Many men were hostages to their fathers until their late twenties or early thirties. Tension, rivalry, and increasing emigration varied directly with household size. And though Olt Landers supported male primogeniture as the ideal, ultimogeniture was usually adopted in practice.

8. According to Cornel Irimie (1948:204), of 3,386 Olt Land village women who entered into exogamous marriages between 1901 and 1945, only 1,344 (40%) left their own villages for their husband's.

Community Social Networks in the Presocialist Years

Before the socialist era, individuals and households in the Olt Land village were linked in one way or another to virtually every other village household. Links forged by kinship, ritual kinship, neighborhood, age, and other principles provided access to resources, labor, mates, and emotional support. Though network relations were mainly between equals, however, they were also cross-cut by hierarchy, and by their operation deepened economic differences even as they provided a patina of social solidarity.

Kinship, reckoned bilaterally, proceeded out from one's *gospodărie* (household) to increasingly distant relatives. Beyond *gospodărie* came the *familiă* (family), comprising one's *gospodărie* and those of married siblings. Separate families formed the *rudă* (bilateral kindred), which included all relatives within memory and was bifurcated into blood relatives (*rudă de sînge*) and affines (*rudă prin alianţă*). Finally, separate *rude* formed *neamuri*, a category that ultimately included all Romanians (*neam romănesc*) and in Olt Land villages was conceptually opposed to all other nationalities (*alte neamuri*).

Given the diversity of kin that composed them, *rude* repeatedly brought together individuals of different economic levels at village social events. Christmas caroling, visiting, reciprocal labor groups, and rites of passage all indiscriminately activated kin ties. No one was distinguished by any sort of honorific title. Still, even in this ideologically egalitarian sphere, wealth received its due. Carolers made it their business to sing at the home of their prominent uncle but were less conscientious with other kin. The rich more often called on their less successful kin for labor assistance (though they also contributed their own). Their voices spoke more loudly in the village. And since marriages were generally made between households of similar economic rank, *rude* of the wealthy were more densely populated by people like themselves.

Like kinship, godparenthood (*naşie*) conflated relations of solidarity and difference. *Naşie*, which had much in common with Serbian and Bulgarian *kumstvo* (Hammel 1968) and *nasz-koma* relations in Hungary (Fel & Hofer 1969:161–67), was an interhousehold relationship inherited over generations; the child of one's *naş* (godparent/ritual sponsor) became the *naş* of one's child. As sponsor at baptisms and weddings, *naşi* had certain expenses and responsibilities for *fini* (godchildren), and they expected labor, support, and other favors in return. Usually households selected coreligionists as *naşi*, but rarely close family members such as siblings or first cousins. The *naş* selected for a wedding depended on whether the couple's residence was viri- or uxorilocal. If it was virilocal, the groom's *naş de botez* (baptismal *naş*) continued as *naş de cununie* (wedding *naş*); if uxorilocal, the bride's. Because *naşie* established relations between households and was related to household honor and prestige, it was shameful to change the household's *naş*.

Because of the prestige involved, all households wanted to serve as *naşi*, but the financial obligations entailed were so heavy that many households could not afford to do so, and a few of the wealthy had many godchildren. Thus *naşie* transferred resources from the wealthy to the less affluent but related the sponsors to the sponsored as patrons to clients. The two wealthiest landowners in Hîrseni sponsored seven and five families each, all of whom served as ready labor during intense agricultural activity. Sam Beck (1979:283–84) also indicates that merchants used *naş* status after World War I to improve their market positions. *Fini*, though, were dependents of their *naşi* and approached them first in times of economic need. The labor that *fini* provided *naşi* was expected, but the grain they borrowed was paid back with interest.

Villagers were also enmeshed in other quasi-kin relations. The parents of a child's spouse were *cuscrii*. People of the same age, year in school, or military cohort were *leaţi*. And many young men between military service and marriage took part in the *ceată feciorilor* (young men's group), with its important social and ritual functions. At Christmas the *ceataşi* sang carols at village houses, received food, drink, and firewood to support their residence with a village host, maintained order at Christmas dances,[9] and visited *şezitoare* (women's work bees) to dance with eligible women. As marriage was mandatory for the *vătăfi mare* (the ceată leader) and common for other *ceataşi* the year after their participation, households that included marriageable daughters had a definite interest in feeding and funding the *ceataşi*. All men of appropriate age were eligible for the *ceată*, and the relations celebrated in the group continued throughout a man's life. Thus

9. In some villages the *ceată* was responsible for discipline among young men through the entire year (Herseni 1977).

the bonds of *ceată* cross-cut kinship and class and solidified community organization by giving people a stake in tradition.

Other community relationships also united economically diverse villagers. Though village neighborhoods were economically heterogeneous, neighbors helped each other extensively with barn raising, house repairs, threshing parties, and the like. In Drăguş, where Saxon influence was strong, neighborhoods were formally organized. These *vecinătăţile* functioned as burial and mutual aid societies, alternated in providing village watchmen, and purchased rights to collect animal manure on village streets (Stahl 1936:23–26). Olt Land neighborhoods were also the base of winter work bees, at which women spun, wove, knitted, sang, danced with the *ceataşi*, and told off-color jokes. Finally, solidarity was engendered and economic competition defused by communal government. Village leaders, selected from the ranks of household heads considered *oameni buni şi bătrîni* (good and old men), included an elected *primar* and *vice-primar* (mayor, vice mayor), an appointed *notar* (secretary), and a cashier responsible for periodic delivery of taxes to a state agent responsible for a *plasă* (network of communities). Elected village councils of up to twelve household heads regulated the crop-rotation system, hired herdsmen, veterinary agents, and barkeeps, and served as local justices. Though all household heads were eligible for the council, usually only middle and wealthy peasants took part. Mayors, too, were almost exclusively upper-middle peasants and in mixed Orthodox-Uniate villages were often selected from the two groups alternately.

Solidarity and Struggle in Olt Land Labor

The social relationships that masked the Olt Land crisis were especially activated and maintained by ongoing production activities. Labor was the raison d'être of the presocialist region, a symbol of individual and regional identity, and the chief topic of public and private discourse. Individuals and households were judged by the quality of their labor, and the ultimate proof of a social relationship was reciprocated work. And work they did. Agriculture demanded constant effort from early March to late November. After manuring and cultivating their many parcels, Olt Landers planted and weeded them three times before harvest. Wheat, rye, and oats were seeded broadcast, but each corn kernel was planted by dibble and hand with a dollop of manure tamped on top. Hay was cut twice a year, occasionally three times, and people worked steadily from dawn into the night to get it in before dew could spoil it.

The region's undercapitalized economy, demography, and land tenure all contributed to labor intensiveness. Hired labor was lacking as the landless were few, surplus labor had emigrated, smallholders had to satisfy subsistence before cash needs, and it was vaguely improper for middle peasants to hire others. Most households that farmed two to ten hectares provided nearly all their own labor, though grain was harvested and threshed with the help of reciprocating neighbors and relatives. Circumstances of the wealthy and the land-poor, however, differed. In Drăguş (Bărbat 1941:54) and Hîrseni all households with more than ten hectares of land hired some labor during the year, usually to help with haying and harvest, but much of this work was supplied by dependent relatives and *fini*. This arrangement was not considered exploitive. One *fin* of a wealthy Hîrseni landowner said that he gladly helped out once or twice a season. Still, two days of labor multiplied by seven households clearly imply the *naş*'s economic advantage. Meanwhile, poor peasants fell further behind. Though their labor was sufficient for their own holdings, one in three had no traction animals and had to borrow them in exchange for labor.

Paradoxically, though labor was mainly a household activity, it was also collective and helped to unify the villagers. Because of crop rotation and the planting of whole fields in the same cultigens, which needed similar treatment at the same time, though members of each household worked mainly on their own parcels, they were still working collectively. Other collective work groups were also common. Reciprocal labor for church and priest, barn raising, house building, fence construction, and mending of village property were notable for their good humor, egalitarian task organization, and copious food and drink. These events provided sociability along with labor, and people looked forward to them.

Religion, Region, and Labor
in Ideology and Identity

Household primacy, contradictions of unity and competition, and the sanctity of labor were also reflected in the villagers' ideology. The church calendar abetted community production by coordinating agricultural and liturgical cycles and offering rituals to bless lands and crops. Corn was blessed after planting, after tasseling, and before harvest. After an Orthodox household's harvest, its young people harvested for the priest and took part in the *Dealu Mohului* ritual, with its *cunună* or *buzdugan* (cornstalk cross) fetish (Ionica 1943). Still, religion was oriented mainly to the here and now; most people, men especially, were skeptical about an afterlife (Cotaru 1938:329). Respect for the clergy, too, depended on their good works and was not automatic, except in fundamentalist sects such as Oastea Domnului (the Army of the Lord).

The household was also ritually celebrated throughout the liturgical year. Both Orthodox and Uniate services had audible prayers for household members, and on *Bobotează* (Epiphany) and *Ziua Sfântu Cruce* (Day of the Holy Cross, September 14) a priest offered mass at each household to sanctify it and ensure its bounty. Economic differentiation was both supported and ameliorated by the leading role played by the rich on church councils and in church proxemics. People stood at services in both Orthodox and Uniate churches, men in front, women at the rear. Some men, however, occupied individual *strane* (pews) along the walls, "purchased" at auction and inherited in the household. *Strane* closer to the altar were more prestigious and usually were "owned" by the wealthy, supernaturally justifying their dominance.

Labor was the major source of regional identity and the prime criterion of respect. Older informants universally described themselves as *harnic și vrednic* (hardworking and industrious), qualities they felt set them apart from other Transylvanian ethnic groups and other Romanians. Labor concerns even extended to forms of greeting. As people worked, others greeted them with *"Mai puteți?"* (Can you do more?) and they invariably answered, *"Mai pot, mai pot!"* (I certainly can!). Similarly, all households, regardless of wealth, were respected so long as their members worked hard, cared for their land and resources, and were honest and forthright in economic and social relations. Such people were considered *cumsecade* (proper) and *ai noștri* (our kind).

Though identity was achieved by such universal qualities, wealth increased one's prestige, which was validated by display and participation in village activities. Though the rich worked on their estates, they hired others to work with or replace them in difficult tasks. They

[47]

participated in the same social events as others, and often organized them as well. People who enjoyed prestige were said to be *oameni văzuţi* (seen people), in testimony to the display basis of prestige (see Verdery 1975).

Regionalism was also a critical marker of Olt Land identity. By the early twentieth century Olt Landers were highly conscious of the Romanian nobility of their past, the civilizing influence of Habsburg rule, the uniqueness of the border regiments and Uniatism, and their emigrant experiences. These images clearly demarcated Olt Land Romanians from Transylvanian Hungarians, Germans, Gypsies, and Jews, and even from other Romanians. Regional media especially expressed this identity. One of the more popular journals was the weekly *Ţara Oltului* (Olt Land). First published in 1907, it went bankrupt just before World War I, resumed publication after the war, and continued through 1942. Before World War I it was a bulwark of economic conservatism and regional chauvinism. A regular column called "Binele Nostru" (Our blessings) described Olt Landers as the most advanced of all Romanians, with great agrarian capabilities. Editorials also favored Olt Land autonomy. A spring 1907 issue blamed the just-concluded Romanian peasant rebellion on "Jewish immigrants, without hearts and without God," spoke out against peasant rebellions in general, and called the leaders of the peasant rebellion of 1784–1785 "liars, rebels, and bad men" (Şerban 1907:1).[10] After World War I *Ţara Oltului* was allied with the National Liberal Party, retained its fierce regionalism (to which it added Romanian nationalism), and declared its purpose to be "to maintain the integrity of our historic Făgăraş County, the cradle of Romanianism and the birthplace of Radu Negru" (Popa 1922:1).[11] The interwar paper had nothing good to say about Saxons and Magyars, whom the editors considered a potential fifth column in Romanian Transylvania.

Common regional and village identities were also forged by linguistic means. The Olt Landers' dialect differed slightly from standard Romanian. Communities conceptualized themselves as within a *vatră satului* (village hearth or boundary), and also used this concept for the

10. In an interesting contrast, this rebellion was held up as a symbol of liberation in socialist Romania, and particular characterizations of it were used to justify a variety of political orientations (Simmonds-Duke 1987, Verdery 1991).

11. Radu Negru, a figure of the late thirteenth century, is said to have been the first person to occupy the Făgăraş Cetate (Fortress), the seat of Olt Land feudalism and later home to the Muntenian dukes. Today the best secondary school in Făgăraş is named in his honor.

entire region, *vatră Oltului*.[12] People used scatological nicknames and jingles to embellish the distinctiveness of regional communities: "Hîrță, pîrță în Toderița / Cară lemnele cu mîță" (Look at the farts from Toderița / Hauling wood with pussycats); "Cîrliuțe din Hîrseni / Face focul cu coceni / Și manînca bîruieni" (Hîrseni curlyheads / Make fires from corn cobs / And eat weeds). Each community household, too, had its nickname, which was passed on through the generations. Nicknames were necessary because there were only a few family names in each village and many people had the same name. Often based on physical characteristics of ancestors (Șchiopoiu, the limper) or a genealogical shorthand (Nica lui Sivu, John son of Joe), nicknames thus provided a common sense of history and belonging in the changing community.

Finally, Olt Lander political orientations also reflected middlepeasant predominance. After feudalism, involvement in local politics was extensive, and people willingly served on village councils and the like. Even after unification with Romania, however, participation in national politics was minimal and people were generally suspicious of national politicians. Of the three major parties in interwar Romania, only the Liberals, the party of the urban bourgeoisie, and the National Party of Transylvania (unified with the Peasant Party of the Old Kingdom) were active in Olt Land villages. The Conservative Party, which supported Romania's large landowners, was next to nonexistent in the region. Religion figured in political affiliation: most of the Orthodox were Liberals; Uniates traditionally joined the Peasant Party. Still, national politics figured little in daily life. State laws were considered legitimate, but people thought they should be left alone to run their own affairs (cf. Cotaru 1938).

Despite widespread indifference, the interwar economic crisis created an audience for rightist radicalism in the region, though socialdemocratic or communist ideals were anathema to the nationalist, upwardly mobile Olt Land yeomanry. Depression, pressure on peasants' livelihood, the expansion of commerce and its role in social differentiation, the visibility of Jewish business interests, and the exhortation of village priests all contributed to the increased popularity of the Iron Guard and its fascist ideology.[13] Though most members of Olt Land Iron Guard *cuiburi* (nests) were middle peasants, the

12. *Vatră* is still a unifying concept for the ultranationalistic cultural group Vatra Românească (Romanian Hearth), founded in Transylvania in 1990.
13. The Guard leader, Horea Simă, was a native Olt Lander from a village east of Făgăraș.

wealthy played a large role in them. In Hîrseni the Guard was led by a prominent teacher, two priests, and some moderately successful merchants. The envy or anger that struggling middle peasants felt toward their economic and social betters was thus somewhat neutralized when they donned the green shirt of the Iron Guard.

Despite conflicting pressures, then, Olt Landers achieved a measure of stability through a wide range of cultural, social, and economic practices that enabled them to keep a tenuous hold on their middle-peasant lives in the years before World War II. To many Olt Landers with cultural memories of feudalism, the struggle for Romanian unification, and war, this time was as good as they had ever had. Pre-socialist Olt Land communities were not idyllic Gemeinschaften, however. "Little community" social relations were extensively cross-cut by emerging class differences, and even in face-to-face interaction and reciprocal labor the bonds of real and fictive kinship and of neighborhood were changing.

Still, Olt Landers had their history to comfort them. From it they developed an appreciation of change, a positive view of development, and even a grudging acceptance of economic differences. These compromises, though, were short-lived, for Olt Land's history, culture, and political economy were soon to be confronted by a socialist system bent on transforming them utterly. And though the socialists achieved a semblance of transformation, doing so required them to widen the fault lines that already cut through the region's society. The costs of this process were tremendous, and nowhere more so than in the public and social lives of Olt Land villagers.

[3]

Romanian Socialism as a
Social and Cultural System

> In the Socialist Republic of Romania the exploitation of man by
> man has been ended for all time. . . . The creation and evolution
> of socialist control over the means of production forms the base
> for social relations of a new type, of mutual assistance and collab-
> oration among all working people . . . united in the process of
> labor, in the work of creating socialism and communism in our
> fatherland.
>
> Preamble, *Labor Code, Socialist Republic of Romania*

> Hence, just as the profit motive leads to the production of waste,
> so plan fetishism too dissociates what is produced from what is
> needed.
>
> Michael Burawoy, *The Politics of Production*

If we are fully to understand the diverse responses of Olt Land
villagers to the state socialist system imposed on them after World War
II, we first have to grasp the essential principles on which state socialism was based and the actual behavior those first principles imply.
Social-scientific examinations of socialist systems have taken diverse
forms and emphasized diverse principles. Such approaches have exposed the class structure of socialist states (Djilas 1955), the role of the
intelligentsia among the socialist elite (Konrád & Szelényi 1979), the
importance of the division of labor in maintaining socialist hierarchy
(Bahro 1978), the nature of socialist bureaucracy (Hirszowicz 1980), its
economic laws (Campeanu 1988; Fehér, Heller, & Márkus 1983), and
socialism as an ideological system (Verdery 1991). Linking these diverse approaches is the recognition, actual or implied, that the organizational principles of particular socialist states, what Rudolf Bahro

(1978) termed "actually existing socialism," bore little resemblance either to the egalitarian utopia of Marxist ideology or, in fact, to each other. They diverged because of historical and international forces at work when socialists captured power, the actual socioeconomic conditions that confronted socialist leaders, the realpolitik that shaped decision making in socialist states, and the constant experimentation with diverse economic, political, and cultural reforms to which socialist leaders were prone in their attempts to perfect the administration of their particular brand of socialist society.

Despite the well-known variations in communist systems and their perpetual socioeconomic experimentation, analysts tend to focus on the state's persistent accumulation of resources and production and its centralized political control as the key principles of the Eastern European socialist state. Each socialist state applied these principles in its own circumstances and in its own way. Even socialist experimentation can be seen as mere window dressing to cover these fundamentals, as Michael Shafir (1985) demonstrates with his concept of "simulated change" in Romania. Thus we must understand the principles and logic of centralized accumulation and its implications for labor if we are to hope to understand what happened to the Olt Land villagers.

The Historic Context of Centralized Accumulation in Romania

Eastern European socialist states varied widely in the degree to which politics, production, and accumulation of resources were centralized. Romania's penchant for centralization must therefore be sought within its particular history, the actual experience of the early socialist state, and the specific features of Romanian society that socialism sought to transform. In this context we see that emphasis on accumulation—that is, the placing of the state's needs above the population's—in fact predates socialism and is a consistent theme throughout Romanian history (Benedict 1953; Jowitt, ed., 1978; Roberts 1951). National political independence and related autarkic economic development were goals of Romanian leaders of all political persuasions well before the 1877 War of Independence. They represented a response to the domination of Romanians by a succession of nations and empires and were the nationalist basis of state power throughout Romania's history. In subscribing to these ideals, Romania's post–World War II leaders stayed well within their national traditions.

The passion for independence was briefly suppressed after World War II, when the Romanian Communist Party was dominated by a faction of Stalinist loyalists, the so-called Muscovites—Ana Pauker, Vasile Lucă, and Teohari Georgescu. It was resurrected with a fury, however, from 1956 to the 1989 revolution under the leadership of Gheorghe Gheorghiu-Dej and Nicolae Ceauşescu. Even Romania's relations with other socialist states and with the Warsaw Pact and the Council for Mutual Economic Assistance (CMEA or COMECON) were shaped by the overwhelming concern for national independence. Though Romania remained a signatory to the Warsaw Pact, it never provided troops and participated only at the general staff level. Romania also had a running battle with COMECON over its attempt to restrict Romanian industry and consign the country to the role of agricultural producer for the Soviet bloc (see Constantinescu 1973). World War II and its aftermath also fomented state accumulation. At war's end every Romanian economic sector was distressed. Agricultural production was half its 1934–1938 level and industry operated at about 75 percent of prewar levels. The petroleum, chemical, metallurgical, and food industries were especially hard hit (Roberts 1951:314–17). The new socialist state was thus faced with a massive rebuilding effort. Furthermore, accumulation was also demanded by the Cold War, state military production to consolidate Communist power, and reparations owed the USSR.[1]

Nicolae Ceauşescu was thus only the latest in a long line of proponents of the nationalist, independent accumulative state, though he carried this proclivity to extremes with his attempts to create a *societate multilateral dezvoltat* (a multilaterally developed society). In a 1965 speech at the Ninth Party Congress, Ceauşescu defined multilateral development as sustained industrialization, intensive agricultural productivity achieved by rationalized production, expanded international trade with emphasis on the export of manufactured goods, self-sufficiency in key raw materials, mass technical education, comprehensive centralized planning and management, and greater popular response to party mobilization campaigns (Gilberg 1975:15–

---

1. Romania, allied with Germany during most of the war, had by June 1948 paid an estimated $1.8 billion in reparations to the USSR (Montias 1967:20). See Sampson & Kideckel 1989 on Cold War influences on anthropological research in and about Romania.

27). Multilaterally developed Romania was thus simply a mobilization state bent on capturing resources to improve the party's control and the state's international economic position.

Though there were respites from accumulation, they were brief. From Ceaușescu's ascent in 1965 until the late 1970s, Romania borrowed Western capital to achieve a high rate of growth and to increase consumption. Mounting debt, world recession, and failure to capture Western markets, however, revived concern about dependence and promoted accumulation for export to repay the debt. By rationing food, energy, medicine, and housing and by placing increased demands for labor on all segments of society, Romania was able to pay its $11 billion debt by late 1989, but this severe austerity turned out to be the prelude to revolution.

Accumulation and political centralization vary directly, and Romanian centralization was the most thorough in all Eastern Europe with the possible exception of Albania (Anderson 1983, Shafir 1985:126). Centralization was intensified in Romania by two factors. First, as Romania's socialist revolution had succeeded mainly by the force of Soviet military power, emulation of the Stalinist model was a foregone conclusion (Jowitt 1971:175–76). Second, the exclusivity of the Romanian Communist Party (RCP) was fueled by its lack of a popular following. Before the war, in fact, communism was a dwarf movement in Romania, rejected by people across the social spectrum. Popular anti-Sovietism and the party's largely Magyar and Jewish membership especially limited its attractiveness, and on taking power in 1945 the party had fewer than 2,000 members (King 1980).

Centralization varied over time. Factionalism in the party leadership limited it in the 1950s, but after purging the Muscovites, and with the ascendancy of Gheorghiu-Dej and then Ceaușescu, the party achieved a great deal of cohesion (Shafir 1985:66–68). Like accumulation, centralization achieved its highest expression under Ceaușescu. State decision making came to be concentrated in fewer and fewer hands in the course of his twenty-five-year rule. Ceaușescu merged the offices of head of party and head of state in December 1967, had himself named president for life in 1974, and thereafter built up a personality cult to rival Stalin's and vested extensive control of state and party in the Ceaușescu/Petrescu clan (de Flers 1984, Fischer 1989).

The Romanian economy was also subjected to centralized political control. In the "mini–cultural revolution" of the late 1960s and early

1970s, large numbers of technocrats were absorbed into the party (and thus subjected to its discipline) and loyal cadres were trained in "scientific management" at party schools and given control of economic enterprises. Centralization was further maintained by *rotaţiă cadrelor* (cadre rotation), which regularly shifted cadres from the state to the party to the economic sectors and back again. Ostensibly designed to "perfect society," this policy effectively prevented the development of separate power centers that might challenge the Ceauşescus.

The chief prop of both accumulation and centralization was central planning. Historically, this was the most comprehensive and centralized system in Eastern Europe. The state oversaw nearly every aspect of society, from university enrollment and books published to the production of steel, tractors, and apartments. Planning became increasingly comprehensive and centralized over time.

> With the 1966–70 plan . . . continuous planning was introduced, which . . . contained sections for each year, sector, ministry, region, and enterprise. The number of targets was increased . . . and at each level of economic activity, responsibility for performance rests at the next higher level and ultimate plan approval rests with the Political Executive Committee of the RCP. [Tsantis & Pepper 1979:35, 45–47]

The plan was so broad that it required all labor institutions and producers to be encapsulated under rigid state control. Such all-encompassing control, however, was impossible from the outset, and as we shall see, the economic and social significance of the state's failure to reach this goal was only magnified by the measure of success the state did achieve in regulating Romanian society.

Property and Production in Socialist Romania

Despite its intent, centralized planning failed to eradicate the state's dependence on local producers. In a curious paradox, centrally planned societies came to depend in extremis on the production decisions and activities of individuals at the local level (Rév 1987), and suffered from a lack of knowledge about and an inability to control local activities and results (Ellman 1979:66–73). Since each level of the plan depended on the results and experience of the preceding level— regional production on local collectives, collective farms on house-

[55]

holds—it was in the interest of the state and its agents to ensure cooperation or at least passivity throughout society. This was the social contract in Eastern Europe (Sampson 1986a), and people there were as fond as the Soviets of saying that "they pretend to pay us and we pretend to work."[2]

Given its overly centralized political apparatus and unwavering accumulative goals, socialist Romania was caught between state control of property and labor and dependence on the capacities and practices of local producers. Property relations, stipulated by law, were heavily weighted in favor of the state's needs and the interests of the ruling group. Because of the state's ultimate dependence on individuals, however, it also had to give minimal support to the interests of its managerial elites and the local labor forces. This was where Ceauşescu failed. The hell-bent-for-leather debt repayment and labor mobilization in the decade before the 1989 revolution skewed these relationships too far in favor of the central apparatus. Even before that nightmare decade, however, socialist Romania was not notably disposed to consider the needs of its work force. The Nationalization Law of June 1948 placed all finance and industry and most commerce and agriculture under state control and thoroughly encumbered the few resources that remained private, mainly in the commercial and agricultural sectors. It was thus in the legal definition of property and its related division of labor that the seeds of socialist Romania's destruction were sown.

Forms of Property in Agriculture

Concerns for independence and autarkic development strategies had especially large implications for agriculture and the peasantry in socialist Romania. Lacking industry, the state had to get capital for development initially by nationalizing and collectivizing agricultural property and channeling private agricultural production into its own hands. As in other socialist states, agriculture was organized into state farms and animal complexes, here termed *întreprindere agricole de stat* (state agricultural enterprises, or IAS), and collective farms, initially called *gospodărie agricole colective* (collective agricultural es-

---

2. In Romania this saying is rendered as "Ei se fac că ne plătesc, noi ne facem că muncim."

tates, or GAC) but later renamed *cooperative agricolă de producţia* (agricultural production cooperatives, or CAP). Once collectivization was completed, in the early 1960s, the proportion of land in each sector remained stable: approximately 30 percent in state farms, 60 percent in collectives, and 10 percent in private hands, mainly in upland zones (Direcţia Centrală de Statistică 1973:214, 1983:116).

The IAS was a state institution and hence a more socialist form of property. All of its workers were state employees and were paid wages; some also received a small garden plot of a few hundredths of a hectare for their own needs. An IAS was organized much like a rural factory and, like the factory, provided services for workers, from children's nurseries to shopping centers. Because IASes produced specifically for state accumulation and export, they received four times the investment allotted to the CAPs and had access to the best available technology. Most IASes had fairly narrow production profiles, specializing in one or another agricultural product.

The CAPs, in contrast, were ostensibly owned and controlled by their members, who pooled their land and resources. Since ownership was theoretically outside state control, the struggle between accumulation and redistribution was more ambiguous on the CAPs than on the IASes. CAPs produced a wider variety of resources, and they were used both for members' subsistence and for state accumulation. CAPs depended more on members' physical labor than on state investment. CAPs' mechanized technology was controlled by state-owned machine tractor stations (MTSes), for whose services the CAPs paid in advance, and their production was determined by regional agroindustrial councils on which MTS directors, employees of the Ministry of Agriculture, played decisive roles. CAP members were not so well paid as state farm workers, and their pay was determined by total farm production as well as by the quality and quantity of their own labor. Though a CAP was ostensibly owned by its members, the state controlled its production by legally prescribing its use, in rank order, to (1) fulfill mandatory state contracts and pay for MTS labor; (2) set up seed and fodder reserves; (3) set up reserve funds for difficult years; (4) provide assistance to orphans, the elderly, and the sick; (5) sell on national "free" markets; and (6) pay the balance to members. A CAP's cash income had to be used to (1) pay state taxes, insurance, and debts; (2) repair machines; (3) fund administration; (4) defray sociocultural expenses; (5) purchase needed items; and (6) remunerate members (Ministry of Justice 1956:65–66).

One benefit of CAP membership was access to a household "use plot" of the collective's land.[3] These plots provided up to three-fourths of rural subsistence needs and were major sources of animal fodder, potatoes, vegetables, and fruits (Brezinski & Petrescu 1986). Sale of the plots' surplus production was also an important source of cash income for the collectivized peasants. Access to a plot's yield was especially critical in the economic crisis of the 1980s. It enabled the peasants to maintain at least a minimal standard of nutrition while urban workers, especially those without strong ties to a rural community, truly struggled. Because access to these plots was so crucial for the peasants, state officials often used it as a bargaining chip to manipulate and mobilize peasants' labor and to ensure their compliance with state policies.

Though private agriculture existed in socialist Romania, it too was legally encumbered. Most private land was in mountain zones where topography and dispersed settlement limited economies of scale and the feasibility of collectivization (Beck 1976, 1987; Randall 1976). Less significant was subsistence gardening in villages and on small urban plots, which was restricted by high tax rates and by laws limiting the ownership of such plots. In zones where available land was scarce, as in the Olt Land, an area equal to a household's private garden plot was subtracted from its use plot unless its members paid the collective with additional production. Private animal husbandry also played a significant role in state accumulation. Collectivized households were allowed a few cattle, sheep, and pigs and unlimited numbers of fowl for their own use. Ownership of horses was first severely restricted and then encouraged in the 1980s, when gasoline prices rose. Households were constantly pressured to contract to sell animal products to the state. Though the state paid independent producers less than they could get on the free market, private sales were heavily taxed and contracting households were allowed to buy feed at a reduced price. The state intensified its demands in 1984 with enactment of the *Program Unic* (Unified Program), which made some animal contracts compulsory, and in some regions denied ration cards to noncontracting households. Some private shepherds became fabulously wealthy. Their mobility and mountain residence enabled them to evade many

---

3. Members' use plots have often been referred to as "private plots," but they were hardly private property; their use was controlled by the state and subject to a variety of regulations and encumbrances.

state demands and their wealth gave them leverage in their dealings with officialdom.

Forms of Property in Industry and Trades

As befitted a classic command economy, Romanian industry was highly centralized and oriented to state needs (Spigler 1973). In the late 1970s each of the 200 or so industrial and mining centrals employed about 8,000 workers; two had 100,000 each (Granick 1975:37, Jackson 1983:493). The party exerted great control over industrial managers, as it either trained them at party institutes or subsumed their enterprises in party umbrella organizations. The agroindustrial councils, developed in the late 1970s, integrated a region's economic enterprises in a single cadre-controlled organization that coordinated the production schedules, planned output, and labor of its constituent institutions, thus circumscribing managerial decision making. The Romanian plan consistently overemphasized production of capital goods, which typically received the majority of investment in each planning period. Transport, agriculture, communications, and forestry combined received only 24 percent of investment in a typical planning period (Jackson 1983:532, Montias 1967:25). Export sectors also received large shares of state investment, had technology superior to that of producers for the national market, were allowed greater profit levels, and paid workers better, though they were also subjected to more rigorous production schedules and quality control.[4]

Aside from export premiums, industrial wages were based mainly on piece rates and on seniority and a performance-based scale, each set for a particular industry. Pay also depended on recommendations by team and section leaders, who controlled the supplementary bonuses paid for achievement of planned production. Thus bonuses were used for political control, as was the retention of 10 percent of a worker's monthly wages, returned only if annual production goals were reached. Industrial pay was further restricted in the late 1970s with passage of the New Economic and Financial Mechanism

4. The extreme emphasis on export gave rise to gallows humor in which the concept of *refuzat la export* (rejected for export) was applied to people as well as products. One joke suggested that only pigs and chickens had the right to passports; another termed pigs' feet hanging in state meat shops "patriots," because that was the only part of the pig that remained at home.

(NEFM), which linked the pay of individual workers to the performance of their work team and factory section, and set limits on energy and raw materials used in production and withheld part of the pay of workers who exceeded them.

Private ownership and control of labor were more widespread in commerce and crafts than in industry and agriculture. This had not always been the case. Private craft production was especially hard hit in the first years of socialism. The number of craftworkers declined from 124,501 in 1955 to 32,923 in 1970 (Brezinski & Petrescu 1986:5). The dearth of goods and services in the state economy, however, prompted more liberal licensing requirements, and gradually the numbers of craftworkers rose. Commercial activity in the villages was organized by *cooperative de consum* (consumer cooperatives), which also operated small-scale local industries and such service enterprises as shoe repair shops, barbershops, and bakeries. Villagers paid a small fee for membership. Though small-scale craft production was carried out privately and often run by single families or households, most craftworkers were formally employed by *cooperative de consum* or *cooperative de meşteşugărească* (handicraft cooperatives). As state employees, craftworkers were subject to state control of their output and practice. Though many craftworkers owned their looms, tools, and machines, raw materials were often available only from state stocks, and access to them was provided first to full-time employees of cooperatives. The need to obtain a license further ensured state control. Still, despite these disincentives, craftwork was viewed positively because of the slightly greater degree of autonomy it implied and the more extensive participation in the second (informal) economy it allowed.

Divisions of Labor in Socialist Romania

State control over property and centralized accumulation of resources and production determined in large measure the division of labor in socialist society and in its production institutions. Three important divisions of labor grew from these practices. As in capitalist societies, the nature and quality of one's work life depended largely on whether one performed mental or manual labor. In addition, socialist development policies reinforced the division of Romanian society and labor along rural/urban and male/female lines. Each of these divisions of labor facilitated the control of the central party leadership and each shaped workers' attitudes toward labor, toward society, and toward their fellows.

To support these divisions of labor and justify its control of property and resources, the socialist state overwhelmingly emphasized labor in its official ideology and sought to make the workplace, whether factory, office, or collective farm, the chief source of social affect in the individual's life. The cult of labor in Romania, as elsewhere in the socialist world (see Bell 1983; Humphrey 1983:7–9, 164–70), elevated production to an end in itself and made work, especially manual labor, the key symbol and central activity of society. (In fact, it was illegal not to work.) These views, promulgated by constant ideological campaigns and media images (Kideckel 1988), were cited as evidence of the state's concern for the working person (Ceauşescu 1983:38–39, Georgescu 1984), though clearly they were intended to justify and maintain workers' productivity and the prevailing socialist division of labor. The shift of social activity from household and community to workplace was also intended to ensure acceptance of the cult of labor and socialist production relations. The emphasis on the workplace as a social institution was reinforced by the control of worker housing, shopping centers, social clubs, and summer camps and health spas by state-dominated labor unions. Not incidentally, by making the workplace the locus of social life, the party enhanced its ability to supervise workers' lives and thoughts.

Mental/Manual Distinctions and the Cult of Knowledge

Despite Romania's formal devotion to *autoconducerea muncitorească* (workplace democracy; see Bazac 1981; Ceterchi 1975, 1979), the organization and control of labor were specifically geared to bolstering the centralized accumulative state. The structures of agricultural, industrial, and commercial organization were thus related to institutions of state power in ways that negated their formal democratic rules and decision-making powers. In deference to workplace democracy, *adunarii generale* (general assemblies) of members or employees were the supreme authority on collective and state farms and in labor unions, consumer cooperatives, factories, and schools. By law they were empowered to debate and approve plans and budgets; elect, supervise, and dismiss management; approve other appointments and dismissals; ensure plan fulfillment; approve contracts; and apportion

[61]

benefits to members. Cooperatives and collective farms were managed by a *consiliu de conducere* (leadership council) and factories, state farms, schools, and the like by a *consiliu oamenilor muncii* (working people's council, or COM). Members were elected by and responsible to the general assembly, and at least 30 percent of COM members were line workers (Ceterchi 1979:121; see also Nelson 1981:238). An executive bureau elected by the council members managed the enterprise on a daily basis.[5] Other institutional procedures also ideally supported workplace democracy. Periodic general assembly meetings had to be called with sufficient lead time to enable members to attend. Agendas were to be publicly posted, and assemblies were open to all members and employees. Presidiums at council and general assembly meetings were elected by members, and time was set aside for members' comments.

Nevertheless, hierarchy was created and maintained in various ways. The constitutional guarantee of the party's leading organizational role enabled its activists to control institutional decisions and divisions of labor (Consiliul de Stat 1975:4). Because many significant decisions were made at the national level, authority in each enterprise necessarily devolved on the executive committees responsible to the highest levels of state and party; and both workers and managers were controlled by central institutions. The National Union of Agricultural Production Cooperatives, for example, which represented collective farmers, was headed by a party secretary, who coordinated and supervised labor in all of a region's farms and industries. Labor unions were even controlled and administered by the Ministry of Labor.[6] Finally, most top managers were trained at such approved institutions as Bucharest's Ştefan Gheorghiu Academy, the party university. Connections to the Ceauşescus or to someone close to them also helped.

The importance of education, training, and knowledge for power and resources produced what might be termed a "cult of knowledge" in socialist Romania. As George Konrád and Ivan Szelényi (1979) suggest, since appropriate knowledge in the socialist state translated directly into position, it was an object of competition in its own right.

---

5. Each type of enterprise was governed by the statutes prevailing in its particular sector. The Labor Code (Consiliul de Stat 1972) summarized general rights and obligations.

6. In what has to be the most egregious instance of the state's domination of labor, between 1977 and 1981 the minister of labor was simultaneously the head of the General Trade Union Confederation.

In Romania, however, power depended as much on informal knowledge as on formal knowledge gained at state and party schools. Extensive centralization randomized the distribution of resources and the availability of desired occupations and objects. In this situation, knowledge of others, of the availability of resources, and of others who knew where resources were available was thus as essential as the formal training that conferred position.

Emphasis on mental as opposed to manual labor and hunger for instrumental and utilitarian knowledge shaped attitudes toward work and class in socialist Romania. Intellectual production of any sort was more highly valued than physical work, even if pay scales formally favored the latter. Denigration of workers and collectivists by intellectuals further separated society into antagonistic social strata (Cole 1985). On one hand, workers were suspicious of the intelligentsia, even those in their own communities and extended families, and of anyone who advocated the most benign reforms. The majority of the intelligentsia, on the other hand, were compromised by state and party, incapable of crafting any meaningful program for political transformation. Out of self-interest they largely supported the prevailing relations of domination (Tudoran 1984).

Rural/Urban Distinctions and the Romanian Peasant Worker

Persisting rural/urban differences also grew from and supported centralized accumulation. On the surface, socialist Romania sought to diminish these differences. First, urban growth was extensive. In 1948 Romania's population was 80 percent rural, but by the mid-1970s it was essentially evenly divided between rural and urban zones (Direcţia Centrală de Statistică 1983:12). The distribution of industry also provided villagers with access to factory work and pay (Hoffman 1972, Ianoş 1981, Turnock 1986:168). Finally, the policy of *sistematizare* (systemization) foresaw the elimination of "irrational" rural settlements (Sampson 1976, 1984, 1989) and improvements to the rural infrastructure.

Despite this surface equality, other data suggest persisting rural/urban differences with significant social and political implications. First, urban growth was illusory (Cole 1981). Through the end of the 1960s migration from villages to cities was so popular that by the

1970s the government officially closed all major cities to immigrants unless they could prove they had a residence and workplace there.[7] The economic crisis of the 1980s intensified rural/urban differences. Lack of food, heat, light, and water in the cities generated resentment of the peasantry, while a return to forced CAP labor in the villages, increased quotas for produce delivery, and lack of processed foods available only in urban areas built resentment of city dwellers among the peasants.

The presence of a large rural industrial work force at odds with their urban counterparts assisted the accumulative state in a variety of ways. Most important, by keeping much of the industrial labor force involved in subsistence agriculture, the state limited demands for urban services and foodstuffs. Second, peasant-workers were tired workers; their interest in politics was restricted by the rigors of commuting and of agricultural, industrial, and household labor (Cole 1981, Halpern & Kerewsky-Halpern 1972, Holmes 1989, Lockwood 1973, Cheetham & Whitaker 1974). Unsteadily integrated into town and village, these peasants were marginalized by both factory and collective farm. Moving between two worlds, they found their social relations fragmented in both.

The Sexual Division of Labor

The sexual division of labor supported centralized accumulation by relegating women to agricultural and reproductive labor. This had not always been the case. In the first years of socialism extensive media campaigns (Kideckel 1988) and the easing of access to divorce and abortion (Nydon 1984) opened all of Romanian society to women. These policies were quickly reversed through the 1960s, however, as rural men flooded industry and women were left mainly in agriculture. By 1973 48.1 percent of able-bodied men worked in industry, construction, or transport and 35 percent in agriculture, whereas 65.7 percent of women were in agriculture and only 16.7 percent in industry (C. Ionescu 1973:101). And though women were the mainstay of CAP labor, they were rarely found among farm leaders, nor were they

7. David Granick (1975) suggests that the need for permission to work in closed cities funneled labor into industries that needed more workers. Furthermore, the large numbers of single men who yearned for city life fostered the development of an active marriage market, and single women with verified urban residence were in great demand.

often leaders in the industries that employed them in large numbers, such as textiles and apparel. Women were not expected to play any role in politics, and in any case their labor in the CAP, in household subsistence activities, and in child rearing—women's "threefold economic role" (Cernea 1978:114)—left little desire, time, or energy for politics.

Among the resources that the state sought to accumulate were children (Cole & Nydon 1990; Nydon 1984; Comitetului Central 1984a, 1984b, 1984c). This pronatalist policy had various sources: official concern about Romania's falling birth rate (itself a function of women's increased economic role); fear of the rapidly increasing Gypsy population; the felt need for a greater Romanian presence in disputed Transylvania; and the Ceauşescus' megalomaniacal desire to make Romania the most populous state in Eastern Europe. Consequently, abortion, except in rare cases, became punishable as a felony. Contraceptive devices were illegal after 1966. Childless couples older than twenty-five paid additional taxes. And women were forced to undergo gynecological examinations at work and were monitored during pregnancy. Other policies also limited women's involvement in working life: maternity benefits were liberal and a family's monthly stipend increased with each child; motherhood was promoted as the feminine ideal; and women were restricted from working in occupations deemed physically hazardous (Nydon 1984).

Still, despite state policies that limited women's political and economic importance, the significance of the informal economy and women's independent wages facilitated a measure of economic independence and ensured them a political voice within the household and community (Cernea 1978:119–20). Precisely because of their disadvantages in the formal economy, women gained significant force in the second economy, which bolstered their informal power in household and community. Because of the rigors of commuting, their household responsibilities, and the continued need for subsistence production, women remained in their local communities and sought employment there. Their roles as producers and clerks in consumer cooperatives and their administrative work with schools and governmental and production institutions gave women access to both consumer resources and knowledge, twin pillars of the informal economy. Their agricultural roles on use plots and in household gardens further increased their influence in household and community. And even the state's pronatalist policies forced village men to consider more fully the needs and circumstances of their wives and daughters, since regulating the number of offspring was a common means used by rural households to improve their economic circumstances.

The Effects of Centralization
on Romanian Labor

Centralization of accumulation, planning, and property and the state's labor policies had large implications for actual work in factories and farms and for the social relations of workers and peasants in their communities. As we have seen, the state was paradoxically overdependent on workers at the local level. The greater the state's control of resources, encumbrance of property, and limitation of economic choice, the greater the meaning of individual acts for the state plan. The more restrictive the state's policies, the greater the political significance of any action or thought (see Rév 1987). Thus as the state became dependent on practice at the local level, formal socialist government and economic institutions were held in thrall to personal decision making, extensive bargaining between individuals at all levels of the economic system, and a widespread informal economy. The rampant economic individualism that centralization created thus furthered the state's domination in the short run but created the conditions to which it ultimately fell prey.

Politicization and Personalization of the Labor Process

Politicization and personalization of decision making radiated from the highest circles of the state down to local factories and farms. In fact, political principles went before all others in the organization and control of labor. Only people with proper credentials and verified political trustworthiness received any advantage from this system, and the most critical decisions were restricted to a few individuals. Within limits imposed by Ceauşescu, these people controlled great power, privilege, and patronage, which they sought to transmit to their families and close associates.

To ensure the social and economic well-being of one's household, one had to establish effective relations with people in a position to help. This was the way to improve one's work assignment, ease restrictions, and get bonuses to boot. In this light, the incredible expansion of membership in the Romanian Communist Party takes on new meaning. By the late 1980s the party had close to 4 million members, about 17 percent of Romania's population. Proportionally it was the largest communist party in East-Central Europe. Michael Shafir (1985:90) suggests that this growth, facilitated by relaxed entry standards, expanded the legitimacy of the Ceauşescu regime and hence permitted a "takeover [of society] from within." Be that as it may, the party's growth resulted from thousands of calculated decisions to seek socioeconomic status through personal connections. The popular joke that PCR (the initials of the Romanian Communist Party) stood for "*Pilă, Cunoştiinţă, şi Relaţii*" (Pull, Connections, and Relations) was really no laughing matter.

Pervasive Bargaining

The pervasive bargaining that personalism promoted encouraged social differentiation, economic opportunism, and the fraying of political unity at the local level. Bargaining is the use of personal relations and informal ties to contravene formal rules and regulations. In Romania it especially concerned the plan and related resources and labor. Plan bargaining was an attempt by "bureaucratic subcenters to block the will of central [accumulators]" by negotiating better enterprise targets and thus better political outcomes for themselves (Szelényi 1988:7). As the plan extended across society, bargaining operated at every level, promoting the divergence of reality from planned priorities. Accumulation targets were generally met at the state level (at least on paper). At the local level, however, bargaining tilted the scales so that some communities gained services while others lost them, some groups escaped change while others did not, and resources capriciously appeared and disappeared. This situation led Steven Sampson to suggest (1984:288) that socialist Romania was "a society with a plan and not a planned society," implying that local groups and individuals had greater potential power than most observers of socialist regimes have recognized.

They manifested that power in their bargaining over resources and labor. Because so many resources were being exported and any production shortfall in one enterprise ramified through countless others, administrators were forced to depend on personal relations to get the resources they needed. They hoarded labor to help "make the plan," to guard against unforeseen demands from the center, and to improve their own political maneuverability and bargaining position. The result was a permanently tight labor market (Burawoy 1985:163, Sabel & Stark 1982:440, Szelényi 1988:7–9) that placed administrators at the mercy of their work force.

Though bargaining over work norms and piece rates brought advantages to some workers (Sabel & Stark 1982:451), it strained relations between workers and supervisors and contributed to a contentious work environment by differentiating segments of the local work force, rewarding some and threatening others:

> The need [for managers] to respond . . . to changing requirements gives great . . . power to the skilled and experienced workers, who over time develop a monopoly of knowledge essential to the . . . enterprise. From the management side . . . extreme uncertainties . . . elicit two strategies. [Managers] can seek to reward cooperation, particularly of the core workers; [or they] can intensify surveillance and control, particularly over the more peripheral workers. [Burawoy 1985:163]

Thus socialist bargaining was not collective in any sense; it was a process of personal negotiation (see Haraszti 1977). Favored workers received bonuses, better work rates, vacation days, medical leaves, and apartments that were denied the politically suspect or those without connections. As a result, bargaining formed dependencies and patron-client relations between supervisors on different levels as well as between workers and supervisors.

The Second Economy

The third factor that fragmented the groups of workers and collective farmers was the extensive second economy, which "encompassed all the activities of the officially accepted private sector, legal or illegal, the kryptoprivate [sic] production [and exchange] of goods within [and between] socialist enterprises and cooperatives, and the illegal economic activities of private households" (Brezinski & Petrescu 1986:1). Though conceptually and practically distinct from the formal socialist system, the second economy was nevertheless a logical part of that system. In fact, as state power became increasingly centralized,

[68]

informal economic relations necessarily expanded. Because the state was unable or unwilling to release resources to the formal economy, people had to turn to informal production and exchange to satisfy their needs. Furthermore, socialist authorities themselves facilitated the second economy by their part in the bargaining process. They provided workers (or looked the other way as workers took for themselves) the time, resources, and facilities to engage in production on the side and thus to maintain a minimally acceptable standard of living. Not incidentally, then, informal economic activity encouraged political quiescence by keeping households and enterprises afloat, by filling the spare time of workers who participated in it, and by providing an illusion of autonomy.

Thus, though informal production and exchange provided a measure of self-validation in the oppressive state political economy, it limited workers' unity and social and political practice. On one hand, it created a curious common interest between workers and administrators. Access to resources at the workplace for a second income outside it ensured workers' commitment to their superiors, who thus received help in their efforts to hoard labor, make the plan, and prosper politically. On the other hand, competition for resources and income pitted workers against one another in a struggle to secure or retain the benefits offered by the dominant. Though workers might momentarily cooperate in some specific informal activity or ruse, the net effect of the second economy was to push them inexorably apart after they had reached their short-term goal.

Centralized Accumulation as a Cultural System

A society needs broad acceptance of common values and meaning if it is to persist over time. In socialist Romania, where personalism, bargaining, and the second economy offered an illusion of economic possibility, Romanian nationalism had to provide ideological justification for the socialist regime. To manufacture internal political support, the regime emphasized the unique qualities and achievements of the Romanian people within a state of their own, deemphasized such socialist images as class struggle and proletarian internationalism, proclaimed the continuity of the socialist state with national historical precursors, and equated service to the state with the preservation of the Romanian nation. As a corollary, though Romania's socialist lead-

[69]

ership regularly referred to the cultural freedoms afforded "coresident nationalities" (officially recognized minority groups), in fact state policy readily fanned the flames of ethnic suspicion and rivalry. This policy not only fed the concern of the Romanian majority for independence but, until the revolution, checked most interethnic cooperation in mounting a challenge to state authority.

The accumulative state consistently evoked certain themes in promulgating its brand of nationalism to the elites and the masses alike. Official historiography emphasized the unique origin and essence of the Romanian people, who were portrayed as distinct in all ways from national minorities. National pronouncements suggested that the party had strengthened the state and won it great international respect. According to the state's ideology, it had bettered the material life of the Romanian people and developed a new Romanian civilization. Though all socialist states used such Promethean claims to justify their dominance (Worsely 1981:105), in Romania these claims were expressed almost exclusively in nationalistic terms.

In view of the revolution, the extent to which this ideology was embraced by either the elites or ordinary citizens is ultimately debatable. Nonetheless, the staying power of Romanian socialism, the support the regime commanded to its very end and beyond, and the widespread nationalism of the postrevolutionary period all point to a widespread societal consensus with it, if not outright enthusiasm for it. Furthermore, the saturation of society with this hypernationalist discourse limited resistance by forcing the equivocation, silence, and marginalization of many who opposed socialism on political and economic grounds (cf. Milosz 1981, Tudoran 1984). It was thus only the extraordinary deterioration in the quality of Romanian life and the Ceauşescus' capricious rule that prompted increased challenges to the state by groups as diverse as multinational aggregates of workers, ever-active miners, and even the party hierarchy (Gabanyi 1987:7–9). Even on the heels of the 1989 revolution, when antisocialist sentiment ran high, a common sentiment heard in city and village alike was that Ceauşescu was right about a lot of things but he just got carried away.

History and the National Essence

Hypernationalist Romania derived its legitimacy in part from an origin myth that emphasized the ethnic purity and originality of Romanians. For millennia the Danubian lands have been home to numerous peoples who mingled, traded with one another, interbred, and occasionally killed one another. Despite this ethnic pastiche, the ideology of socialist Romania emphasized the pure origins of the Romanian people in the interbreeding of autochthonous Dacians and conquering Romans in the first century A.D. (see Cândea 1977:8, Giurescu & Giurescu 1971:80–83). Rome withdrew south of the Danube in A.D. 275 but official Romanian history suggested that the Daco-Roman population remained pure-bred and in continuous occupation of the lands that today constitute Romania. The supposed continuous occupation, of course, justified claims to Transylvania as well as to the uniqueness of the Romanians:

> Left without [Rome's] protection . . . in their contacts with successive waves of barbarian[s], the Dacians maintained their being thanks to forces stronger than arms: their way of life, their capacity for material and spiritual creation, their language, the advantages of a sedentary life, and a superior culture. . . . The migrating populations' inability to nullify or alter the physiognomy, language, and way of life of the inhabitants of Roman Dacia was proved after centuries of invasions. [Cândea 1977:19–20]

Other cultural policies also worked to justify the state's claim to the preservation of the national essence. Ideologues in history and the humanities promulgated the idea of protochronism: the minimal foreign influence on Romania's cultural development, the originality of Romania's culture, its independent development of art forms, music, language, and values before they were known elsewhere (Verdery 1991).[8] The Romanians' ethnology and folklore were also said to express unique themes that distinguished them from neighboring peoples (see Butură 1978:6).

Folklore was considered an especially important means to intensify Romanian national identity. The Institute of Dialectology and Folklore, a branch of the Academy of Social and Political Sciences, was charged to create new folkloric forms and homogenize other elements by eliminating many of its regional specificities. At the instigation of Elena Ceauşescu, a national folklore contest, Cîntarea României (Song of Romania), was organized by the National Council of Cultural and

8. Protochronism was often taken to extreme ends. In the mid-1970s a few Romanian historical linguists even alleged Romanian origins for the Indo-European language family.

Socialist Education, a department of the Ministry of Education. Community and workplace groups competed at local, regional, and national levels (the latter often televised) for modest prizes (plaques, trophies, etc.) and the renown they brought. The forced dances, choral singing, and skits were then proclaimed as the original and creative expression of the people, as implied in the newspeak introduction to the journal *Cîntareă României:*

> The people enable their permanent self-creation by taking control of the historical process and by affirming essential human virtues: work, liberty, creativity. . . . Our nation is . . . the chief work of our living culture, which . . . reestablishes . . . unity among socioeconomic, scientific-technical, and literary-artistic creation, and is today a powerful reflex and stimulus of the deeply humanistic process of social homogenization. [Cernăianu 1983:1]

The Ceaușescuite state also sought to foster a nationalist collectivism in social life. Collectivism, of course, is a cardinal principle of socialism, under which people were expected willingly to place the group's needs over their own and those of their family. In socialist Romania, the group whose needs took priority was the nation, and socialist consciousness was replaced by continued attempts to force national integration. Collectivism was sought chiefly in the labor process, but it was also fostered by practices that ran the gamut from control of architectural styles to homogenization of school curricula and the prescription of uniforms for schoolchildren. Corporate organization of social life was especially important for collectivism (Chirot 1978). Thus the Pioneer groups common in the socialist nations were expanded in Romania to the preschool Șoimii Patriei (Eagles of the Fatherland), and any group not sanctioned by the state was forcibly disestablished. This policy occasionally took on comic-opera proportions, as when Elena Ceaușescu personally undertook to rid Romania of flourishing contract bridge clubs and Transcendental Meditation groups.

Maintaining National Strength and Independence

To support its claims of national autonomy and international respect, Ceaușescu's Romania emphasized a Third World identity and forged extensive commercial and diplomatic ties with the developing world. As *o societate in curs de dezvoltare* (a society on the path of development), Romania joined the largely Third World Group of Seventy-seven, and Romania's leaders regularly excoriated the International Monetary Fund, imperialists, and avaricious capitalists for economic problems in their country and throughout the Third World. Even the debt crisis of the 1980s was used to sharpen Romania's Third World identity: rapid amortization of the national debt and its related human suffering were said to be necessary to maintain the nation's independence and avert control by the imperialists.

Romania's identity as a maverick socialist state that refused to follow Soviet dictates embellished this ideology. Though this idea has been challenged as a ploy to gain access to Western economic credits and technology (Pacepa 1987, Socor 1976), a good body of evidence supports it: Romania's maintenance of diplomatic relations with Israel in the wake of the Six Day War in 1967, Ceauşescu's denunciation of the invasion of Czechoslovakia by the Warsaw Pact nations in 1968, Romania's presence at the 1984 Olympic Games at Los Angeles, and estrangement from Gorbachev's USSR as it implemented *perestroika* and *glasnost* [9] Talk of Soviet intervention in the December 1989 revolution, the aid sent by the USSR to post-revolutionary Romania, and revelations of Ceauşescu's sale of Soviet weaponry to the United States also testify to the reality of Romania's estrangement from the Soviet Union.

Even the Ceauşescu personality cult was expressed in terms of national independence and international recognition. Cult images often emphasized the continuity of Romanian leadership and pictured Ceauşescu as the latest in a long line of national heroes who unified and defended the nation. By showing the Ceauşescus meeting with other world leaders or displaying gifts and awards they received from around the world, the images promoted their role in Romania's acceptance in the community of nations. At the exhibition at the Bucharest Art Museum in honor of the president's sixtieth birthday, images of Ceauşescu were woven together with those of such important figures as Michael the Brave, Mircea the Elder, and Vlad the Impaler. Gifts and honors from various countries were displayed, and one large wall was devoted to tracing the expansion of Romanian diplomatic relations under Ceauşescu's leadership.

9. On the eve of Romania's revolution it was said to be easier to buy a copy of *Newsweek* or the *International Herald Tribune* in Bucharest than a copy of *Pravda*.

The ideological corollary of Romanian independence was the idea that foreigners sought to destroy the nation. This xenophobia justified the Official Secrets Act, which required any contact with a foreigner to be reported within twenty-four hours and spawned rumors of Soviet or Hungarian subversion every few months. Such fantasies, in fact, occupied Ceauşescu until the dramatic end. After Romanians and minorities were mown down together in the streets of Timişoară as they protested their miserable conditions, Ceauşescu, in his last speech, called the victims "foreign-inspired fascist reactionary elements."

Developing the New Romanian Civilization

Despite the material deprivation of most Romanians through the 1980s, the news media constantly displayed graphs and charts to bolster the state's claims of material progress achieved under its aegis. Civilization itself was equated with simple material changes (apartment houses), cultural consumption (newspaper subscriptions, theaters), and the growth of science, technology, and industry. Party officials proclaimed the virtue of "lifting ourselves up" and the need to be "clean, cultured, and civilized."

Related to the obsession with material change was official Romanian culture's inordinate concern for number and size. The social transformation of towns and villages was regularly indicated numerically on community bulletin boards. Colored graphs on large posters indicating recent or planned production adorned the gates of most factories. May Day and National Day parades were replete with numerical depictions of growth in the state, county, or enterprise. The same concern was apparent in state monumental architecture and massive construction projects, such as the Casă Scînteiă (the state publishing house), a typical Stalinist cathedral; the Trans-Făgăraş Highway, which cuts through some of Europe's most rugged mountains to link Transylvania and Wallachia; the Danube–Black Sea Canal; and the Bucharest–Black Sea Canal, which was to turn the landlocked Romanian capital into a major port. Just before the revolution the historic buildings and churches and the commercial and residential zones of central Bucharest were destroyed (see Giurescu 1989) to make way for the massive Boulevard of the Victory of Socialism, lined with hundreds of luxury apartments to house party officials and dominated by

Ceauşescu's House of the Republic

the multitiered House of the Republic (now House of the People) with its thousand rooms and five-ton chandeliers.

In the aftermath of the 1989 revolution it is easy to dismiss Romanian socialism as the product of one megalomaniac and his avaricious relatives. Though socialist practice varied from region to region and over time, however, the principles of accumulation, hierarchy, central planning, division of labor, and egregious nationalism clearly achieved wide support among elites and masses alike. Though the socialist state was designed to serve the interests of its leadership—the group that Pavel Câmpeanu (1988:143–57) termed the "global monopoly" and the "supreme entity"—it nonetheless offered many bureaucrats, workers, and peasants the possibility of competing for privilege, power, and economic well-being within a hypernationalist context. Some groups—regional elites, heads of industries, economic administrators—staunchly defended the system until the last. Others—capable bargainers, second-economy speculators, those who "pretended to work" but received a range of real benefits nonetheless—supported the system with less enthusiasm but were sufficiently compromised to limit their challenge to it. Still others rejected much of it but were cowed by the legions of secret police, their own lack of organizational ability, the fractiousness of community social relations, and the divisiveness of nationalism. All three groups emerged in the Olt Land with the implementation of the socialist system.

[4]

Socialism Comes
to the Olt Land

> Our peasants are joining the collectives en masse. They believe
> strongly in the path charted by the party.
> > Gheorghe Gheorghiu-Dej, December 1961

> After the collective came, no one was proper anymore.
> > Old man's lament, Cîrţişoară village

The social system against which the 1989 revolution was directed
owed its excesses to more than Ceauşescu. In fact, the conditions that
produced the revolution date to the very beginnings of Romanian
socialism and the transformation of political, economic, and ideological life it set in motion. In this process, termed elsewhere "revolutionary breakthrough" (Jowitt 1971), new political and economic institutions came to dominate Romanian communities, at great cost. The
socialist state's policy and practice expanded existing regional social
conflicts and engendered new ones as well. In response to these twin
pressures, social life was set on the course that resulted in the events
of the winter of 1989.

To some extent the contradictions of Olt Land life were due to too
little socialism rather than too much. Socialism, after all, leveled and
improved local economic life. Local life was oriented to socialist institutions and identities as industry and education expanded, private
agriculture gave way to collective farms, and the state extended its
reach into all occupational areas. Many villagers experienced considerable gain as they devised strategies to profit by the opportunities
and overcome the obstacles that the new system presented. Despite
these positive features, however, the way socialist institutions were

put in place was itself alienating and fomented conflicts grounded in presocialist institutions.

Presocialist institutions remained significant for various reasons. Some were deliberately retained by state and party. The dearth of capable activists after World War II, for example, forced the party to rely occasionally on local cadres of dubious qualifications and questionable character. They often pursued their own agendas and worked for their family's benefit rather than society's. Similarly, the lack of economic infrastructure required the state to cooperate with peasant households to guarantee labor and production. Institutions that were considered to conflict with the socialist program, however, were forced to the margins of village life. The church, for example, retained its significance more by the anger its abasement provoked than by its continued activity.

It is reasonable to assume that the social conflicts produced by the socialist breakthrough were desired by Romania's new leaders. Clearly they limited the likelihood of counterrevolution. Yet such conflicts also limited the possibility of developing the nation without constant and forced mobilization. They prevented any possibility of reform and cultural renewal short of the cataclysmic.

Means and Ends of Postwar Socialist Policy

Socialist breakthrough policies were designed to transform society politically, economically, and socially. Political policy sought to ensure centralized party control. Economic policy demanded elimination of dependency by nationalization of resources, rapid industrialization, and collectivization of agriculture. Social policy sought the formation of a new working class oriented away from the family and toward the socialist program (Ionescu 1964, Montias 1967). These were ambitious plans indeed. In view of postwar Romania's economic situation, they essentially implied the simultaneous destruction of an old society and construction of a new one with meager resources.

In the villages three types of overlapping policies were to bring about the new society. *Chopping* tactics were to break up existing institutions to eliminate political resistance and "free" individuals to be remolded as socialists. After the peasant community was fragmented, society would then be reconstituted by *push* and *pull* policies. The former forced the peasants out of agriculture and small-scale production of goods; the latter, through economic and social incentives, drew them into socialist industries and collective farms.[1]

Chopping: Class Warfare and Social Dissolution

As a Leninist party in a society historically marked by extreme differences in land tenure, the RCP sought to foment rural class conflict. This policy is fairly clear: "The poor peasant is the principal support of the working class. . . . We will support the poor peasantry, tighten our alliance with the middle peasantry, and organize an uninterrupted struggle against the kulak class. Don't make mistakes, comrades, and by your actions cause middle and poor peasants to run into the kulak's arms" (Ministry of Justice 1956:8–12).

Fomenting rural class war was easier said than done. In much of the country prosperous peasants were rare, and the Olt Land had few such households to serve as a focus of hostility. No peasants could have been called "rich" before the interwar land reform, and the few who had prospered were still generally well integrated in their communities, where they were sought out as political leaders and godparents (cf. Shanin 1972).

Under these conditions, the party had to focus on weakening the bonds between disparate peasant groups. The first step was conceptually to separate the rich from the others. Villagers called the prominent *ţărani bogaţi* or *ţărani înstăriţi* (rich or well-off peasants); socialist cadres, however, called them *chiaburi*, a pejorative term synonymous with the Russian *kulak* and specifically coined to sharpen their distinctiveness. The rich were singled out for constant political and economic abuse. Their land was confiscated, their possessions were sabotaged, and they were denounced, beaten, or imprisoned in attempts to stigmatize them and weaken their authority (see Enuţa 1952:14). *Chiaburi* also suffered disproportionately from the agricultural quota in effect from 1948 to 1956. Quotas were based on the extent of household holdings and increased precipitously with the amount of land owned. The quota was thus a punitive form of taxation intended to separate rich and poor peasants. *Chiaburi*, who owned a

---

1. Kenneth Jowitt (1971:110–11) suggests that state policies at the time are best classified as constructive (industrialization) and destructive (implicitly, collectivization and class war). This classification is certainly adequate, but I have adopted the tripartite chop-push-pull to distinguish the means and processes of communist policies from their institutional ends.

total of 8 percent of Romania's arable in 1952, delivered up to 13 percent of the grain collected during the operation of the quota (Montias 1967:30).

As the anti-*chiabur* campaign gathered steam, many poor peasants were induced to join the party by offers of low-interest agricultural credit and other economic assistance. The land reform of 1945 was yet another attempt to unify the party and the poor. Under the reform about 10 percent of Romania's total agricultural land was confiscated from the holdings of large landowners and Nazi collaborators (Montias 1967:89). Since the amount of land that changed hands was so limited, the "reform" can be understood as an ideological tactic rather than a true effort to redistribute land. The small-scale, market-oriented agriculture it implied clearly contradicted the socialist policy of centralization, and after the party consolidated its power in 1948, it dismantled the reforms and set to work to collectivize agriculture in earnest (Mitrany 1951).

The party also sought to limit other actual and potential alternative sources of power in peasant communities. Administrative reforms replaced the locally responsive county system with larger, state-oriented superregions. Semi-autonomous, locally elected village councils were replaced by "people's councils" headed by party cadres, and the single village administrative unit was replaced by the multivillage commune (Helin 1967:494). Organized religion was also taken in hand. Some religious groups, such as Jehovah's Witnesses, were banned outright. The Uniate church was forcibly unified with the official Romanian Orthodox church, which itself was placed under firm state control. A wide variety of religious practices were severely restricted. Community-wide ritual celebrations were prohibited. Informal religious study organized by local priests was severely curtailed. And nearly all religious activities outside church walls were prohibited.

Pushing: Collectivization of Agriculture

The collectivization of agriculture was the socialist state's main tactic in its efforts to push the peasants from their old way of life. After collectivization was approved as policy at a plenary session of the party in March 1949, cadres were sent into the countryside to explain its benefits and enroll peasants in the new organizations. This first campaign had mixed results. More than 1,000 farms with some 70,000

households were established by the end of 1950, but resistance stiff-
ened the following year and only 62 farms were formed (Rusenescu
1979:434–35). The party blamed resistance first on the over-
enthusiasm of cadres in forcing peasants to enroll. It also blamed the
peasants themselves, whom it characterized as petit bourgeois, familistic, and unlikely to adjust to collective labor and ownership (Cernea
1974:98).

To counter these problems, the state established a transitional organization, the *întovărăşire agricole* (agricultural association), in September 1951.[2] Unlike collectives, the associations blended private and
socialist relationships. Their members contributed as much or as little
land as they desired, whereas collective farmers were expected to
contribute all of their holdings except for their homes, outbuildings,
and small gardens. Association land was private, though it was amal-
gamated into large plots to facilitate joint labor; collective lands were
joint property. Association members' remuneration was determined
by the amount of land they contributed, but members of collectives
were paid according to their labor. Finally, association regulations still
promoted collectivization by mandating the use of machinery held by
state-owned machine tractor stations, year-round functioning of the
association, joint labor, and formal offices and statutes (Cernea
1974:102, Ministry of Justice 1956:50–52).

The associations proliferated rapidly through the 1950s, encouraged
by state loans to members and reductions in land taxes and delivery
quotas. From 1952 to 1958 their numbers increased from 1,800 to
12,748, with more than a million members (Cernea 1974:106, Montias
1967:93, Rusenescu 1979:433–39). Like the 1945 land reform, however, they contradicted the tenets of state socialism: they did not
centralize production, they permitted use of property by individuals,
they contributed little to the state, and they remunerated members
according to the amount of land they owned. These contradictions,
combined with the intensified push for autarkic development after
Romania's break with COMECON, renewed the collectivization campaign and doomed the associations.

Like class war before it, collectivization was directed as much to
changing peasants' conceptions as to changing the political economy. A
party manual of the time summed up this approach:

2. These organizations were modeled after the Soviet TOZ, the Association for the Joint
Cultivation of Land; the organization's name also derives from the Russian *tovarishch*,
"comrade."

To strengthen the collectives . . . there will be no economic or administrative pressure on the peasantry and the only method to be used is *convincing and explaining.* . . . Convincing the peasantry [will be accomplished by] organizing discussions between peasants who visited the USSR and others, arranging for visits of peasants to existing farms, arranging for regional exhibits, discussions at local culture halls, extensive media campaigns. In addition, special attention is to be accorded women and youth and . . . in regions of high agricultural productivity the Party must send a propagandist to aid in organizing new farms. [Ministry of Justice 1956:47–48]

Full collectivization was announced in 1960–1961, when 80 percent of Romanian land was in the socialist sector (National Conference of Peasant Collectivists 1962). As a push policy it succeeded remarkably. It rationalized labor, restricted household production, and pushed rural cultivators out of agriculture into expanding industry. From 1950 to 1960 the agricultural work force declined by about 10 percent (Tsantis & Pepper 1979:139) and peasant villages were reconstituted as proletarian peasant-worker communities.

Pulling: Industrialism and Related Policies

Along with collectivization, industrial development was the sine qua non of Romanian socialism and the cornerstone of party dogma. Stimulated by policies that made industry attractive to the peasants, Romania's industrial output grew about 13 percent a year between 1958 and 1965 (Gilberg 1975:142, Montias 1967:54, Shafir 1985:107). Labor unions established social clubs and shopping centers as adjuncts to factories. The unions also controlled access to new apartments. A state media campaign sought to create industrial traditions where few had existed (see Hobsbawm & Ranger 1983, Kideckel 1988). All of these activities were designed not only to remake the rural population into a capable industrial work force but to relocate social life from the rural community to the industrial workplace.

Educational expansion complemented industrial and social policy. The extensive reform of 1948 sought to eradicate illiteracy, expand compulsory education, and improve technical training for economic development. The increase in the number of schools and the expansion of the curriculum were particularly impressive. Factory training programs were begun to help new workers master their jobs. Special schools were set up to train people with production and administrative functions, and other schools were established for party personnel. As a whole, school attendance increased about 300 percent between 1938 and 1960, with the greatest increase in vocational education (Braham 1963:13, 32).

The educational reform also sought ideological change. School and university faculties had "spiritual guides appointed by the Ministry of Education, whose task [was] to indoctrinate not only pupils but also their parents" (Seton-Watson 1951:285). "The ultimate objective of this new education [was] the creation of the new socialist man," whose "individual interests" were to be "subordinated to the interests of the state." The schools were "to train youth in the spirit of patriotism and proletarian internationalism" (Braham 1963:14).

Thus was the socialist state established. Chopping, pushing, and pulling its way through society, the RCP set about its program of socialist breakthrough. Policy is only as good as its results, however, and the results of the socialist breakthrough were a far cry from the vision set forth in party documents, particularly in the Olt Land.

Breakthrough in the Olt Land

The unproductiveness of the Olt Land's farms, its middle-peasant socioeconomic structure, and the intensiveness of the industrialization process in the region skewed its experience of the socialist break-through. Poor agricultural production created poverty and famine in the face of the party's economic policies. The middle-peasant class structure produced intense though short-lived resistance to collec-tivization. And massive industrialization had dramatic effects on the region's peasant households. These experiences prejudiced most of the population against the socialist system even as they tore the social fabric of the villages.

Quotas, Kulaks, and Class War

The immense suffering caused by the agricultural quotas imposed on the Olt Landers did more to turn them against socialism than any other government policy, even collectivization. Extreme deprivation

[83]

provoked little sense of shared suffering because the suffering was not distributed evenly. The agricultural quotas were so unrealistically high that many households were forced to buy produce in city markets to sell to the state at a loss. To fill their own needs some households were reduced to collecting wild food in the forests and meadows and gleaning the fields. A household's quota depended largely on its ability to influence the local official who determined it. Some households (including a few of the wealthy) escaped steep quotas by bribing an official to classify them as two or more units. Others who owned more than one house distributed their members among their holdings to limit their compulsory deliveries. Such manipulation provoked envy, suspicion, and an abiding distrust of people once regarded as good neighbors and kin.

The anti-*chiabur* campaign was as disruptive as the quota. Like the quota, the *chiabur* classification was subject to abuse. Some households were so obviously affluent that they could not avoid it. Others, however, were classified as *chiaburi* largely for personal or political reasons, with economic justification provided ex post facto. Many of the nineteen *chiaburi* households in Cîrțișoara village probably did not deserve this fate. Here are the bases for their classification as *chiaburi*:

1. 14-hectare estate
2. 10-hectare estate, blacksmith shop
3. Leasehold and operation of mill
4. Butchershop, leasehold of mill
5. Buzz saw, cereal trade
6. Brandy still
7. 8-hectare estate, shares in bank, position as teacher
8. Thresher and tractor (owned jointly with a brother who was not named as *chiabur*)
9. General store
10. General store, knitting machine
11. 10-hectare estate, servant (and a record of two years in prison)
12. 15-hectare estate, servant, shares in bank
13. 9-hectare estate, servant, threshing machine, brandy still
14. 10-hectare estate, servant, position as forestry supervisor
15. Brandy still, shares in bank
16. Buzz saw
17. Buzz saw, brandy still
18. Brandy still, servant, position as forestry supervisor
19. Threshing machine

Some of these people were petty merchants, but not all small business owners were named, nor were ten to twelve other households with estates of more than ten hectares, which theoretically qualified them for *chiabur* status. In Hîrseni village, too, six of eleven households classified as *chiaburi* seemingly did not warrant this status: they neither employed labor, owned a business, nor rented out agricultural machinery.

Though some of my informants suggested that party cadres had a *"chiaburi* quota" to fill, misclassification appears to have been closely related to interpersonal relations and class-based competition. Public denunciations of *chiaburi*, for instance, depended on the quality of social ties between the wealthy and the informant. In general, villagers were reluctant to admit to any role in the persecution of *chiaburi*. General discussion suggests that witnesses were scarce because the rich still had a long reach in the dissolving corporate community, and the poor peasants who were the focus of the Leninist class-war strategy were still dependent on them. Consider, for example, Nicolae R., a land-poor Hîrseni peasant who occasionally worked as a shepherd for the *chiabur* Iosif Oltean. In 1948 Oltean promised Nicolae 20 kilos of wool and 10 kilos of cheese in return for work but gave him only a small quantity of inferior wool. When party cadres asked Nicolae and his mother to testify against Oltean, both swore he had received full payment. "Oltean was a good man who helped us poor people," they told me, "even if he was greedy." Some informants suggested that it was more common for wealthier peasants to testify against the *chiaburi*; they were the ones who competed with the *chiaburi* for influence, and they were in a precarious position themselves.

The case of Ioan Cioră, the upwardly mobile mechanic whom we met in Chapter 2, reveals how some people avoided *chiabur* status. Though Cioră had built his trucking service into a successful commercial network, his humble beginnings and his gifts of food, drink, and services to local officials initially kept him off the list of *chiaburi*. When collectivization was rumored, he deeded his general store, liquor depository, and bar to the state and sold his brandy distillery to a wealthy Uniate family, but kept his home in the village center, his arable land and orchards, and a tractor and thresher. Despite his calculations, national events sealed his fate. As the first collectivization drive sputtered, some party factions attributed the failure to the "right-wing deviations" of the party leaders Pauker, Lucă, and Georgescu and to the machinations of the *chiaburi*. So the class war intensified and officials had little choice but to condemn Cioră. He split his remaining estate between commune and kin and left for Bucharest, where he lives today.

The new owner of Cioră's distillery also seemed to merit *chiabur* status. Besides the distillery, this household had a twelve-hectare estate, part ownership of a local grain mill, and shares in a local bank. To avoid *chiabur* classification they deeded the distillery to the state (though the family retained functional control over it), split the household into separate units, and sold some land. They also joined the Agricultural Association when it expanded and sought membership in the party.

The anti-*chiabur* campaign was ultimately at odds with the state's aims. Though it silenced the wealthy and eliminated local political resistance, it also provoked noncooperation and deprived cadres of influential voices that might have helped to shape community opinion. Some *chiaburi*, such as Ioan Cioră, did not overtly oppose the new order. Others, such as Traian T., a wealthy sheep owner in Cîrțișoara, who ultimately was proclaimed a hero of socialist labor, were actually sympathetic to it. The campaign against the *chiaburi* thus needlessly furthered social disintegration without promoting socialist aims.

The Road to Collectivization

Despite quotas and class war, Olt Land villagers tenaciously opposed collectivization. As collective farms expanded throughout Romania in the 1950s, Olt Landers deluded themselves that it would not happen to them. The rockiness of their soil, they were sure, would keep them safe. Still, rumors of collectivization spawned local debate and strategizing. Since uncertainty prevailed, short-term opportunism was the order of the day. Those who thought collectivization imminent sold land. Some young people rejected land they might have inherited and sought education instead. Still others took advantage of the anti-*chiabur* campaign and amassed more land. Hîrseni village land records attest to the uncertainty. Of 117 households for which records are available, 58, or 50 percent, participated in some land transaction in 1953 or 1954. Of these households, 32 sold land, 18 bought land, and 8 did both. Those who sold land generally had estates of more than nine hectares and first sold land located in neighboring villages and communes, often to close kin. Those who bought land had estates of five to seven hectares, bought mainly village land, but sold land located in other communities.

By 1952 only three small collective farms had been founded in the region. Regional agricultural associations, however, mirrored the national trend and grew rapidly in size and number, expanding from 111 with an average membership of 53 families per association in 1955 to 410 with an average of 145 families in 1959.[3] These statistics, however, tell only part of the story. Initially the campaign to attract peasants to the associations focused on commune centers where many party cadres were based. These party activists were prompted by regional cadres to form associations in order to attract others later. This tactic often failed, however. Social pressure kept some party members from joining, and many of those who joined were opportunists, and because personal networks were used to recruit members into the associations, reliance on one network often excluded others.

In Hîrseni village, for example, only nine of approximately twenty resident party members joined the association. One young cadre deeded most of his land to a younger brother in order to avoid joining. Another, with no official function to lose, simply refused to join. Many who joined had been in the Iron Guard and apparently enrolled to improve their political standing. Such a shift did not go unnoticed. Hîrseni informants remarked that "all these people did was change the color of their shirts from green to red. You can change clothes, but not character."

Analysis of Hîrseni association members shows the influence of social networks and community status in the decision to join. The ten original members of the Hîrseni association shared a range of social characteristics. All were married heads of households, all but one were middle peasants, and all resided in the Orthodox neighborhood. Such criteria did not specifically select villagers for membership, since others shared them as well; rather, they were a boundary that kept others out. More influential in the decision to join an association was the network of social ties that bound the ten and supported them in the face of community derision (Table 3). The cases of two people, one who joined and one who did not, clearly show the significance of such ties.

Nicolae M. was 46 years old in late 1952 when party cadres encour-

3. This statistic refers to families, not households. Since many Olt Land households comprised two or more families, the number of households in the associations was actually much smaller.

Table 3. Characteristics of original members of Hîrseni Agricultural Association

	Name	Position	Number of hectares owned	Party member	Local origin	Network relations
1.	Ştefan A.	Mayor	5.4	Yes	Yes	Brother-in-law of 10; cousin of 5
2.	Valeriu M.	Vice mayor	10.3	Yes	Yes	Neighbor of 5, 7, 10
3.	Ioan C.	Party secretary	2.5	Yes	No*	Neighbor of 4
4.	Aurel T.	President, Hîrseni Cooperative	9.7	Yes	Yes	Brother-in-law of 5; neighbor of 3
5.	Ioan T.	President, Copăcel Cooperative	5.1	Yes	Yes	Brother-in-law of 4; cousin of 1; neighbor of 2, 7, 10
6.	Gheorghe B.	Custodian	5.8	No	Yes	Neighbor of 8, 9
7.	Nicolae M.	Veterinary agent	9.9	No	Yes	Cousin of 8; neighbor of 2, 5, 10
8.	Simion J.	None	9.2	No†	Yes	Father-in-law of 9; cousin of 7, 10; neighbor of 6, 9
9.	Ioan P.	None‡	5.8	No	Yes	Son-in-law of 8; neighbor of 6, 8
10.	Ilie N.	Party activist	8.8	Yes	Yes	Brother-in-law of 1; cousin of 8; neighbor of 2, 5, 7

*Before his marriage Ioan C. lived in an adjacent village.

†Simion, who had dense village network connections, was under pressure to join the party from a son-in-law who was a highly placed party official in another county.

‡Ioan P. was partially handicapped and had difficulty working. His disability seems to have been relevant to his decision to seek the benefits of membership in the association.

Sources: Registru agricolă, Hîrseni commune, 1951–1955, 1959–1963; Kideckel 1982:329.

aged him to join. He was a likely candidate, as he was employed as the commune veterinary agent and could have lost his job if he failed to join. Still, Nicolae agonized over the decision. His wife and sons, worried that villagers would think it shameful for him to join, were vehemently opposed. For four months Nicolae was called repeatedly to the town hall and pressed to join. He was never threatened, though, and the officials assured him that the association would not lead to collectivization. When he finally joined, he still maintained symbolic distance from the organization. He was the last of the ten to register and contributed only one hectare of land, less than any other member.

Iosif S., a teacher in Hîrseni, was not a native but still should have been a prime candidate for the association, as he shared all other characteristics of the members. Also, though not a party member, he was sympathetic to its goals. Iosif did not join the association because, he said, he was never asked. Even if he had been, he still would not have joined because "the members were wicked. One was a womanizer, another was a drunk, a few were lazy and greedy, and all were thieves who wanted to profit from others' work." All the same, Iosif was impressed by the association's economic success, and later he tried to persuade his in-laws, neighbors, and friends to begin another, but he failed to do so.

The major difference between these men appears to have been their local social relations. Nicolae's network was strong enough to overcome his concerns, whereas Iosif had neither the connections to join the first association nor the support to establish a second. Most of Iosif's school colleagues commuted to the village and his lack of local origins diminished his status. His wife was a local woman, but her family was small and lived in the Uniate half of the village. Though her family was linked to the association (Gheorghe B., no. 6 in Table 3, was her father's sister's husband), the tie was not significant. Gheorghe B. was only a custodian, was not a party member, and lived right on the boundary between the Uniate and Orthodox neighborhoods— whence his usual designation in the village, Gheorghe din colţ (George from the corner).

The associations also failed to promote socialism in the region. The local members ignored most national regulations in favor of practices more suited to them. Mechanized agriculture went first. Members considered the tractor station's services too costly and deep plowing ineffective. Mutual accusations of laziness soon brought joint labor to a halt. When joint labor was eliminated, land was redistributed back in accordance with the amount contributed, but the association members kept the better-quality lands they had received in forced exchange with nonmembers. From 1958 meetings were rare and no elections were ever held.

The Hîrseni association was a financial success and a social disaster. Members had access to the best village lands and profited handsomely from a large flock of sheep. Their prosperity contrasted so sharply with the misery of the other villagers that it fostered animosity and even violence. Fistfights in the fields kept members from working their new lands, their property was sabotaged, and the mayor and local party secretary walked the streets with pistols openly displayed. Because of its divisiveness, the association attracted no new members for four years. Seeing developments in Hîrseni, other villages in the area refused to form associations of their own. Finally, in late 1959, with cadres pressured to show progress, the organization was expanded by about 75 families. A few people joined to avoid *chiabur* status. But the expansion was mainly window dressing to impress officials at the county level. Actually, no meetings were held, no property was worked in common, and some of the listed members were never even informed of their enrollment.

Collectivization and the Regional Division of Labor

The formation of collective farms was less disruptive than that of the agricultural associations, though ultimately they were more socially significant. Again the party played on local social relations to effect its policies. After a few compliant individuals enrolled, they were encouraged to pressure others to join. The vastly expanded ranks of state employees—workers, teachers, commercial agents—were threatened with demotion or dismissal if they failed to join or to persuade their families and friends to do so. Prominent citizens were subjected to special pressure. If they enrolled, the reasoning went, others would follow. Along with the stick came the carrot: villages were promised running water, natural gas mains, and other infrastructural improvements if they collectivized.

Olt Landers parried both promises and threats. Unable to fight politically, they turned to folkloric forms of resistance (see Kideckel 1988, Kligman 1983). People in Hîrseni still laugh about how they confused visiting cadres who pressured them to join the collective. They said they would "rather enroll in Toderan [the nickname for the communal cemetery]." In Cîrţişoara people told of the widow who fed a cadre diseased chicken for a week. And people everywhere promised to join—just as soon as a neighbor or friend had signed up. Still, collectivization was a foregone conclusion. By the end of 1961, as state pressure and threats intensified, people began to enroll in large numbers, and early in 1962 the villagers formally voted the collectives into existence. More than fifty farms were formed in February and March alone. Peasants deeded land and tools to the farms, along with grain and seed potatoes, all horses, and most cattle and water buffaloes.

Records show that villagers were nearly unanimous in forming the collectives. Still, in every community a few households refused. Four households remained private in Hîrseni, sixteen in Copăcel, and three in Drăguş. In a process of attrition, 27 of 450 households in Cîrţişoara joined when the farm was first formed in 1959, 67 had joined by 1961, and by 1964, 409 households had become farm members and only 4 remained private.[4] People paid dearly to remain private. They were denied state employment, their land was exchanged for plots of poorer quality at greater distances from home, and that land was heavily taxed. Most households that chose to remain private had little to lose. Many of these people were elderly and only minimally dependent on the state. The occasional younger household that stayed private had no children of school age and generally was headed by a craftsman who was not employed by the state.

Collectivization had an immediate impact in every area of local life. It transformed social relations, labor, and ideology and had a massive effect on individual career plans and internal household relations. Underlying each of these changes was collectivization's effect on the division of labor. Collectivization was, after all, the state's chief means of separating peasants from agriculture and pushing them into industry. This goal was especially evident in the Olt Land (see Table 4). In Hîrseni village 14.1 percent of all men between 16 and 58 and 22.4 percent of active women left agriculture after collectivization began. In their wake they left a labor force that was mainly aged and female.[5]

Collectivization was the chief factor behind the emergence of the peasant-worker household and its mixed labor strategy. Though many able-bodied workers left agriculture, they continued to live in their villages because the factories were within easy reach and there were no city lights in the region to lure them away. In any case, industrial wages and the socialist marketplace could not supply all the needs of a

---

4. Of the remaining 37 households, 32 were classified as workers and 5 as functionaries.

5. These numbers are even more significant than they appear. Spurred by the agricultural quotas and pressured by the Agricultural Association, many men and some women had left the farms for factories shortly before agriculture was collectivized.

Table 4. Type of work performed by men and women, Hîrseni village, 1959 and 1963, by age group

Age group	1959			1963			Percent change		
	Wage	Agri-cultural	Other	Wage	Agri-cultural	Other	Wage	Agri-cultural	Other
Men									
16–24	18	13	16	11	10	40	−20.3%	−11.3%	+31.6%
25–39	53	26	7	59	16	7	+10.4	−10.8	+0.4
40–54	28	30	7	34	31	5	+5.5	−1.9	−3.6
55–58	2	18	1	6	8	1	+30.5	−32.4	+1.9
59+	1	44	16	3	41	21	+3.0	−9.1	+6.1
All ages	102	131	47	113	106	74			
Women									
16–24	7	34	11	7	20	31	−1.5	−30.9	+32.3
25–39	7	67	3	10	51	19	+3.4	−23.2	+19.8
40–54	1	62	3	0	47	11	−1.5	−12.9	+14.4
55–58	0	23	1	1	19	6	+3.8	−22.7	+18.9
59+	0	31	40	0	24	48	0.0	−10.4	+10.4
All ages	15	217	58	18	161	115			

Source: Registu agricolă, Hîrseni commune, 1959, 1963; Kideckel 1977:47–49.

rural household, so at least one member usually continued to work in agriculture. Of 175 households in Hîrseni village in 1962, 141 (81 percent) were registered as farm members. In more rural Cîrţişoara, fully 91 percent of households were enrolled in the collective. Probably more people would have left agriculture if they had been allowed to do so. Because farm labor was needed and industry was unable to absorb all of the villagers, some people (mainly men) were refused permission to work outside of their home village and remained in agriculture by default. Not incidentally, the need for permission to work in industry was a prime means of political control during the early days of collectivization.

Industry absorbed most men in their twenties, thirties, and forties and many women as well. Equally significant for the division of labor were the educational opportunities available to both men and women. Thus the decrease in both agricultural and wage labor in the 16–24 age groups indicated in Table 4 no doubt resulted from the expanded educational opportunities offered by area factories. Factory schools in Făgăraş, for example, graduated 68 chemical operators, 38 journeymen, and 57 students in general technical education in 1963 and provided basic courses for an additional 300 (mainly local) students each year (Herseni et al. 1972:189). Similarly Cîrţişoara, a village of over 2,000 people, had only 17 skilled workers in 1951, but by 1964, according to an estimate by the village civil statistician, 170 had been qualified for skilled labor.

Pushed from agriculture, Olt Land workers mainly found employment in the expanding chemical industry. The Făgăraş Chemical Combine (CCF), formed from the union of the Nitramonia Chemical Company and the Făgăraş Explosives Society in June 1948, quickly became the region's largest employer. Chemical facilities were also built in Victoria and at Mîrsa in the western region. Other industries developed to service these plants. Several small workshops on the outskirts of Făgăraş, for example, were combined into the Enterprise for Chemical Industry Tools (IUC) to manufacture tools, equipment, and valves for CCF and other nearby industries.

Industrial expansion in the Olt Land was extraordinary. CCF, which employed slightly fewer than 1,000 people in early 1948, by the close of the first collectivization drive in 1953 had 3,603 permanent employees: 3,015 (84 percent) workers and 588 technical and administrative employees. By 1964 it had 4,943 employees, of whom 84 percent were workers. Over half of this work force lived in nearby villages (Herseni et al. 1972:121–91). Services were developed to facil-

The Făgăraş Chemical Combine

[93]

itate villagers' participation in industry. By the late 1950s all of the region's main roads were paved and regular bus service linked the villages with Făgăraş, Avrig, Victoria, Braşov, and Sibiu. Except for some outlying Gypsy hamlets, most of the region was electrified and communications and postal links were expanded.

Breakthrough and Social Reality

Breakthrough policies and institutions were designed to facilitate class homogeneity, end familism, and promote socialist identity and labor relations. In the Olt Land, however, they forged new kinds of inequalities and simultaneously reinforced the preexisting differences in wealth and privilege. Instead of increasing the participation of autonomous individuals in society, the breakthrough policies turned Olt Landers away from the society that socialism had wrought to seek refuge in their own revivified households. As a result, social networks were so eroded that conflict intensified in labor relations.

Changing Inequality

It is unlikely that any revolution instantly eliminates age-old inequities. In Romania, however, the socialist breakthrough not only failed at this task but created new kinds of differentiation. Before socialism, village differentiation was essentially unidimensional, based simply on wealth in land and related property. Such differences were an accepted part of the Olt Land village and did not prevent most villagers from participating in social and political life. Though these communities were internally differentiated, they were culturally unified. Their members resonated to the same values and relationships that defined the rest of the region's peasantry. Even disenfranchised emigrants sought to reproduce those values and relationships.

With the socialist breakthrough, economic well-being became a mark of political status. The quotas and the class war generated suspicion and pervasive envy of the people who escaped them. To many villagers a household's economic stability was thus a sure sign of influence peddling, illegal activities, or political compromise. Those who joined the Agricultural Association were branded as opportunists. And the slightest slip might send one hurtling into a political abyss. In 1956

[94]

twenty-five Hîrseni men and women lost their factory jobs overnight by administrative fiat when their political reliability was questioned. Others were denied permission to leave collective agriculture for industry for similar reasons. Still others, young men and women, were sent against their will to the Romanian Dobrogea for low-paid harvest work. And the *chiabur* Iosif Oltean was hounded, beaten, and imprisoned; he died a broken man. One old Hîrseni man said, "It was completely bad then. We thought everything would be taken away, so we kept quiet and kept to ourselves lest others know too much about us. Almost everybody suffered. We didn't have the wherewithal to escape."

The decisive role of the party thus interrelated political, economic, and cultural differences. Regional differentiation became qualitative instead of merely numerical. The activities that one engaged in now depended on whether one joined the party: only party members made political decisions and headed local agencies. Party members had access to cultural and economic resources that were not available to other villagers. Family and network connections to this new elite further divided people. Connections enabled some villagers to avoid persecution and others to gain wealth.

By cultivation of political ties, strategic distribution of resources, and obeisance, a few upper-middle peasant households (the second tier under the deposed *chiaburi*) were able to retain their wealth and prominence under socialism. Though these people were hardly committed socialists, they joined the party and became village deputies, officials of consumer cooperatives, and administrators of collective farms. All nine members of the first leadership council at the Hîrseni collective farm had prewar estates of over ten hectares. The ranks of the local party and the Agricultural Association were also disproportionately filled by upper-middle peasants.

The process by which many local elites gained or preserved prominence tainted their influence from the outset, and what influence they possessed was restricted by party centralization. Together with the destruction of the *chiaburi*, this situation left the party few effective links to transmit its policies locally. Even local elites who were respected by the other villagers suffered in the troubled breakthrough climate. Informants universally agreed that the first president of the Hîrseni collective farm was an honest man who greatly helped his fellow villagers in his brief five-month tenure. His respect was ensured when he publicly opposed a plan to transfer about 100 hectares of land to the neighboring commune of Ileni. Still, he quit his job because of constant accusations of nepotism. Other members of the first Hîrseni farm administration also quit within months of assuming their posts. Of twenty-five Hîrseni farm leaders in 1962, only four finished their full terms of office. The head of the Hîrseni agricultural brigade summed up the situation simply: "Nobody was ever happy with you."

Transformations of Households and Networks

Nationalization, industrialization, and collectivization changed peasant social relations so suddenly that villagers' responses were uncertain and confused. To limit the role of peasant households in the local political economy, the party sought to eliminate landed wealth, expand educational and occupational opportunities, pay collective farmers according to individual labor, and organize team labor on the farms. The data suggest that in the face of these innovations, Olt Landers clung to what they knew and maintained their existing household structures and internal relations. In doing so, however, they sacrificed their households' larger social networks and paved the way for greater differentiation among households.

This stability in the midst of confusion is first suggested by demographic statistics. Instead of disintegrating under the pressure of industrialization and socialist breakthrough, the three-generation stem family continued to be common in Olt Land villages, though its functions and divisions of labor underwent some modification. This situation was duplicated elsewhere in Eastern Europe (Hammell 1972), though it is a response not noted among industrializing societies in general (see Yanagisako 1979:181). Data from Mîndra village (Cole 1976), five kilometers to the east of Făgăraş, show that in 1961 three-generation households were nearly as numerous as simple nuclear units (98 and 104, respectively). In Hîrseni village the number of three- and four-generation households was the same in 1964 as in 1951 (74 and 5, respectively) but their total frequency increased from 42 to 45 percent of village households. In the same period, the number of simple nuclear families decreased from 55 (29 percent) to 45 (25 percent). The stem family certainly appeared to be gaining in prominence, as nine additional two-generation families in 1964 (seven in 1951) were on the verge of becoming three-generation structures.

[96]

Each comprised two married couples, and all of the younger couples had just entered their childbearing years.

This stem structure no doubt owed its survival to the uncertainty of access to resources and the new socialist division of labor. Extended families had an advantage in these conditions, as their members could be involved in a variety of economic activities, from industry to collective farming. Even when quotas and the need to seek work outside the area forced households to split, the advantages of economic cooperation encouraged their segments to retain their ties with home as links in a long-distance exchange network.

Internal household relations changed little. Party ideology foresaw increased household fissioning as young people acquired their own incomes, but in the Olt Land an income did not make one independent. To be sure, as young people were freed from the need to inherit land, they began to marry earlier than their elders had done before World War II. Age at marriage declined for women from 20.5 in 1931–1940 to 17.8 in 1960–1964, and for men from 24.7 to 23.5. The young couples did not set up their own households, though. Marriage simply brought an additional income into the larger household.

Still, both marital residence outside of Hîrseni and exogamous marriage in general increased in this period. This situation can be traced to the interaction of three factors: with industrialization, individuals made a greater number of contacts with people in other communities; nationalization of the land obviated the need to find a marriage partner with land resources close to one's home; and an increase in social conflict made it easier for some people to leave the village. The proportion of exogamous marriages rose from 35 percent in 1919–1945 to 47.3 percent in 1946–1962. And spouses were now sought farther afield. In forty-one known exogamous marriages, eighteen of the spouses were from neighboring villages, nine from Făgăraş, and fourteen from out of the region. Between 1919 and 1938, thirty-four spouses in comparable marriages were from neighboring villages, one from Făgăraş, and only eight from out of the region.

As households became overly concerned with their survival and animosities developed over perceptions of "improper" differentiation, community networks experienced contradictory pressures. In a process that foreshadowed developments just before the 1989 revolution, concern for basic survival increased the perceived importance of Olt Land networks. At the same time, however, people's inability to give the help that others asked of them strained those relationships and

[97]

hastened their dissolution, as did increased political control. Social relations with fellow workers at the factory began to fill the gap.

The quotas dealt an especially severe blow to network relations, as they required most households to struggle on their own. A household that was forced to deliver produce to the state had few resources to exchange with other households. Though people sympathized with those who suffered extreme hardship, few came to their aid. Most were in no position to help. A middle-aged Hîrseni worker told me:

> We [Olt Landers] are honest people. But in the time of the quota, people had to steal because we had no money and needed every potato or bit of bread. The poor P. family. The man drank, the woman was sickly, and they had a lot of children, but no one helped them. I remember him eating wildflowers. It was a great famine. We had produce but it was all delivered to the Făgăraş train station. At the station there'd be a line of horse carts loaded with potatoes stretching [about half a mile] across the tracks.

The agricultural associations aggravated the situation. Many feuds broke out in Hîrseni after the association was formed and the members set out to enroll their friends, neighbors, and relatives. Contrary pressure was applied by people who wanted the association to fail. Whether one joined or rejected the association, the decision generated conflict. Aurel T.'s brother and Nicolae M.'s stepfather and brother stopped speaking to them after they joined. In Nicolae's case the estrangement lasted well into the 1960s, and rapprochement was still tentative in the 1970s.

Association families were also held at arm's length after collectivization. Ştefan A. and his entire family left the village in 1962. Valeriu M.'s two daughters and a son married out of the region and one son never married. Ioan C.'s son married locally but was soon divorced. Four of Aurel T.'s six children left the region, one married in Făgăraş, and only one married in Hîrseni. All of Ioan T.'s three children left the village. Two of Gheorghe B.'s three children married out of the region. Five of Ioan P.'s six children married out, and Ilie N.'s only daughter married in Bucharest and his two sons never married. Only Nicolae M. and Simion J. diverged from the pattern. Four of Nicolae's seven children married locally (though one into the only Hungarian family in the village), two in Făgăraş, and one not at all. One of Simion's two children married locally. Of thirty-five children only eight (22.9 percent) married endogamously, and all twenty-three (65.7 percent) who married exogamously left the village.

The Reorganization of Ideology and Identity

The political and economic changes affected perceptions of self, others, and society. At this time the tensions between collectivism and individualism which marked socialist life began to emerge. The precariousness of most people's political position and the struggle for economic survival prevented a dawning recognition of class from being manifested in action, but we can observe a shift in attitudes. Before World War II, successful persons were expected to be socially active; they were *oameni văzuți* (seen persons) (Jowitt 1978; Verdery 1975, 1983). Community involvement varied directly with prominence and agricultural success. Now a proper person was *cineva care n-are treabă cu nimeni* (someone who minds his own business). In the presocialist village there was a surfeit of candidates for government and church councils. Now people refused to serve in any public capacity and resigned quickly from any position to which they were named, unless they feared that resignation would jeopardize their political status. At a time when all of life had become politicized, when to be prominent was to be condemned by one's fellows, when visibility could be dangerous, people simply withdrew from public life.

Religious change also promoted social atomization. Religion had been somewhat divisive in the past, but the split between the Orthodox and the Uniates had little significance in the interwar period. Intermarriage was frequent and religious intolerance minimal. The forced unification of the two churches in 1948, however, exacerbated religious conflict. In Hîrseni mass was said in the formerly Uniate and Orthodox churches on alternate Sundays, and many people refused to attend when the service was held in the church to which they did not belong. Church council positions went begging, and in some villages church-sponsored activities, such as cemetery maintenance, were increasingly avoided.

Certainly other elements of the Olt Landers' identity countered individualism. Regionalism and nationalism were enlivened by the socialist transformation. Regional identity was often expressed in stories contrasting village and region to state institutions and cadres (Kideckel 1988), and fables of wily peasants who tricked local officials

[99]

were popular. So were jokes about people who came from other regions to work in Olt Land industries. The Moldavians, it was said, were so poor that they traveled on the tops of the trains to avoid the fare. So how can you identify Moldavian immigrants? Answer: Shout "Wire!" in the town square and count the people who duck.

Intensification of nationalism appears to have been directly related to party policies that favored such marginal social groups as Gypsies and by the large numbers of Jews and Magyars in the party. Though Gypsies had always been tolerated in Hîrseni, in the early 1960s a group of villagers torched the home of a Gypsy elder after his family moved into the village. Ten to fifteen Hîrsenites were arrested, tried, and fined. Informants routinely referred to regional party cadres and factory officials as *jidani* (yids), *bozgori* (bohunks), and *țigani* (gypsies). Though the identities of these people were never traced, it would be surprising if all or even most were minorities.[6]

The implementation of socialist power in the Olt Land generated a massive social transformation with far-reaching consequences for sociability and class identity. Not all of its effects were negative. The revolutionary transformation expanded economic alternatives, modernized the villages, and equalized conditions of life. It created a base for a modern, rational, economistic, self-interested, class-oriented population. The process by which the new institutional arrangements were implemented, however, had unintended results. The ability to organize the region's communities was eroded, for the breakup of local leadership forced the party to rely on the egregiously self-interested. Though social networks were maintained, cooperation waned, households drew in upon themselves, and the differentiation of households was intensified in the socialist political economy.

Thus the socialist breakthrough both weakened local political unity and homogenized the conditions of most people's lives. Homogenization was evident in the shared suffering of quota and class war, but especially in the conditions under which Olt Landers worked. It was socialist labor on collective farms, in regional factories, and in local cooperatives that encouraged economic strategies that focused simultaneously on the individual and on the household. And it was socialist labor that left this fragmented people unable to respond to the Ceauşescuite state in any but the most passive-agressive manner.

6. Sam Beck (1986) relates a similar story about the pejorative use of "gypsy" to describe an official of another Olt Land village.

[5]

Working for Self,
Working for Socialism

> Labor, in the conditions of socialist society, creates and develops new interpersonal relations of collaboration, mutual assistance, and reciprocal respect—corresponding to the principle of "all for one and one for all"—and actively contributes to the formation and multilateral evolution of the human personality.
>
> Article 5.1, *Labor Code, Socialist Republic of Romania*

> The ox works while the horse eats.
>
> Olt Land proverb

The essence of socialist labor was evident nearly every afternoon in Olt Land villages. After 3 P.M., when workers returned home from the factory shift that began at 7 A.M., they sat with their families to speak about the workday just passed and to decide together what activities all needed to accomplish. Over cups of tea, glasses of *rachiu*, sweet red onions, and bread with jam or mustard and fatback, men and women, young and old, were assigned the various tasks they agreed had to be done. These meetings, often presided over by women, were usually notable for their good humor as the corporate household juggled its own needs and the state's demands. Though occasional disagreements surfaced, a typical meeting of a four-generation household sent one man to work on the collective, another for wood or chicks or utensils at the consumer cooperative at a nearby village, one woman to prepare food, and another to resolve an administrative problem at the town hall, while the grandma watched the children, gathered garden vegetables, or kept the fires burning. Even I was sent to the bakery to queue for scarce white bread.

Household corporatism was even more noticeable on the first and fifteenth of each month, when workers were paid. Then many men and women, married and often parents themselves, gave their pay to their mothers and fathers, with whom they lived, ate, and planned for the future. If they wanted to buy cigarettes, pastries, or a glass of brandy, couples in their thirties and forties had to request funds from household seniors, who kept the purse and guarded the future. These dependent younger couples thought this practice perfectly acceptable and in their own interest. They were amused by young couples who chose to keep their money separate from their parents', and often critical of them as well.

The persistence of the rural corporate household within the mobilization state created the dynamic of socialist labor. As state and household, by definition, worked at cross-purposes, socialist labor must be understood as the product of the attempts of each to control and manipulate the other. At the same time, the struggle also produced accommodation and interdependence. Politicized labor, workplace bargaining, and the second economy were useful to the centralized socialist system in its efforts to control labor, but households used them too to turn the socialist system to their own ends. Taking advantage of these socialist processes, however, demanded an appropriate household structure, training, and resources.

The socialist breakthrough was responsible for the emergence of the mixed peasant-worker household, and the state's strategy of multilateral development in combination with persistent shortages and politicization of labor relations ensured its survival. Unlike peasant-workers in capitalist societies, who use industrial wages to supplement their agricultural income (Holmes 1983, 1989), and workers in peripheral societies who are forced into subsistence agriculture by lack of industry (de Janvry 1981, Roseberry 1989, Smith et al. 1984), the Olt Land villagers sought to maximize all economic and political possibilities simultaneously, chiefly through the division of household labor.

They did not achieve this goal simply by distributing household members among a variety of occupations, however. The specific positions household members occupied, the tasks they were assigned, and the relations they established also were factors for households to consider in their efforts to control their members' labor in the planned but unpredictable socialist state. The diverse household resource base achieved by a diverse household division of labor (Cole 1976, Kideckel 1977, Randall 1983, Sampson 1984) thus countered Romania's economic shortages, allowed rapid response to shifting state wage and labor policies, and enhanced opportunities to procure resources from the ubiquitous second economy. In agriculture a household's ability to control its labor enabled its members to participate in the culturally suspect but economically necessary collective farm in their own way and at their own time. In industry it provided better tools, easier and more healthful jobs, and timely leaves.

Even as diversified households were preserved, the economic role of individuals was diminished. Individuals adrift in the socialist labor system were at the mercy of their own economic and political limits. If they were to survive and succeed, they had little choice but to submerge their will in the household's goals and decisions. Some individuals did ultimately limit or even cut their ties to their larger households, but they were few.

Though individuals were diminished, household social networks were just as important as they had always been. Networks, in fact, mediated the struggle between household and state. Individuals representing each institution used networks to adapt to the demands and restrictions imposed by the other: householders to secure access to the resources of the socialist economy and state agents to secure adequate production in formal socialist institutions.

The status of the household was recognized and synergistically supported by state and party cadres. Though state policy officially sought to eliminate household production and only individuals were formally employed by factory and farm, in actuality the need for labor to fulfill the plan prompted administrators to allow members of households to work together or spell each other at work. In fact, it was often a household's ability to deliver its members' labor that determined an enterprise's ability to meet the state's demands.

Household labor played a role in every socialist economic sector. Members of employees' households informally substituted for them in many nontechnical industrial jobs, as when the son of a worker at the water pumping station of the Făgăraş Chemical Combine helped make repairs at the station. When a factory's schedule conflicted with a worker's household demands, supervisor and worker reached an accommodation. To retain their workers and ensure their productivity, supervisors regularly looked the other way when workers left on a shopping trip in the middle of the day. They gave workers consecutive days off to cut hay on a household garden plot, or a week off to buy corn in Wallachia. Household cooperation was especially common in services, commerce, and crafts. The husband-wife teams at the general stores in Hîrseni and Cîrţişoara, the bar in Hîrseni, and the Cîrţişoara gas station were only a few of the family groups that worked together. Private ownership of tools and the practice of teaching skills (carpentry, weaving, tanning) to children and grandchildren mandated a household role in craft production. In Cîrţişoara and the western Olt Land, for example, skill at weaving and embroidery brought a woman prestige, and she shared her knowledge only with members of her household.

Even cadres and functionaries were assisted by their households. Cadres' political success and promotion depended on their ability to mobilize labor, and their own household members and close relatives were the ones they turned to first for assistance. Commune mayors, secretaries, and tax collectors relied so often on the help of their spouses, in-laws, parents, and children that the People's Council offices at Cîrţişoara and Hîrseni communes seemed like family reunions when I visited them on business. [1] People whose jobs required them to handle large sums of money would trust no one outside the family. When the Hîrseni Postal, Telephone, Telegraph, and Radio office needed an additional operator, the director in Făgăraş told the woman who ran it to "hire a close relative, someone I trusted, because we always have to adjust work hours in the village, I have things that I sell [such as lottery tickets], and I don't want anyone to steal anything."

Like everything else in the socialist state, labor was intensely political, and a household's control of it was thus related to its ability to establish good relations with the appropriate people in the political hierarchy. It was the joint responsibility of the mayor, vice mayor, secretary, presidents of the collective farm and consumer cooperative, school director, and party activists to deploy labor, determine work schedules, impose penalties for improper work, approve requests for leave, and even provide access to scarce foodstuffs. Officials personally selected the people to fill well-paid jobs with pleasant work conditions and menial, poorly paid jobs. Thus any outcome the villagers desired—avoiding a pig contract, getting the right day off at the factory, getting the right job assignment at the collective or a scarce commercial license without delay—demanded some quid pro quo.

Local leaders found these informal promises essential, for they were

---

1. In this light, the Ceauşescus' use of family members for the operation of state and party seems quite normal.

often under intense pressure from their own superiors. In the press of the harvest or the rush to make annual plans to satisfy the state's demand for animal contracts, or to deal with unforeseen emergencies, leaders needed ready participation by locals, who in turn attempted to manipulate relations with leaders for their own purposes. Politics thus involved complex and constant negotiation between leaders, individuals, and their households, and the advantages that accrued to some were withheld from others. This bargaining contributed to the Olt Landers' perceptions (if not the reality) of pervasive local inequality, sanctioned the use of second-economy principles in the operation of the formal economy, and further diminished the importance of formal economic relations by encouraging a positive view of illegal activities.

Cooperation and Conflict
on Olt Land Collectives

Bargaining, the second economy, and the persistence of household labor had especially pernicious effects on collective farms. Because factory jobs were widely available in the region and the agricultural environment was marginal, Olt Land CAPs always depended on the labor of entire households, especially the part-time labor of people employed in industry. Their development was thus shaped by the bargains their administrators could strike with households to secure their labor. Such bargains, however, ensured neither a household's identification with the farm nor its cooperation with other households. As the state continued its demands for labor and resources, the constant bargaining contributed to a pervasive sense of influence peddling and favoritism, and promoted conflict among households and between household and farm (cf. Sampson 1983b).

Bargaining on the Early Olt Land Collective

The bargaining at the inception of Olt Land CAPs may have been a response to the villagers' resistance to collectivization. Regional CAP administrators essentially ignored the national policy limiting the roles of the household on collective farms and sought to retain workers by structuring their labor to meet their cultural expectations. Though

[105]

households were forced to deed animals and tools to the farms, they continued to keep them in their own barns and sheds (since the collective had none) and so retained de facto control over them. The permanent brigades and work teams mandated by the state (National Conference of Peasant Collectivists 1962:663–64) existed pretty much in name only in the Olt Land. When state cadres first divided Hîrseni village into work teams, for instance, the villagers rejected their plan because it brought together people with few social linkages. When the cadres later divided the Hîrseni village collective into two production brigades of five work teams each, some team leaders simply parceled out land to member households, and the households worked them as "work teams."

Whatever enthusiasm for farm labor these bargains generated was negated by conflict over livestock. Though households were able to use the manure, milk, and power of the expropriated cattle and water buffaloes they cared for after the collective's needs were met, the treatment of horses—ideologically anathema to the socialist state but local status symbols—provoked incredible resentment. As the collective took hold, horse ownership was prohibited and expropriated horses were worked and starved to death or destroyed outright. The number of horses in Hîrseni village decreased from about 200 in the early 1960s to 64 in 1965 (Annual Report, CAP Bujorul Carpaților, 1965). The destruction of horses also caused considerable inefficiency and tension among farmworkers. Though households were informally responsible for labor organization, they now had to bargain with individuals named as *conductori* (animal drivers). Scheduling the *conductor*'s service created animosities and bottlenecks, and the situation was little affected by reversion to team labor later.

Collective farmers were paid according to the *zile muncă* (workday) system, and the fact that the workday was also subject to bargaining produced considerable resentment. The *zile muncă* system formally contradicted household production, as only individual labor was remunerated, and pay was linked to the performance of the brigade and team. Each farm task was assigned a point value based on its difficulty and the special skills, training, or danger it involved. Picking fruit (few skills, minimal effort) had a point value of 0.75; spreading manure (hard, but safe and needing no training) was evaluated at 1.00; and spraying fruit trees (physically easy but requiring special skills and exposure to pesticides) was assigned 1.50 points. Though one's pay increased with the points one accumulated, bonuses were paid only if the work team and brigade fulfilled their production plans.

This system was eminently equitable on paper, and controls such as independent verification of accounting and limits on credits earned by farm officers were built in to prevent favoritism. All the same, the point value of a task seemed to rise when it was assigned to a person high in the village hierarchy, and the same number of credits were awarded whether one worked conscientiously or lackadaisically. And despite accounting controls, farm officials still rewarded favored workers and their family members disproportionately. An early team leader summed up the situation this way: "Many came to work early and worked hard all day while others would come late and work like this [he mimed hoeing while he gazed off in the distance], leave early, and still get the same credits."

Policy in regard to use plots assigned to households by the farm also promoted the second economy and bargaining. Restrictions on the size and use of plots limited household production and increased villagers' competition for appropriate plots. According to informants, all households that entered the collective were promised 15 ares (100 ares equal one hectare) for each member, but the promise was never kept. Almost from the first, CAP administrators claimed that contract requirements and a shortage of land forced them to restrict the sizes of plots. All farm members except pensioners had to satisfy minimal work requirements to get a plot, households were limited to 45 ares without exception, and those with courtyards or gardens larger than 10 ares had the excess subtracted from their plot. Furthermore, the plots were not assigned until all CAP fields were planted, so their growing season was shortened appreciably.

Farm leaders, pulled in all directions by the households and the state, were expected to satisfy them all, again by negotiation. In their first years the CAPs were usually headed by respected local men elected by their peers with the party's approval. Despite the anti-*chiabur* campaign, all of the administrators elected in February 1962 in Hîrseni were prominent upper-middle peasants. The Hîrseni and Copăcel CAP presidents had estates of slightly more than 14 hectares and slightly less than 10, respectively. The eight members of the Hîrseni leadership council owned an average of 8 hectares, nine of ten work-team leaders owned between 5.5 and 8.5 hectares, and the two brigadiers owned 8.5 and 9.5 hectares.

As mediators between state and community and between local households for access to farm favors, administrators had to satisfy all at once. Satisfying particular households, however, opened them to accusations of favoritism, while acceding to the state's demands deprived them of local legitimacy. The first president of the Hîrseni farm lost much of his local support and quit after just a few months' service when a state land requisition forced him to take an unpopular action. To equalize the sizes of collective farms after 200 hectares were expropriated from Rîuşor village for a new state farm for Făgăraş, Rîuşor was ceded 200 hectares from Ileni village, which in turn received compensation from Hîrseni. There the chain stopped. The Hîrseni president first vetoed the expropriation from his farm but was ultimately pressured by the regional officials to accept it. He reluctantly approved the transfer and then resigned. "I quit," he later explained, "because I was needed at home and the job took too much time. There were people coming to see me all the time, complaining about everything—work credits, the size of their plot, their work teams. . . . There were too many meetings and I was always at the town hall."

Such difficulties multiplied after 1964, when village farms were unified into commune-wide organizations with specialists provided by the Ministry of Agriculture. This unified structure precipitated tensions between Drăguş and Viştea and between Copăcel and Hîrseni, among others. In the latter case, a president who ruled with an iron hand was brought in by the Ministry of Agriculture because, according to informants, this was the only way to prevent household and village influences on the collective.

These competing pressures played havoc with CAP labor, which was extensive in the first years of collectivization but steadily declined through the 1960s. In 1963, for example, the 57,777 work credits earned in Hîrseni exceeded the planned 52,000 credits by 11 percent (Kideckel 1979:127). Adult men were so active in the collective that their full-time and part-time labor together accounted for close to 60 percent of all labor. After 1964, however, labor of both men and women declined steadily (Tables 5 and 6). Even though the minimum number of labor points to qualify for a use plot had increased from 75 to 80 for women and 130 to 140 for men, actual labor performed fell 9.3 percent below the amount planned in 1966 (213,621 work credits realized of a planned 230,000) and 9.1 percent below in 1969 (156,963 realized of a planned 173,000).

Table 5. Full-time and part-time participation in CAP labor by adult men, Hîrseni village, 1965–1970, by age group

Age group	Full-time		Part-time		Total	
	N	%	N	%	N	%
1965						
16–24	1	1.2%	2	2.4%	3	3.6%
25–34	1	1.2	0	0.0	1	1.2
35–44	4	4.8	0	0.0	4	4.8
45–54	8	9.6	3	3.6	11	13.2
55–60	16	19.3	2	2.4	18	21.7
61–65	17	20.5	0	0.0	17	20.5
66–75	25	30.2	1	1.2	26	31.4
76+	2	2.4	0	0.0	2	2.4
Unknown	1	1.2	0	0.0	1	1.2
All ages	75	90.4%	8	9.6%	83	100.0%
1968						
16–24	0	0.0%	0	0.0%	0	0.0%
25–34	0	0.0	0	0.0	0	0.0
35–44	2	4.1	1	2.0	3	6.1
45–54	4	8.2	0	0.0	4	8.2
55–60	13	26.6	3	6.1	16	32.7
61–65	9	18.4	1	2.0	10	20.4
66–75	15	30.6	1	2.0	16	32.6
76+	0	0.0	0	0.0	0	0.0
Unknown	0	0.0	0	0.0	0	0.0
All ages	43	87.9%	6	12.1%	49	100.0%
1970						
16–24	0	0.0%	0	0.0%	0	0.0%
25–34	0	0.0	0	0.0	0	0.0
35–44	0	0.0	0	0.0	0	0.0
45–54	3	7.3	0	0.0	3	7.3
55–60	5	12.2	7	17.1	12	29.3
61–65	6	14.6	2	4.9	8	19.5
66–75	11	26.9	6	14.6	17	41.5
76+	1	2.4	0	0.0	1	2.4
Unknown	0	0.0	0	0.0	0	0.0
All ages	26	63.4%	15	36.6%	41	100.0%

Source: Evidenţa zilelor, CAP Bujorul Carpaţilor, 1965–1970.

The Contract Payment System

The decline of farm labor was a problem throughout Romania. To counter it the state introduced a new policy that allowed the household a greater role in CAP labor (Cernea 1975:929, Sandu 1973). This policy, the Acord Global (or contract payment system), remained in

Table 6. Full-time and part-time participation in CAP labor by adult women, Hîrseni village, 1965–1970, by age group

Age group	Full-time		Part-time		Total	
	N	%	N	%	N	%
1965						
16–24	10	6.1%	6	3.7%	16	9.8%
25–34	23	14.0	5	3.1	28	17.1
35–44	38	23.2	5	3.1	43	26.3
45–54	27	16.5	4	2.4	31	18.9
55–60	20	12.2	2	1.2	22	13.4
61–65	12	7.3	1	0.6	13	7.9
66–75	3	1.8	4	2.4	7	4.2
76+	0	0.0	1	0.6	1	0.6
Unknown	0	0.0	3	1.8	3	1.8
All ages	133	81.1%	31	18.9%	164	100.0%
1968						
16–24	4	3.5%	2	1.7%	6	5.2%
25–34	15	13.0	5	4.4	20	17.4
35–44	28	24.3	5	4.4	33	28.7
45–54	23	20.1	4	3.5	27	23.6
55–60	10	8.7	2	1.7	12	10.4
61–65	12	10.4	2	1.7	14	12.1
66–75	2	1.7	1	0.9	3	2.6
76+	0	0.0	0	0.0	0	0.0
All ages	94	81.7%	21	18.3%	115	100.0%
1970						
16–24	1	1.0%	0	0.0%	1	1.0%
25–34	15	13.9	5	4.6	20	18.5
35–44	23	21.3	8	7.6	31	28.9
45–54	20	18.5	7	6.1	27	24.6
55–60	7	6.1	8	7.6	15	13.7
61–65	4	3.8	4	3.8	8	7.6
66–75	2	1.9	4	3.8	6	5.7
76+	0	0.0	0	0.0	0	0.0
All ages	72	66.5%	36	33.5%	108	100.0%

Source: Evidenţa zilelor, CAP Bujorul Carpaţilor, 1965–1970.

effect in one guise or another from 1971 until the 1989 revolution, and over time was generalized throughout the Romanian economy. According to Nicolae Ceauşescu (1971:246–50), the system encouraged individual initiative, gave CAPs greater flexibility, and took advantage of the productive powers of households. Despite the envisioned increase in household autonomy, however, it was a perfect example of simulated change: it maintained the old production relations, and other administrative changes even strengthened centralized control.

The collectives were merged in intercooperative councils controlled by the Ministry of Agriculture, and daily oversight of farm activities was given to the directors of the machine tractor stations. Thus adjacent Hîrseni, Recea, and Lisa communes, with over 7,400 hectares of arable land, were now dependent on a single organization that controlled ninety tractors based in three locations.

The Acord Global set up a sharecropping system by which cooperating household groups, work teams, and brigades contracted with a farm to work a specified amount of land in return for a percentage of production or its cash equivalent. As further incentives the Acord called for a guaranteed minimum agricultural income, better pensions, and other industrial-style amenities for collective farmers.[2] At the same time, however, it foresaw increased state accumulation of produce by monetizing pay for agricultural work, increasing CAP taxes and state procurement contracts, raising the charges imposed by machine tractor stations, and further restricting access to farm use plots.

Each region implemented the Acord Global in its own way, depending on ecological and economic conditions. Olt Land farms practiced three variations of the scheme. The most common was termed "global" by informants, but I shall call it "team global" to distinguish it from other "global" systems. Team global was vaguely like the informal household-based production of the collective's first years, though now it was formalized and contractual. Such crops as potatoes, maize, turnips, and beets were planted on the farm's land, the farm provided seed and manure, and the machine tractor station did initial cultivation and harvesting. Plots were apportioned to work teams, and households within each team contracted to care for a specific number of rows. Each team was paid 30 percent of its total production (minus a percentage for MTS services), which was credited to cooperating households as work norms in cash and kind according to the number of rows contracted.

The second type of production, locally called *global cu atelaje* (global with animal teams)—here "plot global"—was practiced when a farm had a labor shortage and had to attract more part-time workers from the nonagricultural labor force. It gave households near-total control over a plot of land and let them choose the people they wanted

2. The minimum income was put into effect in the mid-1970s but was negated in 1983 when it was tied to achievement of planned production.

A farm work team breaks for lunch. Note the hierarchical arrangement: the team leader sits facing the group and the agronomist stands.

to work with and the way the work would be divided up. Participating household groups, along with an animal *conductor,* contracted to perform all production tasks except harrowing on a plot of 1 to 1.5 hectares, with manure, seed, and fertilizer furnished by the CAP. The group then received 30 percent of their production less the cost of mechanized services. Payment was initially to be in kind, with a bonus for production beyond the contracted amount. The related third variant, *împarte* (sharecropping), was practiced on farms where labor and resources were in extremely short supply.[3] Again households contracted to perform all necessary production tasks on a parcel of land, but they supplied their own manure, seed, and traction in return for 50 percent of their production. Only a few households were able to take advantage of this option.

The Acord Global initially accomplished its main objective of increasing farm labor. In Hîrseni, as Tables 7 and 8 indicate, the figure for full-time labor was higher in 1971 than in earlier years (Tables 5

3. *Împarte* was often allowed after years of particularly poor harvests.

[112]

Table 7. Full-time and part-time participation in CAP labor by adult men, Hîrseni village, 1971 and 1974, by age group

Age group	Full-time		Part-time		Total	
	N	%	N	%	N	%
1971						
16–24	0	0.0%	0	0.0%	0	0.0%
25–34	0	0.0	0	0.0	0	0.0
35–44	2	3.9	2	3.9	4	7.8
45–54	2	3.9	0	0.0	2	3.9
55–60	6	11.8	4	7.8	10	19.6
61–65	13	25.5	2	3.9	15	29.4
66–75	12	23.5	6	11.8	18	35.3
76+	2	3.9	0	0.0	2	3.9
All ages	37	72.5%	14	27.4%	51	99.9%
1974						
16–24	0	0.0%	0	0.0	0	0.0%
25–34	0	0.0	0	0.0	0	0.0
35–44	1	2.7	1	2.7	2	5.4
45–54	1	2.7	1	2.7	2	5.4
55–60	2	5.4	2	2.7	3	8.1
61–65	8	21.6	8	10.8	12	32.4
66–75	7	18.0	7	24.3	16	43.2
76+	2	5.4	2	0.0	2	5.4
All ages	21	56.7%	21	43.2	37	99.9%

Source. Evidența zilelor, CAP Bujorul Carpaților, 1971–1974.

and 6) in nearly every age and sex category. Three years later, however, team global began to unravel, and the popular plot global, which had been designed to address problems related to bargaining and the second economy, actually intensified them. In Hîrseni the number of households active in plot global declined from 67 in 1974 to 48 in 1976 and to fewer than 20 in 1980; by 1984 the practice disappeared altogether.

The ebb of plot global reveals the social costs of farm bargaining, which in this case centered on access to animal traction and internal group organization. Since plot global required the group to link up with a *conductor* unless they had their own draft animals, and since the households that wanted to participate were more numerous than the animal teams available, *conductori* were enticed by kin, neighbors, and friends to sign on with them. Households also had to bargain with each other over their own division of labor. Of the fourteen groups on the Hîrseni village CAP in 1976, eight were made up of

Table 8. Full-time and part-time participation in CAP labor by adult women, Hîrseni village, 1971 and 1974, by age group

Age group	Full-time		Part-time		Total	
	N	%	N	%	N	%
1971						
16–24	0	0.0%	0	0.0%	0	0.0%
25–34	17	16.0	4	3.8	21	19.8
35–44	23	21.7	7	6.6	30	28.3
45–54	20	18.9	8	7.5	28	26.4
55–60	10	9.4	5	4.7	15	14.1
61–65	7	6.6	2	1.9	9	8.5
66–75	1	0.9	2	1.9	3	2.8
76+	0	0.0	0	0.0	0	0.0
All ages	78	73.5%	28	26.4%	106	99.9%
1974						
16–24	0	0.0%	0	0.0%	0	0.0%
25–34	6	6.7	0	0.0	6	6.7
35–44	24	26.7	2	2.2	26	28.9
45–54	27	30.0	4	4.5	31	34.5
55–60	12	13.3	1	1.1	13	14.4
61–65	3	3.3	6	6.7	9	10.0
66–75	3	3.3	2	2.2	5	5.5
76+	0	0.0	0	0.0	0	0.0
All ages	75	83.3%	15	16.7%	90	100.0%

Source: Evidenţa zilelor, CAP Bujorul Carpaţilor, 1971–1974.

neighbors and one of three related households; four shared both neighborhood and kin ties; and one consisted of two friends who were former members of the Agricultural Association. Though members of these groups liked the system, people who were unable to participate saw in plot global the same favoritism that characterized all of life since the breakthrough. People left out of the system typically phrased their criticism in terms heavy with sarcasm: the plot-global people were such good farmers that nobody else could keep up with them; plot-global households were the most respectable in the village and they deserved the opportunity to profit. Further complicating plot global was the state policy of paying for most CAP labor in cash. In the industrial, cash-saturated Olt Land, this practice destroyed the only rationale, aside from the use plot, for collective farm work, and it was not popular elsewhere in the country either (Fulea & Cobianu 1972:222). People who signed on for plot global thought they would be paid in kind and were angry when their 30 percent share turned into 22 percent (1 percent to the MTS, 1 percent to the plant-spraying service, 6 percent to the *conductor*), of which two-thirds was paid in cash.

Of all the factors that shaped the household response to collective farming, none was so important as access to a use plot, which over time became increasingly restricted and conflictful. Every year on the Hîrseni farm, for example, the number of workday credits required to earn a plot increased and the maximum amount of land that a household could own before land was subtracted from its plot decreased. Furthermore, demands for state contracts on the CAPs and the uncertainty of access to tractors forced the farms to plant grain and team-global crops before they distributed land for plot global and *împarte*. Use plots were distributed last of all, late in the region's short growing season (Kideckel 1976). Finally, whenever a question arose about a plot, it was invariably settled in the CAP's favor. One collectivist who had accumulated more than the required number of work credits died a few weeks before plots were apportioned, yet his widow was denied a plot. Worry about use plots echoed through village life. Everyone suspected that the neighbors would get a better plot. Plots were the chief topic of conversation throughout the spring. As I often worked at farm headquarters, people expected me to know when plots would be allotted. They didn't understand why all of the farm's land could not be worked at the same time. Farm leaders, however, had their own ideas. As Comrade G., a representative of the Ministry of Agriculture office in Braşov, said, "If you gave people the plots now, you'd never see them again in the fields, because here they don't work the way they should, they care for nothing but themselves." The lateness of the season when the plots were finally apportioned called for frenetic activity, but people often found themselves at a standstill as they waited for the *conductor* to decide to bring his animals to their plot.

All these conditions, then, influenced household work on the farms and intensified both bargaining and second-economy activity. In their efforts to combat constant labor shortages, CAP administrators often begged friends, relatives, and neighbors to sign up for team global. The Hîrseni husbandry brigadier, told to go door to door to enroll her kin and neighbors, spoke of her frustration one February afternoon. In the homes she visited she spoke at length about responsibility but could promise little except to make sure that the rows people received were not rocky or weedy. It was not surprising that most people refused to sign up for more than the minimum number of rows required to qualify for a use plot. Leaving one home, she complained, "People here don't want to work anymore and the CAP makes it hard to convince them. This CAP isn't going well and most of my work is what you see—trying to convince people to do what's necessary and proper."

Securing labor for unique and unplanned farm needs (digging a lime pit, removing the carcass of a dead animal, bagging oats) also presented problems. To get the work done, administrators had to offer favors—a guarantee of payment in kind, extra work credits, a promise of the first chance to buy bottled gas or firewood. So many people refused such work that many administrators stopped asking and relied instead on their kin and friends; then they were accused of favoritism. The Hîrseni agricultural brigadier Vasile R. regularly asked his two older brothers and their sons for help. According to them, they helped him only with some reluctance. Yet others still asked why they should work "when only the Rs benefit," and jokingly pointed to the large stomachs of the three brothers as evidence of their unfair advantage. Though the brothers did benefit in small ways, they still complained about the burdens of kinship and the jealousy of their neighbors.

The CAPs' labor problems were compounded by lapses in communication between the farms and the tractor stations when tractors broke down, as they frequently did, and no spare parts were available. Furthermore, because CAP production was under the control of inter-cooperative councils and tractor stations, the farms were at the mercy of these state employees, who lived outside the communities for which they were responsible (the head of the Hîrseni-Recea-Lisa MTS resided in Braşov and commuted to the area twice weekly) and rarely took any part in farm decision making. To ensure access to tractors, CAP leaders assisted MTS officials with personal services and treated them with deference and extreme respect. As the CAP gave precedence to mechanized tasks, however, alienated local workers were quick to criticize MTS employees and cultivation practices. The teenage tractor drivers from such less developed counties as Bistriţa-Năsăud and Botoşani, they said, were careless; they ruined the land, and they were more concerned with drink than with work. The tractor drivers, too, were dissatisfied; they complained that the CAPs overcharged them for food and rent and that the local people treated them shabbily and were hard to work with.

CAP Labor in the Years of Crisis

In the decade before the 1989 revolution the failure of the Acord Global to stem the decline in farm labor, in combination with the rising national debt and the state's insistence on exporting ever more food, increased the pressure on village households. Unless one were aged or infirm, CAP labor became mandatory, no matter what one's job or whether one had joined a collective. Ration cards were withheld from farm members who failed to achieve 140 annual labor credits; 70 credits were required of workers in other occupations. Once again the state put into force an agricultural delivery plan, the so called Program Unic, requiring all households, CAP members or not, to provide specified amounts of agricultural production. A Hîrseni wall poster summed up its demands:

> *Commune households!* Measures must be taken to ensure accentuated household contribution of produce to provision the population and satisfy national economic needs. Therefore each household comprising 2 or 3 persons is obligated to raise at a minimum: 1 cow, 5 sheep or goats, 1–2 pigs, 10 laying hens, 60–80 chicks for poultry, 5–8 other fowl (geese, ducks, or turkeys), 10–15 rabbits, 1 beehive, and enough silkworms for 4–5 kg. of cocoons, to sell to the state fund. Households larger than 2 or 3 persons must grow a greater number of animals and fowl, in accordance with the number of family members. *We will fully realize and exceed this charge of the Program Unic.*

The economic crisis also affected local stockkeeping. As the tractor stations were hobbled for want of gasoline and spare parts and the Program Unic imposed its demands, the number of people who owned cattle declined while those who owned horses, sheep, and goats increased. Officially, only full-time CAP members could own horses; nonmembers had to sell theirs to the farms. But most people were able to avoid this regulation by personal arrangement. Horses served a variety of functions in this scarcity economy dependent on personal connections. They hauled wood from the forest, transported goods to market, and even provided taxi service. Copăcelers said that one in three households owned a horse to help with their *afacere* (affairs; that is, thefts from forest or collective); in Hîrseni, where only three households owned a horse before 1979, at least fifteen and possibly twice as many owned one by the mid-1980s. The CAPs even

[117]

sought to profit from the situation by requiring local horse owners, farm members or not, to cart manure from barns to fields. The decline in cattle ownership, meanwhile, represented attempts to escape from state contracts. A pregnant cow was a calamity, because a contract for both the calf and the cow's milk inevitably followed the birth of the calf. Many people tried to abort calves or killed them at birth. As one informant said, "Only the plan matters. It's more serious if a cow dies than a person."

Effects of Village Society on Farm-Household Relations

State policies, bargaining, and the second economy were the prime sources of the CAPs' labor difficulties, but normal village social relations also influenced farm life. The CAPs' need to rely on often problematic village social relationships to get their work done constantly affected the quality of farm labor and villagers' attitudes toward the farm, socialism, and one another. In Hîrseni two brothers who had not spoken since a dispute over an inheritance in the 1930s continued their conflict on the CAP. The elder resigned the vice presidency of the farm in the early 1960s in part because his brother accused him of theft. In a similar case of sibling rivalry, a CAP *conductor* used his influence to prevent his younger brother from joining a plot-global group.

Farm administration, too, intertwined with household affairs and intrigues. One decade-long conflict involved three Hîrseni households, all active in CAP administration and dependent chiefly on agriculture for their income. One of their number, Dma. P., a large, earthy woman given to joking and flirting, was a true power in the CAP. Her many siblings had strong ties to the party, she often served on the farm leadership council and as work-team leader, and was consistently named *fruntaşă* (leading worker) at farm assemblies. For a time she was a close friend (and possibly lover) of her neighbor across the street, one of two blacksmiths in the village. She supported his election as work-team leader, helped him gain most of the farm's smithing business, and encouraged him to seek appointment as farm brigadier.

As such things go, the two had a falling out, and she switched her friendship and support to her next-door neighbor, who was subsequently appointed brigadier. In his fury the jilted work-team leader publicly criticized the new brigadier, accused him of illegalities at farm assemblies, and complained that his own CAP blacksmith work and pay had declined. During the brigadier's absence at one assembly, he tried to get his own work team to back his demand that the brigadier be fired, but attracted only minimal support. When the brigadier heard of the attempted coup, he had the smith dismissed. The smith was alienated from both his neighbor and Dma. P. until his death in the early 1980s.

Other tensions that began during the socialist breakthrough also lingered on. Five of the ten original members of Hîrseni's agricultural association figured prominently in CAP conflict. In 1975–1976 two of three cases of verbal abuse heard by the farm's judicial commission, one of which had escalated into fighting, involved former associationists. CAP members accused other associationists of petty theft, shirking, and improper use of farm horses. Former association members were also separated from most other villagers by their assignment to work in the CAP animal barns; the families of two-thirds of the members of Hîrseni's zootechnic brigade from 1976 to 1979 had belonged to the association. CAP officials claimed that work assignments were random, but some villagers were sure that these "first communists" were being given a good deal: barnwork brought a regular monthly salary and the right to purchase grain from state stocks at reduced prices.

The Questionable Moral Economy of Collective Farming

Thus far the portrait of collective farming shows it to be suffused with narrow individualism and familism. Still, as its success depended on some degree of cooperation and reciprocity, in fact farm members often suppressed their own interests in favor of the common good. At farm assemblies members often begged people to put aside their petty differences and cooperate for the larger good, and they always took great interest in and spent considerable time evaluating the people hired as herders and nonmember barnworkers and fieldhands. A ready sociability and friendly banter often characterized women's work groups as they sorted potatoes or threshed grain. People cooperated during natural disasters. When the Hîrseni flax harvest (a major cash crop) was threatened by a month of rain, villagers readily worked overtime to harvest the muddy fields by hand. When Hîrseni's sheep

[119]

were menaced by a heavy snowfall, two dozen men hiked up the mountain to help the shepherds protect the rest of the flock. When an infestation of potato beetles threatened Olt Land collectives, villagers in both Cîrţişoara and Hîrseni, many of them people who worked regular factory shifts, voluntarily mobilized for a week to apply insecticide to the fields.

Though these efforts were clearly in the spirit of collectivity, they were frustrated by socialist labor principles. The insecticide mobilization is a case in point. It was announced by the bugle and drum of the village crier and his son one Monday morning. Villagers were told to bring old nylon stockings to apply insecticide to the fields by 2 P.M., but so great was local concern that a clutch of villagers showed up even before the appointed time, and soon more than sixty people were assembled, including twenty-two full-time factory workers. But the impressive turnout was for nothing, because there was no insecticide. The CAP *ghestionar* (quartermaster), the only person entrusted with a key to the storeroom aside from the farm president (away at a spa for medical treatment), was nowhere to be found. It was rumored that he had fallen asleep in the Copăcel animal barn. He pedaled up on his bicycle two hours later, but by then half of the villagers had left.

The only other kind of natural cooperative sentiment on Olt Land collectives is best described as a kind of mass paranoia. Any random event or natural disaster was likely to be laid at the door of the socialist state. Thus the death of a 36-year-old Hîrseni tractor driver who was felled by a heart attack in August 1984 was said to have been caused by overexertion brought on by the national petroleum crisis: earlier he had been allowed to drive his tractor home from the Recea tractor park, but gasoline rationing had forced him to walk. Many people blamed collective agricultural practices for any event that disturbed them: changes in the weather patterns were attributed to crop spraying; ill health was traced to the use of chemical fertilizers. But like the weather, the CAP was something one talked about but did not think of changing.

Cooperation and Conflict in Socialist Industry

Factory labor was more satisfying and less socially disruptive to Olt Landers than collective farming. Despite the revolutionary sentiments of recently proletarized peasants (Thompson 1966, Wolf 1969), a wide range of factors kept Olt Land workers and factories politically quiescent. The region's early and extensive industrialization provided many Olt Landers with opportunities to qualify as skilled or semi-skilled laborers with better wages, perquisites, and job conditions than those generally available elsewhere in Romania (cf. Herseni et al. 1972:250, Hoffman et al. 1984:62–90). Factory work also fed Olt Landers' sense of themselves as modern, technologically advanced, forward-looking, and orderly people.

Nor were Olt Land households permanently pulled apart by the rural/urban division of labor. Elsewhere in Romania factory workers typically worked so far from their homes that they saw their families only sporadically (Filip et al. 1972:85–87); but in the Olt Land most villages were within 15 kilometers of a city or town, most roads were paved by the early 1970s, and regular bus service operated between villages, factories, and towns most of the day and night. Almost 40 percent of the workers at the Făgăraş Chemical Combine commuted from villages in the early 1970s (Herseni et al. 1972:247), and no doubt the percentage was higher at factories in Victoria and Mîrsa, which had fewer residential areas than Făgăraş.[4]

Proximity of village and town, farm and factory had drawbacks and advantages, both of which encouraged stability in the factories. For one thing, Olt Land workers were tired. Commuting time extended the workday over two hours, and village residence subjected them to the demands of both the CAPs and their households. More than once during spring planting I saw a man rest his head on the rump of a water buffalo as he plowed. Still, most Olt Land workers found the daily commute worthwhile. With access to both industrial wages and agricultural produce, they maintained a reasonable standard of living while many Romanians were enduring unspeakable suffering in the economic crisis of the 1980s. Commuting was also fairly sociable. Young men played cards at the bus stop. As Christmas approached, *ceataşi* from different villages playfully competed in singing carols as they rode the bus. And the bus schedule gave workers time to shop in the city after their shift.

Unlike the CAP workers, the factory hands spoke positively about their co-workers, even though the New Economic and Financial Mechanism (NEFM) held their wages hostage to the performance of

---

4. I do not have more recent data, but the percentage could not have changed significantly in the late 1980s, as the debt crisis limited rural migration in any case.

Young men play an impromptu card game as they wait for the bus that will take them to their factories.

an entire team and section and aroused resentment against malingerers. Team members were called *băieți buni* (good guys) and *oameni de treabă* (serious or trustworthy people), and shared an ethic of mutual assistance expressed by the phrase *ne ajutam între noi* (we help each other). Ethnicity was rarely a factor, and family metaphors abounded in descriptions of factory colleagues:

> As a parts assembler I'm in a small team with three other guys. We're like a family because we help each other with all our troubles. Like, if one guy has someone sick at home, we'll even do some extra work for him. All of us come from different places—Șercaia, Hîrseni, Recea, and Șinca—but that's OK. . . . I like all my team. The guy from Șercaia is a Saxon and not so capable as the rest of us. We always show him how to correct his mistakes. We do it because we're all close, but with Global [NEFM] it costs.

Though workers' relations were generally good, they rarely developed into political unity or went much beyond appropriate shop-floor behavior. For one thing, the hours required for commuting, CAP work, and household chores left no time for fast friendships to form.

All of the workers preferred the first shift (from 7 A.M. to 3 P.M.) because "it gives more time to work at home." Many workers said that they rarely or never visited other members of their work team and that their closest factory friend was a village neighbor, *naş*, or relative.

Village loyalties were even stronger in the factory than in the collective. With few exceptions, Olt Land workers said they would rather work with fellow villagers than with others. One welder explained: "In the factory you have to know the people you work with. The work is more dangerous, things are always breaking down, and because of the Acord we always have to help each other get materials to do our jobs. And we have to be able to trust each other to take a break, borrow equipment, or just get by."

Thus some of the emphasis on trust was necessitated by the numerous illegalities in which people participated; these activities called for far more coordination than the petty larcenies on the collective farm. To steal factory materials was glossed as *să copsi* (to paint); there was no special term for stealing from the CAP, perhaps because the practice was so general. On the farm bags of grain, carts of hay, and fatted lambs were taken by people who worked alone at night. Theft of tools, raw materials, and food or improper use of transport was harder and required cooperation to circumvent the controls on workers and inventory. Truck drivers, inventory technicians, and gatekeepers were especially valued accomplices because they stood at critical nodes in the factory distribution chain and had information about the plant's resources and personnel movements. A fairly well-developed code of honor kept people from informing on colleagues at the factory, but not on the CAP. Workers might complain if a teammate failed to do his share, but not to their superiors. A work-team leader at the Chemical Combine explained, "It's not *omenesc* [decent] to go to the *maistru* [master technician], though it's the *maistru*'s job to control labor. Everyone makes mistakes and life is difficult, so we should just *să facă şi să tacă* [do the job and shut up]!"[5]

State accumulation, labor control, and the pressures of the second economy reinforced the tendency of village loyalty to erode solidarity among factory workers. They had few opportunities to craft affective relations on the shop floor. Workdays were filled with work. Few informants recalled games, jokes, gossip, or the other interchanges

---

5. CAP members, in contrast, said that theft from the farms would have been far greater had it not been for the fact that people were certain they would be turned in by their neighbors if they were found out.

that lighten the load in Western factories, except when team members failed to pull their weight. Malingerers became the butts of factory horseplay: their food or cigarettes disappeared; their machinery and tools somehow became coated with salve; they were told that the section chief wanted to see them.

Money, too, got in the way of factory friendships. Manipulation of workers' pay and bonuses was a chief source of conflict. Bonuses, determined by work-team and section leaders, were awarded for production in excess of the plan and, under the NEFM, for reductions in the use of energy and raw materials. Their distribution was subject to bargaining and was often based on favoritism. One common ploy of the *maistrii* was to request time budgets of 1,000 worker-hours for tasks that required only 600 or so, so that they could reward cronies and clients with extra pay. As one manual laborer put it, "Only factory leaders and their dancing bears get bonuses. They have a subscription to them."

Though workers recognized the manipulation of their pay, they still allowed it to come between them. A quality-control inspector at the Făgăraş Chemical Combine and four of her co-workers were ostracized after they received bonuses. The other workers avoided them, spread sexual and other rumors about them, and said they had "their hands in the same pockets as the *maistru*." This experience, however, had no effect on her political consciousness. She only insisted that she deserved her bonus, and that "the quality-control teams on the other two shifts got more than their share because their team leaders have connections with the higher-ups." A woman office worker said that "if it weren't for the bonuses, my work in the accounting office would be completely satisfying. But there are always problems between co-workers because the bonuses break up our relationships."

A related problem was competition for work assignments and leaves. In contrast to industrial workers elsewhere in Romania, the Olt Landers had stable work histories and most remained at one workplace until they retired.[6] Instead of seeking more congenial work elsewhere, Olt Landers bargained for the jobs they wanted in the factory. Though specific procedures were mandated, work assignments were so often subject to personal influence that any promotion was suspect. When a spot for chief technician opened up at the Chem-

6. Job hopping was discouraged by the fact that one lost seniority and its higher pay rate by switching workplaces, even in the same industry.

ical Combine, five people applied for it. Selection was based on a two-phase process that included a written essay and a practical exam. Though the woman who won the promotion passed with a high score, she said, "My colleagues spread rumors about me—that my husband [an engineer in the plant] gave me the answers, that I'd stolen the answers, that someone else had written the essay for me. When I heard all this, I cried and wanted to quit. These are decent people, really. It's just that they're so envious."

Bargaining also operated in the selection of people for in-country travel delegations and foreign work assignments. Work abroad with pay in Western currency was particularly prized, but few Olt Land villagers had such opportunities. I knew only two men who worked in West Germany in the early 1970s and heard of another who worked in Iran. According to the first two, they were chosen for their skills, but some others said they got the jobs because one was related to a commune mayor and the other to a party secretary.

Delegations to workplaces elsewhere in Romania were more common. Short-term assignment to Bucharest, Braşov, or some other city on factory business was usually welcomed. The expense allowance was minimal, but the assignment provided a day away and access to contacts and goods elsewhere in the country. These jobs were mainly for managers and skilled workers. Appointment to them was generally considered a favor dispensed by team and section leaders, and occasionally provoked jealousy among the favored ones' colleagues. Manual workers, in contrast, were subject to long-term reassignment, since their skills were readily transferred from one job to another, and they sought to avoid such transfers at all costs. Two metalsmiths of my acquaintance at the Chemical Combine were dismayed to find themselves facing transfer to a mining station in Argeş County. The pay, they said, never covered living expenses, and working and living conditions were always substandard. Efforts to avoid such assignments did much to curtail worker politics: the troublesome were transferred, the compliant remained. Leaves to shop for a scarce commodity or for a day of harvest were also subject to whim. Medical leave was especially problematic, because workers needed verification of disability from the physicians at both the commune and the factory.

Competition and bargaining at the factories were even more pervasive during the decade of crisis before the 1989 revolution. Underproductive factories were pressured to transfer out surplus labor (one of the issues behind the strike and riots in Braşov in November 1987), opportunities for promotion were rarer, and speculation about jobs, bonuses, and factory resources was extraordinary. In contrast to the stability of previous years, workers now based their decisions about whether to take or quit a job on the influence they had with superiors and the availability of resources in the second economy. The critical factor was *pilă* (pull).[7] Paradoxically, as the state tightened its grip on labor, bargaining and black-market operations became more extensive at the workplace, with a corresponding loss of unity and the spread of apathy and atomization. The complaint of Ioan M., a Hîrseni welder, when his son was denied extended home leave to care for him when he was seriously ill captured the spirit of the times: *"Cu pilă mare, pilă mică, / Fără pilă, nu faci nimică* [With big pull or with small, / Without pull you do nothing at all]."

Domestic Economy and Second Economy

To a great extent, agricultural and industrial work was evaluated according to the opportunities it provided for production for the second economy. The restrictions and shortages of the socialist economy made such work a virtual necessity for most households. The second economy did not merely supplement a household's industrial wages and subsistence agriculture; it gave access to key resources, exchange partners, and cultural objects considered necessary for a proper life. And so almost every household dabbled in the second economy in one way or another. Electricians made a second career of repairing TVs, radios, and cassette players. Welders made rabbit cages and fixed bicycles with factory equipment. Bakers used the consumer cooperative's ovens to bake for their friends. Local officials had first choice of scarce food and bottled gas delivered to the communes. And some people even took a job because of the access it offered to the second economy. In fact, this was a chief rationale of CAP brigadiers and quartermasters. Ilie P., a Combine tinsmith, clearly expressed the importance of this informal production: "The work I do isn't important, like an engineer's or even a turner's, but I can double my income when I have the time and materials to make gutters. . . . You have to have something on the side."

Most definitions of the Eastern European second economy

7. *Pilă* literally means "file"—a tool that rounds off sharp corners.

(Brezinski & Petrescu 1986, Sampson 1986b) emphasize production activities carried on outside the purview of the state. In Ceauşescu's Romania, however, so many things were outlawed and so many demands made on rural producers that the definition of the second economy must be broadened to include practices that helped households *avoid* state production. We have already seen Olt Landers' efforts to escape state milk contracts by aborting calves or destroying them at birth. And according to local physicians, the demands of the Program Unic caused an increase in applications for medical leave to evade work on the collective farm.

Like so much else about socialist life, the second economy inevitably had paradoxical effects on social relations and political possibilities, as it both encouraged and destroyed cooperation and unity. Though access to resources in the second economy often depended on one's position in the formal economy, the illegality of many such practices required organization, mainly within the household, between related households, or among two closely cooperating individuals; *între patru ochii* (between four eyes), as Olt Landers say. The tools and techniques that these activities required tended to be small-scale and easily passed across generations, and production was largely subsistence-oriented. In this light the second economy can be seen as a kind of resistance to the state and a source of reciprocity in the socialist village. Furthermore, production for the second economy often counteracted the effects of the socialist rural/urban and sexual divisions of labor. The buses that ran between village and town were regularly filled with people taking fruits, vegetables, and small animals to town and bringing bicycle parts, electronic equipment, and canned goods to the villages. The household base of the second economy made women and the elderly important producers, for they spent more time than the male workers in the village. As domestic production was so critical for Olt Land life, the division of labor in village households tended to be quite often egalitarian (Table 9).

Though it contributed to egalitarianism in the household, the second economy contradictorily gave some households a competitive edge in the socialist economy, despite the equalizing pressures exerted by industrialization and collectivization. Though nearly every village household engaged in some activity for the second economy, training, employment, or connections offered opportunities to some households that were not open to others. Two households that once had owned *cazane* (brandy stills) and now operated them for the

Table 9. Sexual division of labor in Olt Land households

	All men	Mostly men	50/50	Mostly women	All women
Household, general					
Institutional relations			x		
Budgeting			x		
Organization of others' labor				x	
Child care				x	
Shopping			x		
Household, internal					
Food preparation					
Before cooking				x	
Cooking					x
Cleaning			x		
Tending fire			x		
Laundry					
Preparation			x		
Washing				x	
Rinsing			x		
Hanging			x		
Folding			x		
Household, external					
Carting wood	x				
Splitting wood		x			
Carrying wood			x		
Carrying water			x		
Beating rugs		x			
Husbandry/gardening					
Feeding animals			x		
Cleaning stalls			x		
Collecting eggs				x	
Collecting nuts, fruits				x	
Cutting hay	x				
Hoeing garden			x		
CAP use-plot activity					
Handling oxen			x		
Carting manure	x				
Spreading manure			x		
Plowing	x				
Weeding			x		
Digging potatoes			x		

Hîrseni CAP in exchange for work credits complained bitterly about the long autumn hours they put in at the *cazane*. One or another household member had to be present to supervise and keep track of the succession of villagers and their brandy production, as seven of every ten liters were owed to the CAP. Yet neither was willing to give up this work because it enabled them to limit other work on the CAP, gave them access to a desirable commodity, and thus brought other villagers into their exchange network.

Still other households persisted with production for the second economy because of the autonomy it allegedly conferred. Masons, carpenters, photographers, tailors, seamstresses, weavers continued to pay their licensing fees, sign animal delivery contracts, and put up with other demands of local officials in order to ply their trades. Of all the resources that contributed to success in the second economy, however, none was more important than good relations with the appropriate people in the hierarchy.

The Meaning of Hierarchy for Olt Land
Peasant-Workers

Since so much of their working lives and economic success depended on their links to superiors, Olt Landers often devoted as much time and energy to these relationships as to those with their neighbors and colleagues. Yet their dependence on superiors and the bargaining implicit in the relationship also provoked an abiding fear that superiors might intervene at any moment to make their lives more difficult and their work more onerous. Ambivalence toward leaders fostered political inaction. Anger over their economic lot was mitigated by the respect they felt for some individuals, and the struggle to change the conditions of their labor was coopted by supervisors' entreaties and favors, which dissolved workers' solidarity into individualistic and familistic compromise.

Running from Responsibility

Ambivalence toward superiors and toward politics was ensured by the pervasive refusal of Olt Landers to participate in political and economic administration. Informants often said that Olt Landers ran from responsibility. This notion, of course, represented a realistic understanding of the limits of their influence. It was shaped by the bitter experience of the socialist breakthrough, reinforced by arbitrary authority, and cemented by the demands of peasant-worker life and the second economy. Though many workers were well trained, had

[129]

high technical competence, and considered themselves more capable than their supervisors, it was a rare worker indeed who desired to be a work-team leader or a *maistru*, who helped workers with their technical problems and supervised the pace of production. Of the more than 600 workers who commuted from Hîrseni commune to Făgăraş in 1979, I heard of only three *maistrii* and four work-team leaders.[8] A Hîrseni welder in his mid-thirties rejected a promotion to team leader when it was offered because "I have no appetite for that kind of work. You have to be involved with people too much. There are too many questions of influence [*pilă*]. In any case, with my mother sick and old, I have too much to do at home." And a factory work-team leader who moved to Făgăraş from Hîrseni two years earlier said, "I couldn't take the job when they offered it to me because it would have been too hard. To be a work-team leader means responsibility, and to be responsible you have to be on the job every hour of the day. As it is, all my free time is still taken up by the scythe and the queue"; that is, haying for his parents and standing in line for food.

The numbers of Olt Landers in administrative work were proportionately greater on collective farms than in industry but equally insignificant. Since the late 1960s farm presidents and members of the leadership councils were almost exclusively local residents, as were the work-team leaders (elected by their teams), agricultural and husbandry brigadiers (appointed by the leadership councils), and farm clerks, bookkeepers, and cashiers. Despite the large number of positions to be filled, scrutiny of leaders' identities revealed that only a small number of politically active households actually served in farm leadership. Between 1962 and 1979, for example, only 87 people actually filled the 203 CAP administrative positions, exclusive of team leaders and brigadiers. The fact that eighteen of those names appear four or more times suggests that farm administration was dominated by a small nucleus of households. Except for these "households of hierarchy," finding other people to serve in farm administration was a real struggle. Potential team leaders were reluctant to volunteer. The limited rewards and power of these positions could not make up for the pressure and demands by fellow villagers. The Hîrseni CAP president said: "The hardest part of my job is to get other people to work. There are never enough team chiefs, so I have to go jawing from house

8. Two other work-team leaders at the Chemical Combine had recently moved out of the commune.

[130]

Waiting for the herd of water buffaloes to return on a summer afternoon

to house, making promises to get people to be chiefs. This one needs bottled gas, that one wants meat. I can't satisfy them all, but we need chiefs." Those promises only reinforced people's jaundiced view of responsibility and the domination of the farm by that core of households.

Administrators as Contradictions

Although Olt Landers' educational and technological backgrounds encouraged appreciation of the skills of leaders who were directly involved in production, the constant need to bargain with supervisory personnel promoted biting criticism of those who avoided production and of all supervisors so far as money issues were involved. Factory team leaders and *maistrii* were lauded for their production roles and described as good guys or as capable, understanding men. An IUC metal cutter said that *maistrii* were "people like us who rose from the

[131]

ranks" because they were better prepared and more capable than others. To the extent that the workers socialized, they and their immediate supervisors were often together in social situations. They all drank at Făgăraş or Victoria bars, attended weddings, funerals, and name-day celebrations together, and more rarely went on outings to mountain meadows. Team leaders were popular choices as godparents, and chiefs and *maistrii* from one's own village were especially valued for their help. All the same, they drew intense criticism over money and authority issues. Even the metal cutter who voiced his respect for the *maistrii* said that "*maistrii* can't be trusted because they talk out of both sides of their mouths about pay and bonuses."

Relations with top factory bosses, in contrast, were marked by social distance and extremes of respect and derision. Though many workers spoke of compassionate treatment when they appealed directly to top administrators for changes in work assignments, workers still approached the IUC director in the classic pose of submission—eyes down, head bowed, voice muted in formal speech—and caricatured him among themselves. Factory bosses were the butts of proverbs: "Never stand at the rear of a horse or in the face of your boss"; "Never raise your hand against your boss, or the bread will drop from under your arm." The Făgăraş Combine director provoked a new round of jokes when he appeared in a worker's smock for the first time during a visit of Nicolae and Elena Ceauşescu.[9] The increase in labor and decline in consumption during the economic crisis of the 1980s and the widening gulf in status between workers and supervisors intensified the criticism. One worker said: "It would be better for everyone to have a hoe in their hands than to be an engineer or a section chief in these times. Those guys only shuffle papers and contribute nothing to society. No one asks anything of them except to be there and collect their money. People should contribute something to society. That's the law, and that's right and honest."

Villagers took equally contradictory views of the collective farm leaders. They blamed farm problems primarily on the leaders' bureaucracy—the seven people with briefcases for every person with a hoe. As in the factory, however, views of leaders depended on their positions. Work-team leaders, elected by the members, were "people just

9. Elena Ceauşescu, allegedly a Ph.D. in polymer chemistry, also provoked laughter when she revealed her ignorance of factory procedures during the visit.

like us," but appointed brigadiers were reviled for their refusal to respond to legitimate local issues (Kideckel 1976, 1979). Farm technicians, such as agronomists and veterinarians, drew the same responses as factory team leaders and *maistrii:* they were lauded for their production roles, education, and expertise but attacked over issues of pay and labor control.

The contradiction between respect for leaders and rejection of hierarchy was highlighted one summer evening when the Hîrseni agronomist gave a slide show on pomiculture at the school. The agronomist greeted the members of his audience warmly as they arrived, and when they had all squeezed themselves behind the small desks, he told them what to look for in the slides. The showing of the slides took about thirty minutes and elicited some favorable comments. Then the agronomist asked for questions. After a long pause, two men asked about the increase in production that could be expected if adequate insecticide were used. Before the agronomist could answer, the mention of insecticide drew a question about its toxicity and complaints about people's headaches and nausea. Then, almost on cue, the men began to criticize the agronomist for other farm policies. "Why don't the animal brigades store manure better?" "How come pay for cutting hay is so low?" "Why are we cultivating land that's so prone to flooding?" All joined in, and questions came so quickly that the agronomist had no time to answer. His calls for order only further incensed the audience. A worker's complaint about the care of farm horses prompted two others to comment about poor farm labor in general, to criticize some other villagers, and to charge that administrators were never seen in the fields. Yet the men's anger faded as quickly as it flared. As the meeting broke up, a sea-change overtook them as they spoke to me about the agronomist's knowledge and decency. All agreed when one said he was a good man. Another said he really knew a lot, and spoke of the importance of education for agriculture. A third thought the meeting helpful, and all said they had learned much of importance. So had I. Clearly, state-sponsored events designed to encourage the cult of labor, rational production, and socialist consciousness conveyed other messages. In short order, discussion of a simple technical matter had turned into an exercise in recrimination and frustration. Efforts to force the villagers to concentrate on the state's message invariably provoked criticism of the system and perhaps a hard-to-swallow recognition of their own compromises with it.

[133]

Olt Landers in the Hierarchy

Not all Olt Landers rejected responsibility. Though many outsiders assumed leadership roles in socialism's early years, by the early 1970s local leaders (mayors, vice mayors, CAP presidents, and school directors) were usually men born and raised in the region, and usually in the commune in which they served. The participation of these local elites was critical to the state. They gave it a patina of local legitimacy, and their knowledge of and membership in local networks helped to maintain order and sped the flow of resources to the state's coffers. Despite the importance of their roles for the state, most of their fellow villagers treated them with respect or at least with equanimity, for they realized that many elites were forced to serve and pitied them for their ultimate impotence in the face of higher-level state and party cadres. Still, their positions tended to shunt them to the margins of local social life, and when they were not working they could usually be found with their relatives or with each other.

Eastern European centralization has often been seen to provoke feelings of inadequacy at the bottom of the status pyramid (Bahro 1978, Haraszti 1977). Its effects on local leaders have tended to escape notice. Centralization made their work difficult and destroyed their effectiveness. Most decisions, and all of those of real importance, were made far from the local community. And because their work was constantly controlled from above, local administrators feared to make the trivial decisions entrusted to them and constantly second-guessed themselves. Furthermore, local leadership was physically exhausting; nearly every petty decision that affected them was passed on to them by a subordinate in another office, so that they had to be everywhere at once. They quickly wore themselves out in the process; alcoholism, ulcers, and ill health became occupational hazards.

One day in the lives of the Hîrseni CAP president and the farm's head agronomist reveals their predicament. As neither had a valid driver's license and their regular driver was ill, I was pressed into service. Our day began just after six o'clock on a spring morning, when the two men cochaired a meeting with farm *conductori* to schedule the transport of manure to the fields. The matter had been discussed earlier in the week, and now the plans were gone over again for an hour and twenty minutes. Then the president met with the commune veterinarian, who doubled as head of the CAP's party executive committee, while the agronomist and I drove just south of the village to a field where potatoes were to be planted. A tractor had broken down and the agronomist, two tractor drivers, three village men, and the agricultural brigadier discussed alternatives for over an hour. We had no way to contact the tractor park, so the agronomist and I drove there to bring back a mechanic, tools, and spare parts. The agronomist then spent another hour directing the mechanic's efforts, to no avail. He dismissed the group and told them to return in the afternoon.

We arrived back at CAP headquarters at 9:45. While the agronomist chatted with the farm accountants, three people sought the president's help with various problems. One needed a horse and cart to get firewood in the next village (permission granted, contingent on the *conductori*'s hauling the planned amount of manure for the day). Another complained about being denied permission for a medical leave to a health spa (dismissed brusquely). The third complained about the poor quality of the land her family was allotted in team global (dismissed, nothing he could do about it).

Just before 11 A.M. we drove to Făgăraş for a meeting at the state bank about a loan for the farm. I was not allowed to sit in on this meeting, so I sat in the bank lobby awaiting my next assignment. Their meeting lasted about an hour and we were back in Hîrseni by one o'clock for lunch at the CAP canteen with the Hîrseni brigadier and more discussion about the broken tractor. At 2 P.M. both men had to be in Recea commune, five kilometers to the west, for a meeting of the Intercooperative Council's farm presidents and agronomists, chaired by the head of the Braşov County office of the Ministry of Agriculture. They had planned to go directly from Hîrseni to Recea, but a call during lunch sent us first to Copăcel village to investigate the death of a water buffalo.

Now, a water buffalo's death was no small matter; the animal was a critical means of traction and represented a sizable capital investment. Bovines had been known to be killed for their meat from time to time, so before this animal could be butchered, the cause of its death had to be determined and an investigative report filled out. Two groups of Copăcelers disagreed about the matter—one maintained that the animal was poisoned and the other claimed natural causes—so our stop in Copăcel took longer than we had expected. The president shouted at the group around the carcass, paced the ground, and demanded

[135]

that a complete accounting be delivered to his office later that day. At 1:45 we finally left for Recea.

Fifteen minutes to travel three kilometers left us plenty of time, but both men were nervous about the possibility of being late. They constantly looked at their watches, shouted "Faster!" and despaired at my pusillanimity when I stopped at stop signs. Surely, I said, the ministry official would understand if they were a moment late. Oh, yes, they said—he would understand that they were disrespectful and undependable. Their nervousness was in direct contrast to their attitude toward punctuality at CAP general assemblies. There they typically showed up one to two hours after the villagers and sauntered slowly down the center aisle, stopping to greet people along the way (Kideckel 1982).

We reached Recea on time, and I visited people there and talked with the other chauffeurs for the three hours the meeting lasted. We returned to Hîrseni in near silence. They had been criticized for the slow pace of the agricultural campaign and were not in a talkative mood. We arrived in Hîrseni about 5:30 and I was excused until the next morning. The two men, however, remained at farm headquarters, no doubt to consider strategies to deal with the Intercooperative Council's complaints and to ponder the mysterious death of the water buffalo.

In sum, the workings of the household and the network were determined in large part by the need for constant bargaining in formal socialist institutions—the factories and collective farms—and in the second economy, in which all households had to engage to cope with the ubiquitous shortages. It would be an oversimplification to equate the workings of the Olt Land household under socialism with Edward Banfield's amoral familism (1958), but not by much. Despite its forty-year campaign against the household, the socialist state depended on individual households, especially in rural peasant-worker communities, to provide the labor that its economic institutions required. And households' struggle against the state for control of their own labor paradoxically fragmented the local social fabric and bolstered the state's dominance.

Ultimately, labor was an antagonistic process both between levels in the region's hierarchy and especially within the rural labor force. Though cooperation shows up now and again, the structure and demands of Romanian socialism, whether on the farm, in the factory, or in informal production relations, ultimately limited cooperation and encouraged division, disagreement, and differentiation. These results then carried over into regional and village social relationships, and encouraged intracommunity differentiation and competition, rather than challenges to the logic and legitimacy of centralized accumulation.

[6]

Community and Conceit:
Social Life and Change
in the Socialist Village

> The Romanian Communist Party has care of the family as a funda-
> mental objective. . . . The socialist village community . . .
> promotes the grounding and strengthening of the family eco-
> nomically, socially, and legally. Supporting and consolidating the
> family . . . are essential features of Romanian Communist Party
> policies and of the socialist community.
>
> Nicolae Ceauşescu, October 1966

> Long live my mother and father so that they can care for me in my
> old age.
>
> Hîrseni worker

The socialist economy of shortages and demands for labor rarely
dampened the Olt Landers' economic spirit. Despite their difficulties,
Olt Landers remained intent on surviving ("getting by") and prosper-
ing ("lifting ourselves up"). These goals were reinforced by the state
itself. Its mobilization campaigns and exaggerated claims of material
achievement intensified longings for abundance. Both survival and
prosperity were to be achieved by household strategizing and maneu-
vering, graphically expressed by a quivering hand moving forward in
snakelike fashion. Households evaluated the possibilities and obstacles and then developed social and economic strategies to gain any
economic advantage they could. Such strategies were manifested in
household structure, demographics, internal organization, and external relationships.

Household Socioeconomic Strategies

It is difficult to fit any household into a typology, let alone a socialist household (see Netting, Wilk, & Arnould 1984, Sanjek 1982, Yanagisako 1979). Efforts to classify households or domestic groups frequently focus on readily observable differences in structure (Fortes 1958, Hammel 1972, Halpern & Anderson 1970), occupation (Pasternak, Ember, & Ember 1976), or ownership and transmission of property (Freedman 1958, Goody 1976). It became common to categorize households in socialist villages solely by demographic (Cole 1976, 1981; Hann 1980:140–41; Randall 1976, 1983) or occupational criteria (Sampson 1984:203–5), as nationalization and collectivization eliminated most property-based class differences. The sources of a household's income were supposed to indicate its relation to the means of production and hence its economic and social standing. A classification of sample Hîrseni households by these criteria clearly shows the importance of the peasant-worker strategy and a slight decline in the three-generation stem family by the end of the 1970s (Table 10).

Of course households considered the sources of their members' incomes and their demographic structure as they maneuvered within their social universe; but, as household theorists suggest, reliance on these categories alone obscures the relation of the household to its community, let alone the national and international political economies in which it is embedded (Fernandez-Kelly 1983, Pahl 1984).

Table 10. Sources of income of sample households, Hîrseni village, 1979, by household structure

Household structure	Agriculture only		Mixed occupations		Wages, pensions		All sources	
	N	%	N	%	N	%	N	%
Four generations	0	0.0%	2	2.5%	0	0.0%	2	2.5%
Three generations	3	3.7	17	21.0	2	2.5	22	27.2
Married couple with parent(s)	0	0.0	5	6.2	2	2.5	7	8.7
Married couple with/ without children	9	11.1	13	16.0	20	24.7	42	51.8
Single person	3	3.7	0	0.0	3	3.7	6	7.4
Other	1	1.2	0	0.0	1	1.2	2	2.4
All households	16	19.7%	37	45.7%	28	34.6%	81	100.0%

[139]

Rather than view households as units bounded spatially and temporally by their structures and sources of income, we must consider them as historically situated and changing "loci of activity and interaction" (Sanjek 1982:58). We must also consider the "continually shifting relationships of authority, influence, emotional solidarity and conflict" (Yanagisako 1979:185) within the household and between households of diverse political standing and possibility if we are to understand their place in their society.

I term the internal and external relations and diverse economic goals of households in socialist villages their socioeconomic strategies. Because the strategy a household chose shaped its social relations and because the significance of common resources (cash, agricultural produce, automobiles, kin ties) depended on its goal, the several strategies available resulted in divergent household relations with both state and village institutions. Households with similar occupational profiles did not necessarily occupy the same economic niche or make the same consumption choices; those of similar demographic structure mobilized different links with other families and might participate intensively, nominally, or not at all in the local Communist Party organization.

Along with the Romanian socialist political economy, a range of factors provided the overall context for the elaboration of household socioeconomic strategies. Any household's strategy reflected first its perceptions of its own position, prestige, and possibility within the village. Some previously prominent households with long pedigrees thought high social status their due and sought prominence in the socialist village, while some descendants of impoverished smallholders hoped for little. Such demographic variables as the number and ages of a household's members also influenced its strategy, as did their health, ambition, vocational interests and qualifications, and personalities. The social network in which any household was embedded also figured in the picture in many ways. Access (or lack of it) to politically connected neighbors or relatives, the size of the kin group, the diversity of occupational and residential situations, and the quality of the relationships among network members all influenced perception, choice, and action.

Five strategies, named to give a sense of their dynamic, processual nature, can be identified among Olt Land households. *Aggrandizing* households sought to expand their social and economic statuses within the village. *Mobile* households also aimed for upward mobility, but they sought it by increasing their spatial or symbolic distance from the village. *Integrated* households, like aggrandizers, were committed to village life but were less successful economically and politically, and thus sought a precarious balance in their economic activities. *Transitional* households moved in and out of villages in the region and were committed instead to people outside of them, but in any village in which they settled, however temporarily, they played important integrative political and economic roles. Finally, *marginal* households existed on the periphery of the community's socioeconomic life and at best made a meager living.

Such strategies were neither static nor mutually exclusive; they changed in response to political, economic, demographic, and cultural conditions. Furthermore, more than one strategy could often be found within a single household consisting of two or more related families. A typology of local households based on these strategies (Tables 11 and 12) is not as cut and dried as one based on structure or occupation, but ultimately it provides a clearer picture of a complex, differentiated local social reality and its dynamic over time.

Aggrandizing Households

Aggrandizing households occupied or sought a niche high in the community's socioeconomic hierarchy, though not necessarily in the party-state hierarchy. Most aggrandizing households were content to profit economically with little actual political involvement but sizable political influence. Still, at least one of their members was usually in the Communist Party and also participated, if only nominally, in local governmental commissions, people's councils, and other volunteer organizations. Aggrandizing households were well integrated and well connected. They were active in all state economic sectors and in the second economy. Though some of them were assisted in their economic and social pretensions by members who chose political careers, party membership and local office placed political and economic burdens on them as well, especially in the last years of the socialist state.

Though all aggrandizing households had at least one CAP member (and rights to the use of at least one CAP plot), on the CAP they often controlled their own labor inputs and were frequently hired to perform nonfarm tasks in return for credits that relieved them of work in the fields. They rarely participated on the CAP as team leaders, brig-

Table 11. Socioeconomic strategies of sample households, Hîrşeni village, 1979, by household structure

Household structure	Aggrandizing		Mobile		Integrated		Transitional		Marginal		All strategies	
	N	%	N	%	N	%	N	%	N	%	N	%
Four generations	1	1.2%	0	0.0%	1	1.2%	0	0.0%	0	0.0%	2	2.4%
Three generations	0	0.0	8	10.0	12	14.8	1	1.2	1	1.2	22	27.2
Married couple with parent(s)	1	1.2	2	2.5	3	3.7	0	0.0	1	1.2	7	8.6
Married couple with/without children	2	2.5	14	17.3	17	21.0	2	2.5	7	8.6	42	51.9
Single person	0	0.0	0	0.0	0	0.0	2	2.5	4	4.9	6	7.4
Other	0	0.0	0	0.0	0	0.0	0	0.0	2	2.5	2	2.5
All households	4	4.9%	24	29.8%	33	40.7%	5	6.2%	15	18.4%	81	100.0%

Table 12. Socioeconomic strategies of sample households, Hirseni village, 1979, by source of income

Source of income	Aggrandizing		Mobile		Integrated		Transitional		Marginal		All strategies	
	N	%	N	%	N	%	N	%	N	%	N	%
Agriculture only	0	0.0%	0	0.0%	8*	10.0%	0	0.0%	8	10.0%	16	20.0%
Mixed occupations	3	3.7	11	13.6	22	26.7	0	0.0	1	1.2	37	45.2
Wages, pensions	1	1.2	13	16.1	3*	3.7	5	6.2	6	7.4	28	34.6
All sources	4	4.9%	24	29.7%	33	40.4%	5	6.2%	15	18.6%	81	99.8%

*Although the occupations of members of these households were found in a single sector, they regularly secured resources in other sectors, either through ties with other families or through the part-time work of some of their members.

adiers, or members of the Leadership Council. If only to maintain their political links, they regularly contracted to deliver animals. The adult men were skilled workers or local administrators; the women were employed as office workers or teachers. Aggrandizing households had ties to the consumer cooperative, since success in the second economy often depended on commerce and trade.

Aggrandizing households were ideally multigenerational, and their members pooled their income, saved for common goals, and made joint spending decisions. Even if one of the families left to set up its own household, the separate units continued to cooperate, even to the point of joint budgeting. The younger people had considerable respect for their elders and even for their siblings. The household members participated in extensive networks of cooperation and exchange and, as leaders in their networks, sought to be the arbiters of community style. They either invested their savings in income-producing resources or used them in village display, especially in the artistic elaboration and technological modernization of their homes, though such modern status symbols as automobiles were less highly regarded. Aggrandizers were of two minds about the value of education. Though they recognized its importance for achievement, supported the education of their offspring, and took an interest in the functioning of the local school, they saw education as best directed to practical ends.

An Aggrandizing Household   The gates of the Voievod household, which occupied a quiet corner on a back street in the northern, Uniate half of Hîrseni, opened onto a sumptuous complex of vegetable garden, orchard, hay lot, chicken coop, large barn, animal stalls attached to a summer kitchen, a separate two-room house rented to a CAP specialist, and a functioning distillery purchased from Ioan Cioră in the 1950s but now operated for the CAP. These buildings and the Voievods' well-appointed home with its new furniture, new television set, and semifunctional tiled bathroom, complete with sink, tub, toilet, and bidet, were set around a vast courtyard with bountiful grapevines and flowers. Tracing their origins to one of the seven original Hîrseni families of the fifteenth century, and with teachers and Uniate priests among their forebears (Figure 3), the Voievods were among Hîrseni's largest landowners before World War II, yet they avoided *chiabur* status during the socialist breakthrough.

In the late 1970s the household had seven members. Ilarie, 54, worked at a water-pumping station for the Făgăraş Chemical Com-

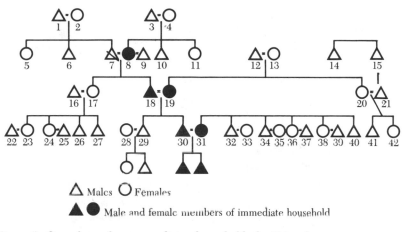

Males △ Females ○

▲● Male and female members of immediate household

Figure 3. Genealogy of an aggrandizing household: the Voievods
1. Teacher at Uniate school, Hîrseni
3. Uniate priest
6. Teacher and Iron Guard activist
7. Wealthy pre–World War II landowner
10. Uniate priest
12. Former *chiabur*; rents rooms to CAP agronomist
14. The *chiabur* Iosif Oltean
16. Former CAP quartermaster
18, 19. Ilarie and Elena
21. Skilled worker in Bucharest; Communist Party member
22, 23. Skilled workers (39 and 40 in Fig. 4)
24. Assistant head CAP accountant; Communist Party member
25. Master technician, IUC; Communist Party member
28, 29. Ana and Nicolae
30, 31. Ioan and Maria
32, 33. Skilled workers
34. Commune civil statistician; member of Communist Party Executive Committee
35. CAP accountant; last commune mayor before revolution of 1989
36. Schoolteacher
37. Orthodox priest
39. Communist Party activist; head of Făgăraş region agroindustrial council

bine, monitoring gauges and doing small-scale repairs. The ease of the work and the proximity of the workplace (one kilometer from his home) made it a fairly desirable job. A member of neither party nor CAP, Ilarie was still regularly appointed to village judicial commissions. He rarely attended church, though his ancestors were prominently interred in the high-status north (formerly Uniate) churchyard, rather than in the communal village cemetery. Ilarie's wife, Elena, 50, was from an upper-middle-peasant family classified as *chiabur* in the 1950s. She was one of the first to enroll in the CAP and the party, however, and regularly served as a deputy on the commune people's council. Though listed on CAP rolls, she rarely worked in agriculture. Working at home, she made knitwear on her own loom for the consumer cooperative. After satisfying her contract, she also made goods for private sale.

The Voievods' oldest son, Ioan, was a party member and skilled lathe operator at the IUC. He often traveled with factory delegations throughout the country. He loved his work, thought himself a technological savant, and was an avid reader of technological journals. He despised agriculture and avoided both CAP and household gardening, though he still earned work credits by doing occasional odd jobs for the CAP. Maria, Ioan's wife, was the youngest daughter of a mid-ranked village family that owned over ten hectares of land before the war. Employed as a bookkeeper at the Făgăraş consumer cooperative, she later transferred to the Hîrseni school as its secretary. Maria had useful political ties. An older brother was commune clerk and a member of the local party executive committee. An older sister was the wife of a party official who headed the Făgăraş agroindustrial council in 1979. Another sister was married to a priest. There were also three dependents in the home: Ilarie's mother, who was a CAP pensioner with the right to an annual use plot, cooked and did other household tasks, and together with Elena cared for Ioan and Maria's two sons, one in first grade and one in third. The boys wanted to be a soccer player and an airline pilot, but their father and grandfather hoped they would become engineers.

Life under socialism was good for the Voievods. Their pooled household income was garnered from a wide variety of sources (one pension, four salaries, the CAP, animal contracting, odd jobs, child allowances, rent, and the second economy) and brought in between 8,000 and 9,000 lei in an active month. Their expenses were relatively low because the family had a use plot and participated in plot global. Food (including fodder), taxes, utilities, clothing, transportation, medicine, wedding gifts, and miscellany totaled between 5,000 and 6,000 lei a month. The balance was put aside to build a new home for Ioan, Maria, and the boys. Ioan's brother, Nicolae, and his wife and children wanted to return to Hîrseni from Braşov, where they lived with her family, so another home was needed.

Nicolae's situation reveals some of the pressures on aggrandizing households and the strategies they adopted to relieve them. Nicolae was a constant source of heartache to his parents. Though he was expected to inherit the household, after he married he decided to live with his in-laws in Braşov, whose *naş*, confusing things further, was a Saxon. Ilarie and Elena were angered by the marriage; it seemed to threaten their household's reputation, for some villagers called Nicolae "a nomad" and "not one of us." The Voievods pressed Nicolae to return to the village, and increased the pressure after his daughter was born. To facilitate his brother's return, Ioan used his seniority and reputation at work, his party status, and his tie to his brother-in-law to get an apartment in Făgăraş for his own family. He toyed with the idea of moving there permanently, but said that even if he didn't, it was still a decent place to stay until the problem of Nicolae was resolved.

The Făgăraş apartment reveals other aspects of the relationships and options of an aggrandizing household. Ioan and his family first moved there after the birth of their second child but continued to contribute a large portion of their income to the household pool. When Nicolae decided to remain in Braşov, Ioan and Maria returned to the village to help with the household's various activities. Though they were now village residents again, and obligated to return the apartment to the factory, they apparently used their connections to retain it. A year in the village proved to be more problematic than they had expected: care of the two young boys was too much for mother and grandmother, and Ioan and Maria's daily commute to Făgăraş was expensive and burdensome. So the young couple returned to Făgăraş but left their elder son in the village and took their younger son and Ioan's grandmother to care for him. After another six months in town, Maria was offered the job of secretary at the Hîrseni school. If she no longer had to commute, she would be able to participate more extensively in the household, so they returned permanently to the village.

The situation with Nicolae, however, was still confused. He and his wife had another child and his parents showed their continued displeasure with him by refusing to attend the baptism. Stepping up the pressure on Nicolae to return to the village, the family began work in earnest on the house for Ioan and Maria. They moved in just as Nicolae's marriage was fraying. He and his wife, Ana, separated for a time and Nicolae returned to Hîrseni with his infant son. Later in the year he returned to Braşov, stayed for a month, and then moved back to the village for good, bringing his son and leaving his daughter with his wife and in-laws. After six months apart, however, and under pressure from her parents, Ana and their daughter also moved to Hîrseni, and there the family remains.

Mobility

Mobile households actively sought to change their social status through emigration or social distancing. Mobility occasionally resulted from or precipitated the breakup of a multigenerational household into separate units. It thus approximated the ideal of the socialist transformation, for the importance of the family was expected to decline as socialist values undermined the old social structure. In census documents mobile households may appear as a three-generation stem family, but actually their nuclear units often had little to do with one another. They maintained separate budgets, cooked separately, slept in separate areas, and considered themselves to be separate units. In local parlance, the household was *dechilin* (divided).

Many mobile men and women were skilled industrial workers or were employed in service occupations as schoolteachers, health-care paraprofessionals, or buyers or contractors for state agencies. Most were state employees and many were Communist Party members. They avoided animal contracting and collective farm labor as best they could and some groused over the need for village network relations to get access to food resources. Mobiles were especially oriented to education and were the harbingers of new cultural patterns. They wanted to buy automobiles and they decorated their houses in a simple style that contrasted with the involuted patterns of the aggrandizers. Members of mobile households rarely attended church, though three Protestant families in Hîrseni did evince characteristics of mobility.

A Mobile Household The plain white-plastered Muntean household stood out for its simplicity along the southern stretch of Hîrseni's main street. As one entered their courtyard one immediately sensed the family's cultural distance from Hîrseni's peasant-workers. Here the usual functional area for animals and tools had given way to a lush flower garden laid out in an elaborate geometric pattern. There was a small vegetable garden in the back, however, and the family also kept a few chickens. The interior of the house was understated. The furniture and TV were not new and the walls were decorated more simply

[148]

than those of most Olt Land houses. The family had many books and took pride in being the first villagers to have their own telephone.

The Muntean family consisted of Gheorghe, Ana, and their two teenaged daughters (Figure 4). Gheorghe was the former head book-keeper of the commune's consumer cooperative, pensioned as a result of illness. Before World War II his family had owned about 7.5 hectares of land, but neither he nor his siblings saw agriculture as a worthy career. In fact, Gheorghe was proud that he gave up his inheritance for help in financing his education in the early 1950s. At that time, he often recalled, he bought a motorcycle and traveled throughout Romania. Ana Muntean, the youngest of three children, was also from a local middle-peasant family. A tireless worker, she was a baker at the Hîrseni consumer cooperative. Because of Gheorghe's illness, she was responsible for most household work, including the flower and vegetable gardens. She kept the vegetables because "the family must eat," but "the flowers are my passion," she said. Each of the Muntean daughters was at the head of her class at school and hoped to study mathematics and law at a university. Both hoped to leave the village after university, and their parents supported their ambitions.[1] In fact, plans were afoot for the younger daughter to live with a relative in Bucharest to receive extra tutoring.

This was a family in the village but not of it. Respected by others and earlier involved in local affairs through the consumer cooperative, the Munteans still saw their future as lying elsewhere. Gheorghe was now marginal in the village because of his illness, which kept him close to home, but also because of his critical approach to life. He saw himself as an intellectual with dispassionate understanding of his own life and of the lives of the other villagers.

The Munteans had greater economic problems than many other families. Their income was restricted by Gheorghe's disability, which required a special (and expensive) diet and costly medical treatment. Though basic health care was free in Romania, people paid bribes or brought gifts to ensure the best possible treatment. They also had to pay for transportation to and from the doctor and for special medi-

---

1. By the mid-1980s the elder daughter, having failed to enter university, became a bookkeeper at the Hîrseni CAP, married the president of the commune's consumer cooperative, and moved in with him and his family in Sebeș. His father was the former CAP president. Thus, Gheorghe's daughter shifted her position from mobile to elite. The younger daughter did attend university, married a construction engineer, and now lives in Făgăraș.

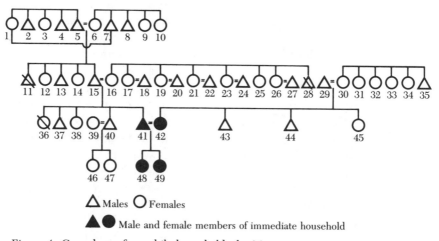

Δ Males O Females

▲ ● Male and female members of immediate household

Figure 4. Genealogy of a mobile household: the Munteans
1, 7. Émigrés to Bucharest
5. Owner of small sawmill; middle peasant
6, 8, 9, 10. Early Adventists in region
14. No. 4 in Fig. 6.
15. Buzz-saw operator for consumer cooperative; middle peasant before World War II
20. Second president of CAP
21. CAP activist; Communist Party member (27 in Fig. 5)
22. Pensioned factory worker (28 in Fig. 5)
23. CAP activist; Communist Party member
25. Married out of village
27. Member of Agricultural Association; vestmaker for consumer cooperative (3 in Table 3)
29. Adopted from Copăcel village
31, 33, 34. Married out of village
32. Married in village
37. Permanently disabled
38. Bookkeeper in Braşov
39, 40. Skilled workers (22 and 23 in Fig. 3)
41, 42. Gheorghe and Ana
43. Skilled worker; Communist Party member
44. Skilled worker
45. Married to brother of 20
48, 49. Maria and Elena

cines. As they were not CAP members and their close relatives participated in the CAP only marginally, they had little access to agricultural
products. In nine months they earned as much as the Voievod family
did in three, but they had fewer mouths to feed, fewer social relations,
and fewer pretensions. Their major concern was their children's education, and these expenses dominated the household budget (Tables
13 and 14).

Mobile households had mobility-related networks. Thus the Munteans were close to Gheorghe's sister in Braşov and to cousins in
Bucharest, where the children went for vacations and where their
younger daughter lived while attending university. Despite his illness,
Gheorghe still contributed to the village's intellectual life. He wrote a
brief volume of village history and an essay on the history of the
consumer cooperative, which he read at a commune assembly organized by the Committee for Socialist Education. Gheorghe and both
daughters were party members, but Ana never joined.

Their crises were also related to mobility. One ended tragically.
Gheorghe's younger brother, Ilie, who worked at the same Combine
monitoring station as Ilarie Voievod, was to inherit the natal household. Ilie and his wife chafed at village life, however, in part because of
their household responsibilities. Gheorghe and Ilie's parents were
elderly and infirm (though their father was still vigorous enough to
operate a buzz saw for the consumer cooperative) and a younger
brother was still at home, partially paralyzed and basically dependent.
Ilie and his wife came to feel increasingly burdened. Over time they
became estranged from his parents and siblings, and curtailed the
income and labor they contributed to the household. As Ilie and his
wife drifted from his family, there were constant arguments.
Gheorghe was caught in the middle. He understood Ilie's desire for
independence, but as the eldest child he felt duty-bound to side with
his parents. He was disgusted and shamed when the family arguments
broke out in public. His brother, he said, "had an ugly mouth and was
extremely self-centered." After a particularly bitter argument, Ilie and
his family packed most of their belongings and moved to a small house
at the monitoring station. The evening they left, the mother hanged
herself. The brothers have not spoken since.

Though this was an extreme situation, the lives of families that
chose mobility were normally filled with travails. Both Gheorghe and
Ilie were mobility-oriented. As an elder son who had come of age with
the socialist breakthrough, Gheorghe was better able to pursue his

Table 13. Sources of income and savings of a sample mobile household, January–September 1977 (lei)

Month	Pension	Salary	Seniority bonus	Night-shift bonus	Prizes	Stipend for children	Gifts, items sold	Total income	Deposited in bank
January	1,121	1,008	45	—	—	—	115	2,289	—
February	1,121	1,288	45	—	—	330	166	2,950	—
March	1,121	1,243	45	—	—	170	285	2,864	—
April	1,121	1,379	45	—	275	—	366	3,186	600
May	1,121	1,479	45	—	—	340	183	3,168	900
June	1,121	1,521	45	—	—	170	219	3,076	300
July	1,121	1,333	45	—	—	170	551	3,220	—
August	1,121	1,378	46	—	—	90	633	3,268	—
September	1,121	1,316	45	75	—	230	713	3,500	—
All months	10,089	11,945	406	75	275	1,500	3,231	27,521	1,800

Table 14. Expenses of a sample mobile household, January–September 1977 (lei)

Month	Food, drink	Health care*	Bus, train, phone	Enter- tainment†	Gifts	Taxes	Dues	Clothing	Heat, light	Items for home	Household maintenance	Reading, writing materials	School expenses	All expenses
January	774	151	162	12	188	—	12	616	152	51	31	44	—	2,193
February	870	61	92	12	42	523	37	103	24	20	8	22	—	1,814
March	1,068	64	174	10	70	75	54	224	1,595	150	33	125	—	3,642
April	1,062	70	126	20	26	8	23	1,131	162	25	88	37	—	2,778
May	994	100	145	11	288	—	20	367	60	127	133	25	—	2,270
June	801	78	116	4	—	75	12	906	29	122	36	58	813	3,050
July	822	14	22	14	1,082	—	15	143	25	163	29	36	638	3,005
August	2,004	15	46	8	243	—	13	209	131	221	90	54	—	3,033
September	900	102	105	9	72	—	12	642	25	6	51	27	1,140	3,091
All months	9,295	655	988	100	2,011	681	194	4,341	2,203	890	499	428	2,591	24,876

*Medicine, consultations.
†Films, dances, lottery tickets.

goals, and he approached his daughters' pending emigration with equanimity, if not joy. With Gheorghe gone, Ilie remained at home to see his pretensions frustrated by the demands of his parents and his paralyzed brother and by the resource-poor environment in which his goals took shape. His future seemed so limited that the only way out he could envision was to precipitate a break with his family.

Integration

Integrated households were the majority in the Olt Land. Like aggrandizing households, they combined diverse sources of income, but their emphasis was on agriculture. They lacked the aggrandizers' social standing and economic possibilities because their resource base was smaller, their education was weaker, their connections were fewer, and their work experience was less helpful. Unlike mobile households, however, they were committed to village life and approximated the ideal three-generation household. Their component families considered themselves to be a single unit, pooled their incomes, ate together, and shared agricultural labor.

Integrated households were conservative, attended church regularly, and were not likely to be party members. To them as to aggrandizers, education was valued but suspect. The best training, they said, was practically oriented and locally applied. If their children attended high school, it was likely to be the village school; a few went to the Agroindustrial High School in Făgăraş. Whatever their education, they became workers in local industries or on the CAP. The young women of integrated households were the core of CAP fieldhands, and the few local tractor drivers were also members of these households. All CAP work-team leaders and *conductori* were members of this group. These households held most of the contracts for animals and most of the privately owned animals in the village; some even kept their own horses or oxen. Even as the agricultural work force aged and the industrial work force expanded, many young people in integrated households still viewed farmwork favorably.

An Integrated Household   Many people considered Octavian Marciu the foremost farmer in Hîrseni. They said so both out of respect for his hard work and out of jealousy of his success. Marciu, too, rarely failed to mention his extensive work on both the collective farm and

[154]

on household plots, and his name often appeared on the lists of commentators in the minutes of CAP assemblies, where he often chided
others for their poor work effort. In the late 1970s Marciu owned one
of the few private teams of horses in Hîrseni. He regularly signed up
for as much plot global and hay lots as he could, and all members of his
household, even his old stepfather, participated in agriculture as extensively as possible. Located right in the middle of Hîrseni, at the
intersection of its two main streets, the Marciu house was like most
others in the village in appearance and size. Its courtyard bustled with
the sights and sounds of farm life: hay wagons coming and going;
implements, boots, and aprons lying about; and the regular cacophony
of pigs, chickens, water buffaloes, and horses.

The Marciu household comprised four generations: Octavian and
his wife, Reghina; their youngest son, Viorel, and his wife, Elena;
Viorel and Elena's infant son; and Octavian's aged stepfather, Constantin (Figure 5). Octavian had been poor as a boy. His father died in
World War I and his mother's second husband was another poor lad.
By the 1940s, however, he had amassed a 7.5-hectare estate. Though
he said he vehemently opposed collectivization, he nonetheless was
determined to make it work. Octavian served two terms as agricultural
brigadier and was regularly on the CAP leadership council. Reghina
also served once as a CAP work-team leader. He and Reghina worked
actively on the CAP through the 1970s. His stepfather ceased field
labor in the middle of the decade. (Pensioned in 1967, Constantin still
earned credits averaging 220 workdays for the next six years.)

With two adults active in the CAP and one pensioner, the Marciu
household annually received a 45-are use plot. They also kept a horse,
one cow, two water buffaloes (one contracted to the state), five pigs
(two on contract), and eight sheep. The household also derived income
from Octavian's pension (he had been employed at the Chemical Combine before the war) and Viorel's and Elena's IUC wages. Viorel was a
welder and earned about 2,000 lei a month in 1976. Elena was at home
on maternity leave and collected about 1,000 lei a month in benefits.
Agriculture was also important to Viorel. He preferred the open fields
to the factory, but he recognized the necessity of an industrial income.

To farm their CAP lands successfully, the Marcius often needed
additional labor; Constantin could no longer work steadily and the
factory took much of Viorel's time. In this regard, Viorel's marriage to
Elena was a godsend. Her family was poorer than the Marcius and her
father had recently retired from the Combine. With Elena in the

[155]

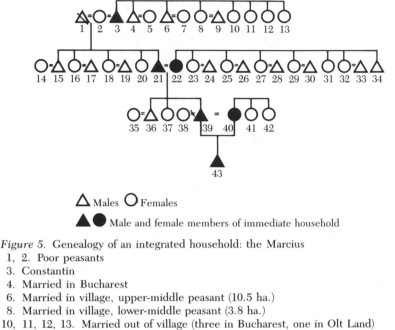

△ Males ○ Females

▲● Male and female members of immediate household

Figure 5. Genealogy of an integrated household: the Marcius
1, 2. Poor peasants
3. Constantin
4. Married in Bucharest
6. Married in village, upper-middle peasant (10.5 ha.)
8. Married in village, lower-middle peasant (3.8 ha.)
10, 11, 12, 13. Married out of village (three in Bucharest, one in Olt Land)
15. Commune veterinary agent; member of Agricultural Association (7 in Table 3)
16. Cook, Hîrseni CAP
18. Married in Făgăraş
20. Left for Bucharest, married there
21, 22. Octavian and Reghina
22–34. See 16–28 in Fig. 4
35. Worker at Chemical Combine
36. Married in village, worker at Chemical Combine
37. Worker at Chemical Combine
39, 40. Viorel and Elena
41. Married in village, CAP
42. Married in village, CAP

home, the Marcius had another factory salary, and more important, they had her parents' help on their various CAP lands. Elena's parents, for their part, now had access to farm produce through their in-laws. Still, the honeymoon between the two households was brief. The new in-laws helped the Marcius for one season, but the relationship quickly soured. The in-laws wanted to be involved as much as possible with all of the Marcius' CAP activities and, according to Marciu, expected a steady supply of hay, potatoes, vegetables, and grain in return. But Marciu needed only occasional help, so when he signed

A three-generation family takes a break during work on the CAP

up for plot global, he never thought to include his in-laws. Meanwhile, the in-law alleged, Marciu asked for help only on poor-quality hay lots where poor production limited his share of hay. Tension grew between the two households, and by the end of that year they were no longer speaking. The conflict threatened Viorel and Elena's marriage, and they split up for a time a year after their baby was born.

Here we see the inherent difficulty of integrating agriculture and industry without major political connections. Since the Marcius' industrial income was so limited, agriculture was their main source of income as much by necessity as by choice. Success in this strategy, however, demanded a wide variety of activities and the constant labor of household members and others. These labor requirements were intensified by industry's demands on the young and the lack of agricultural machinery. Further, limits on agricultural pay intensified Marciu's penuriousness and ultimately precipitated conflict between the newly allied households. Though this conflict was not inevitable (produce could have been divided more equitably), the contradictions that caused it were not uncommon and often prevented any large-scale cooperation between households.

[157]

The Puia household, whose demographic and occupational profile differed slightly from the Marcius', offers a contrast. The Marcius were so thoroughly committed to agriculture that they were more peasants than peasant-workers. The Puias balanced agriculture and industry more judiciously. Puia's son-in-law, who lived in the household, was older than Marciu's son and had higher wages from his Combine job. Furthermore, although Puia was a CAP animal *conductor* and work-team leader, the household still limited their involvement in agriculture (and their need for cooperation with others) by keeping only one water buffalo, so that their need for fodder was not great. These differences enabled them to participate in agriculture but avoid the pitfalls that ensnared Marciu and his in-laws.

Transition

Transitional households made up in importance what they lacked in numbers, for they linked disparate households to one another and to state institutions. Though such households were transients, spending only part of each year in a community or residing there for a few years and then moving on, they filled a variety of important social and economic functions, which depended on the nature of the transitional group to which they belonged.

Transitional groups were exceedingly diverse. In the Olt Land they included seminomadic Gypsies,[2] party and state functionaries, and some schoolteachers. It may seem absurd to lump such disparate groups, but they all played analogous roles in village life, and they saw themselves and were seen by Romanian Olt Landers as people apart. Socially, except for economic transactions and the performance of official duties (for which they were roundly criticized), transitionals generally kept to themselves or interacted mainly within their own networks. Most Gypsies, tractor drivers, and state functionaries were actively avoided (though for different reasons), and they themselves thought it improper to become involved in local social life. Transitionals owed their allegiance, their identities, and usually their incomes to individuals and institutions outside the village, and thus

2. The Gypsy population is highly diversified. Many Gypsies are permanently settled in Romanian villages, are married to Romanians, and regularly work in factories or on CAPs. This group is excluded from the transitional category.

sought to use relations with local households to achieve ends defined by this external community, be it Gypsy autonomy or a party career.

At any one moment from seven to twelve households of semi-nomadic Gypsies lived in Hîrseni village as itinerant craftworkers, odd-jobbers, part-time CAP laborers, and animal traders. They filled important and necessary economic roles, and Olt Land communities could not function without them. But outside of those roles they were largely invisible. They lived on the outskirts of the village, sat by themselves in local bars, and, except for the Gypsy children who came begging at funerals and at Easter, moved through the village with little contact with others. Yet their presence was still felt, for they provided a common focus for the Romanians' enmity, not unlike the function served by Communist Party officials. The circumstances of Gypsies are, in fact, reprised in those of local party and state function-aries.

A Transitional Household Dan and Eugenia Cloca were agron-omists from a village near Braşov. Both attended the university in Bucharest, and to stay together near their natal community after they graduated, they took two vacant positions on the Hîrseni CAP—Dan as chief agronomist/vice president and Eugenia as chief of the CAP agricultural sector. Though they had lived in Hîrseni about six years, the Clocas never became integrated into community life. They rented rooms from a widower near the village center and spent most of their nonworking time there. They never attended the Christmas dances, weddings, or other village social events. On holidays they returned to their home village, where their child remained with Eugenia's par-ents, and planned for the day when they could move back. They finally did so in the mid-1980s, when Dan received a fellowship to study potato cultivation at a Braşov institute.

Despite their social distance, they had great influence on local life. As CAP agronomist, Dan taught scientific agriculture to fieldhands, team leaders, and others and tried to persuade hesitant villagers to participate in CAP production and administration. Eugenia had sim-ilar responsibilities, though she was less visible than her husband. Soft-spoken and somewhat withdrawn, she preferred to work with farm brigadiers and team leaders. According to the Clocas, they re-stricted their local involvement to avoid personal entanglements and thus do their jobs more equitably. Though some people interpreted their reserve as a sign of disrespect, most villagers still looked up to them as educated people, even if older men and women sometimes questioned their agricultural expertise.[3] Both were formally employed by the National Ministry of Agriculture, but their CAP positions also gave them the right to a farm plot. Not wanting to work the plot themselves, they arranged for a lower-level CAP administrator to farm it on a sharecropping basis, fifty-fifty. They also had the free services of MTS tractor drivers, an advantage that many villagers resented.

Marginality

Alone among Olt Land households, marginals were unable to compete for resources and position. On the margins of the community's social and economic life, they subsisted on resources garnered by unskilled labor, small pensions, and community assistance of various sorts, including kin exchanges and outright charity. This category comprised a variety of households. Most common were surviving spouses or elderly couples whose children had either left the village or themselves were in a precarious economic situation. Other marginals included the few drunkards who squandered resources brought in by other household members. Some of these households had many children, though their marginality never enabled them to form the ideal three-generation household, as they suffered high rates of divorce and household dissolution.

The chief interest of marginals was day-to-day survival. Lacking training, motivation, and energy, they were generally unskilled workers or collective farm laborers and rapidly consumed all their income. Though they sought broader social relationships, they were generally spurned, as they had little to exchange in the instrumental environment of late socialism. Some pensioners and CAP workers with rights to use plots, however, did have effective exchange networks and wavered between marginality and integration. Marginals were patronized and often treated as children. Like children, they showed little constraint in their actions, nor did political decision makers worry about controlling them. For them, as for Janis Joplin, "freedom" was "another word for nothing left to lose."

A Marginal Household One Hîrseni marginal household was headed by Ioan Grosu, nicknamed Johnny Communist by fellow vil-

3. Recall the pomiculture slide show described in Chapter 5.

lagers. His nickname derived from a day in the early 1960s when he went through the village in a drunken rage, swearing loudly and telling the world what he'd do to the Communists if they tried to collectivize the village. In the mid-1970s the Grosu household consisted of Ioan, his wife, Elena, and five children between 10 and 17. Three other children were there occasionally, two boys in the military and a girl in a training program near Sibiu (Figure 6). Ioan worked at a Făgăraş construction workshop, but was often absent because of drunkenness and other health problems. Elena, from a lower-middle-peasant family, was the cleaning woman and "gofer" at the Hîrseni CAP offices. As unskilled laborers, together they brought in about 2,700 lei a month plus a few hundred lei in allowances for their minor children. Thus their income was only slightly less than that of the mobile Munteans, but the standards of living of the two households were worlds apart.

All of the Grosus were physically dirty, and their appearance and that of their disheveled home caused much comment. Ioan was sel-

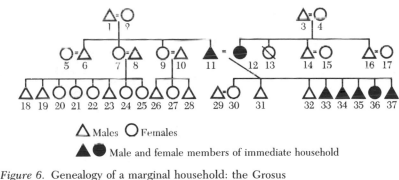

△ Males ○ Females

▲● Male and female members of immediate household

Figure 6. Genealogy of a marginal household: the Grosus
1, 2. Pre–World War II poor peasants
3. Immigrant from Olt Land village
4. No. 14 in Fig. 4
6. Married in Hîrseni; worker at Chemical Combine
7. Married in Hîrseni to member of Agricultural Association (4 in Table 3)
9. Married in Hîrseni; housewife
10. Worker at Chemical Combine
11, 12. Ioan and Elena
14. Married in Sebeş
16. Disabled worker
17. Cook, Hîrseni CAP

dom clean-shaven, Elena and the children often wore rags, and the younger children were frequently barefoot. Much of the plaster was chipping from one section of their two-room house, and another section remained bare brick and roughly finished. This was the case in 1973, when I first visited Hîrseni, and nothing had changed by 1990. The garbage-strewn courtyard evinced a lack of economic activity, though they did have a small vegetable garden and kept a few chickens and pigs. As Elena was a CAP employee, they usually contracted one pig every two years. Elena earned occasional labor credits for various tasks she performed for the CAP as well as for work in the fields, so the family qualified for an annual use plot. Elena worked it with little help from her husband, and it was their main means of sustaining life. Elena also received occasional gifts of food from the other women who worked in the CAP offices, who pitied her. Ioan's only work on the collective was occasionally to spell his wife. In the early 1970s he had worked regularly, and helped qualify the family for two 15-are plots. By the late 1970s, however, his fondness for alcohol not only kept him out of the fields but was estimated to consume between one-fourth and one-half of the household's monthly income. Ioan often begged other people to buy him a drink. They rarely did, but the local barkeeps occasionally gave him a glass of brandy.

Though Ioan was politically irrelevant, it was politics that sealed his fate. As rationing took hold in the early 1980s and work requirements and consumption regulations became more stringent, Ioan again took to acting out his drunken rage. One night he railed at length at state, party, and Ceauşescu without realizing that two security officials were in the bar. When someone warned him of their presence, he ran out in panic. Though repercussions were hardly likely, he hanged himself that night.

Socioeconomic Strategies and Cultural Practice

Whether their consequences were tragic, mundane, or economically effective, these diverse strategies not only influenced the structure and behavior of Olt Land households but also helped define the social and political relationships between households. Such relationships were not based on class. Since the socialist breakthrough, most Olt Landers engaged in much the same kinds of work and were related to the means of production in similar ways. All gained resources through state or collectivist corporate organizations and all, except a few transitionals, had minimal control over others' labor. The particularistic strategies they adopted, however, inhibited cooperation among households, promoted conflict, and encouraged a variety of attitudes, actions, and values. Despite similarities in class, households differed in their ability to control their own labor and time within socialist institutions, the diversification of their resource base, the goals they sought, and their access to information and resources. It was these differences, then, that prevented them from expressing any common political concern or recognizing common interests.

Aggrandizing households seemed to be in a superior position, but their exposure made them vulnerable. As their prominence increased, so did the demands on them by relatives and friends with party and governmental functions. In return for work credits and discount grain for nonagricultural CAP work, they had to serve on committees, contract for animals when they were asked to do so, and take on other production responsibilities as the need arose. With their wide range of resources, contacts, and influence, aggrandizers were often importuned for assistance by nonpolitical relatives and neighbors. Finally, the aggrandizing strategy was hard to maintain. Constant effort was required to validate the household's status in others' eyes. Network relations were crucial, yet the effort to maintain them ultimately led the aggrandizers away from their goals. When their strategy forced them to favor one person over another, they were immediately seen as greedy and out for themselves.

Because they were compromised by the connections with the official hierarchy on which their strategy depended, aggrandizers never attained the prestige and respect of wealthy households in the presocialist era. Though some Olt Landers named an aggrandizing household as "the most proper people in the village," by and large aggrandizers were looked down on as *lacom, mai bagăreți*[4] (greedy), or *afaceriști* (economic manipulators). Some informants even contrasted the uprightness of the aggrandizers' forebears with the sorry state to which their descendants had fallen. Others, particularly members of integrated households, referred obliquely to socialist egalitarianism to suggest the impropriety of the aggrandizers' behavior and criticized them for their use

4. *Mai bagăreți* is rarely used in this context. It connotes the action of putting other people's valuables in a sack and came to be a popular epithet for Oltenians, people of southwestern Romania. It thus was a veiled reference to the Ceaușescus, who came from that region.

of collective farm resources without corresponding agricultural labor.[5] Mobile households, frustrated in their attempts at mobility, saw the apparent success of aggrandizers as limiting their own.

Mobile households tended to find their socioeconomic strategies frustrated first by the housing shortage and then by the urban living standard in general, by restrictions on educational opportunities, and by the constraints of Romania's economic stagnation. Other villagers tended to consider them as pretentious ("not like us"). Trapped in the village or in uncomfortable family circumstances, they frequently found themselves unable to make firm decisions about their futures, to the cost and chagrin of their families.

One young man who was intent on leaving Hîrseni was Mircea, a soccer star and highly regarded bachelor until he married a Moldavian woman whom he had met at the Chemical Combine. They wanted to move to Făgăraş after their marriage but no housing was available there, so they spent their first six months together with Mircea's parents, his elder brother, and the brother's wife and three children. The young couple found this situation intolerable, and after a few months decided to build their own home in the village. Construction, financed by the entire household, was begun on a vacant lot purchased through the People's Council. Within a few months a front fence was built, the foundation was poured, and the exterior brick walls and roof were erected. After this investment in time, money, materials, and social capital for reciprocal labor, the couple were informed that an apartment was available in Făgăraş. Against the family's wishes, they renounced their new house and left for the city.

Integrated households were in the most tenable position so long as they limited their desire for social mobility. As their outlook was geared to local possibilities and they were dependent on local resources, they could pursue their goals without the tensions of mobility or of the aggrandizing strategy. But as their success depended on a judicious mix of CAP resources, industrial wages, and household husbandry, integrated households consciously had to maintain their multigenerational structure or gain the regular cooperation of their kin, which was becoming increasingly problematic. Since their incomes were tied directly to the CAP, tension arose in their village rela-

5. The Hungarian villagers studied by Peter Bell (1979, 1983) also criticized emerging status distinctions by appealing to socialist ideology.

tionships: they frequently accused other CAP members of not pulling their weight and in turn were criticized for being too greedy for farm resources. Since their members often occupied lower-level CAP administrative positions, they were blamed for much that was troublesome about socialist agriculture and charged with theft from the farm; if they were women, they were said to have gotten their jobs by sleeping with the farm leaders.

Transitional households, too, came in for criticism. People low in the local hierarchy, such as Gypsies and tractor drivers, were reviled for their otherness, but the very fact of their mobility made all transitional households suspect. Even in the contemporary period it was shameful to sell one's home and patrimony or to be constantly on the move. Thus transitionals were both pitied and blamed for being far from home and family. In any case, they did not figure in local community life, as they were willingly uninformed about local social traditions and economic practices. The Gypsies, of course, were scapegoated and condemned for their commercial transactions and their alleged penchant for gold.

The tensions aroused by these conflicting strategies prevented local leadership from emerging and thus limited joint social action. People in positions of potential community leadership were members of aggrandizing households, and those were the households that were most criticized. At the same time, the very nature of their interests made members of such households ill disposed to leadership. Mobile households, the cultural avant-garde, had no interest in local affairs, and in any case were disqualified by a cultural orientation that put them at odds with the other villagers. Finally, the vast majority of integrated households were struggling so hard to maintain themselves that they had little energy left over for political concerns.

Household Strategies and Changing Social Networks

Despite divergent interests, Olt Land households still had to cooperate and exchange resources and labor. People with large hay lots but insufficient labor to keep animals traded hay for milk. Mobile households needed child care and potatoes. A parent's death required quick access to food, candles, and brandy for the wake and funeral. And everyone needed bottled gas. Network ties had to be mobilized to

[165]

satisfy all of these requirements. Yet the diversity of household strategies and the socialist political economy brought massive changes in the operations of local networks.

Aggrandizing households made most frequent use of network ties in their quest for socioeconomic predominance. Integrated household networks were mobilized slightly less often and mainly to secure resources from an economic sector in which members were not strongly engaged. The networks of mobile and transitional households lay largely outside the village, and the transitionals avoided any local relations that were not absolutely necessary. Marginal households relied on a still more restricted network of relations to fill a more restricted set of needs.

Olt Land networks under socialism were formed by shifting sets of kin, ritual kin, agemates, neighbors, and friends made at work, at school, and in the army (cf. Barnes 1972, Sanjek 1978). Structurally they resembled the networks of the prewar era, but the socialist political economy wrought major changes in the meanings, behavior, goals, and significance of these quasi groups. Networks were both more ubiquitous and more heterogeneous than they had been before. Networks of relationships within the region, among fellow villagers, or with a few urban workers were enlarged (especially by aggrandizers and mobiles) to include others throughout the country and across the socioeconomic range. The functions of networks also expanded. Once they had served as leveling mechanisms and social cement; now they provided the information, resources, and connections that fostered social mobility and differentiation. Given the importance of networks under socialism, household decisions were rarely made without consideration of network-related issues. Networks dominated village life so thoroughly that personal relations became shaped by what can only be characterized as an ethic of socialist calculation.

A variety of factors lay behind these changes. Most important was the scope and structure of the state bureaucracy, which created a nationwide social organization in which all participated. Urbanization and migration for employment, education, and marriage also linked people from all parts of the nation. Economic development, media images, and contact with other societies opened people's eyes to the availability of occupations and resources their parents had never dreamed of and expanded the perceived needs of households and individuals. Even as desires expanded, however, shortages put the things one wanted and needed out of reach and encouraged the cultivation of people who had access to them. Ceaușescu's attempt to pay off Romania's foreign debt and such related policies as the Program Unic also encouraged the use of networks for personal ends. Though many of these laws seem to have been designed to restrict networks, the mechanisms by which they operated actually promoted them. Food rationing, for example, inevitably led to occasional alteration and forgery of ration cards and to efforts to get commodities by other means. Restriction of market purchases to one's own community guaranteed the persistence of extensive subterranean exchange networks. Increases in requirements for collective farm work and animal contracts, rising taxes, and restrictions on bonuses also encouraged people to use their personal ties to get around these difficulties.

Thus network exchange was ubiquitous and constant in socialist Romania. Any exchange of goods or favors was preceded by a long chain of previous exchanges and generated a ripple effect itself. My gift of cigarettes to a soon-to-be married friend initiated a chain of transactions: he traded the cigarettes for meat, for medical care for his future father-in-law, and for assistance in procuring an imported wedding gown for his fiancée. People in government and party bureaus, with control over state resources and information, were especially valued network partners; so were visiting foreigners—West German Saxons, American relatives, even the occasional anthropologist.[6] As sources of many new goods, foreigners were resources in their own right. In fact, the presence of Western goods probably intensified network behavior, even as my own presence heightened the possibilities and desirability of exchange. One friend became extremely excited about importing a central heating unit when he heard that my father-in-law was in the building trades. He constantly made me offers and suggested ways the unit (which he saw in a catalogue a Saxon colleague received from a West German relative) could be shipped to Romania.

The Sociocultural Implications of Networks

Many scholars who have focused on socialist societies view social networks as having integrative effects (Ash 1989, Wedel 1986). In

6. Resident foreigners, such as Arab and African students, who had access to hard-currency shops, were significant network partners in Bucharest and other cities but rarely figured in Olt Land exchanges.

Romania they made scarce resources more widely available, stream-lined the workings of the state bureaucracy, and masked the imper-sonality of the hierarchy, turning it into a ramification of "friends of friends" (cf. Brezinski & Petrescu 1986, Ronnås 1986, Sampson 1983a, 1986b). In this view, with which I agree, network relations contributed to political inaction by making a horrendous life marginally passable. By emphasizing the advantages of networks, however, these explana-tions overlook the less salutary calculations involved and thus do not fully explain the limits that such relationships placed on political pos-sibilities in Romania (cf. Hann 1990).

Though life was made tolerable by network exchanges, such ex-changes required relationships to be judged mainly by instrumental rather than affective criteria, and thus they objectified and weakened the social bonds on which they were based. To be sure, many network relations retained considerable affect. Even when affect originally out-weighed instrumentality, however, the socialist political economy and the scarcity of resources readily created conflict among friends. When Ioan and Maria Voievod vacated their apartment in Făgăraş to return to the village, for instance, a soon-to-be-married first cousin asked them to turn it over to him. But the Voievods thought they might need it again, and their refusal sparked a feud that lasted for months.

Network-related social distancing is also seen in the decline of re-ciprocal labor. Though this was the Olt Landers' chief means of getting barns and houses built, informants from all types of households men-tioned the increased difficulty of getting people together for such projects. Typically it took three or four attempts before they could get enough people together, and even then the helpers grumbled about the inroads on their time. One Hîrseni mechanic who had twice begged off a job for a cousin—the second time because he had to go to Făgăraş to get meat from the son of an official at the consumer cooper-ative—himself complained that "relatives today are never there when you need them and always around when you don't. They're as useful as a seventh spoke on a wheel."

Though network exchange cut across class lines and linked diverse socioeconomic groups, it promoted social differentiation and dishar-mony. People more favorably placed in the socialist system could more readily control the behavior of their network partners. By alternately withholding and bestowing favors, they manipulated their partners and set one against another. Thus the need to use networks to satisfy a household's minimal needs probably reinforced hierarchy and fostered

Friends and relatives help with a household construction project. Though reciprocal labor groups are increasingly hard to organize, they are still the chief means of getting such projects done

a vicious dependency in social relations to boot. At the same time, the surface relations of cooperation and extensive webs of friendship that networks facilitated were charged with tension and jealousy. Since maintenance of these relations required constant exchanges of goods and services, concern was pervasive that the things one wanted would be given to someone else who could offer something better in exchange. Failure to keep the exchanges going resulted in frustration and ruptured relationships.

Distrust also grew from the kinds of activities that network exchange entailed. Because centralized accumulation, legally or de facto, restricted access to so many resources, frequently the only way to gain them was to engage in one petty criminal act or another—theft of farm or factory property, "purchase" of admission to the school of one's choice, general influence peddling. Because network exchange depended on such criminality, the trust that it allegedly prompted can just as easily be understood as the distrust of people who shared mutually incriminating knowledge. In socialist Romania, then, access

[169]

to positions and possessions certainly depended on what and who you knew, but it also depended on what you knew about who you knew.

Network Transformations Illustrated: Godparenthood

The changes in network principles are clearly seen in the institution of *naşie* (ritual parenthood). Before the 1989 revolution the *naş-fin* (godparent-godchild/sponsor-sponsored) relationship was in turmoil and its ability to link Olt Land households in a common purpose waning. The criteria by which godparents were selected had been considerably modified. In the past, sponsors were almost universally selected from within one's village. Recently, however, godparents were as likely to live outside the village as in it. Of twenty-three sample Hîrseni households that selected godparents to sponsor their children at baptism or marriage between 1973 and 1976, ten bypassed the households with which their own were traditionally linked in *naşie* and chose someone else. Five of the new sponsors were close friends or work colleagues in the village and five were relatives or friends who lived elsewhere. As Table 15 indicates, ten of the thirteen households that maintained their old ties practiced an integrated strategy. It was primarily mobile households that sought new relationships in the changing socialist political economy.

This change implies others in the function and meaning of godparenthood. Whereas *naşie* traditionally linked diverse village kin groups and neighborhoods affectively, spiritually, and economically, the modern relationship seems to have been used mainly for instrumental purposes. The relatively large number of work colleagues selected as sponsors suggests that godparenthood was increasingly influenced by political and economic considerations, such as the need for

Table 15. Godparent choices of sample households, Hîrseni village, 1973–1976, by household strategy

Sponsor	Aggrandizing (N = 2)	Integrated (N = 14)	Mobile (N = 6)	Marginal (N = 1)
New	1	4	5	0
Traditional	1	10	1	1

work-related ties and for cooperation in the second economy. Even party and state cadres were frequently asked to be *naşi*, despite their overt rejection of the religious aspects of the relationship. According to a former mayor of Hîrseni, soon after he assumed office he became *naş* to four families, and by the end of his first year in office over twenty families requested his sponsorship. Factory foremen, engineers, and people well connected in the network of resource distribution were also popular as sponsors. The costs of sponsorship could be considerable (up to 10,000 lei for a wedding), but an official was compensated in prestige and connections he could exploit for his own ends.

Instrumentality is also implied by the frequent selection of new sponsors. In the past it was shameful for either party to bow out of the *naşie* relationship without compelling cause (illness, say, or lack of heirs, or financial need). Furthermore, the other party had to agree to any proposed change. Lately, however, shame rarely figured in such decisions. Many young parents requested new sponsors for their infants, and young spouses also readily selected other *naşi* regardless of preexisting relations. The obvious political and economic motives for selecting new *naşi* were not the only justifications for forging new bonds of *naşie*. Some godparents asked to be relieved of the responsibility for financial reasons. Though this excuse was thought legitimate and was common during the difficult years of the socialist breakthrough, some informants opined that the people who claimed sudden financial difficulties were merely being greedy and trying to avoid responsibility. Some expected sponsors declined to serve out of resentment at a personal affront. I witnessed an argument between a husband and wife over whether to sponsor the baptism of their *fin's* child after the shabby treatment they felt they had received at the *fin's* wedding. They had given "proper" gifts, they said, but the family had paid little attention to them at the reception and the *fin* had not given the husband the traditional shirt. I was also present when an aggrandizing *naş* castigated his mobile *fin* and threatened to break off the relationship because the *fin* had failed to bring back some household equipment for the *naş* from a trip to Braşov and also failed to use his influence to help a relative of the *naş* gain entrance to a good school. Whether *naşie* had been marked by such sensitivities and pretensions in presocialist days is hard to gauge, but certainly socialist ambiguities lent a sense of touchiness to the relationship. *Naşie*, like so much else, had suffered as the golden past gave way to the leaden present. As one middle-aged Cîrţişoara worker said, "Nowadays shame has kind of disappeared as a custom. Interest and money have taken its place."

The economic conditions spawned by the accumulative state thus coincided with widespread change in the social lives and relations of Olt Land villagers. Household differentiation took on new dimensions when the peasants became peasant-workers. The diverse ways in which households positioned themselves in their efforts to take advantage of official and unofficial opportunities influenced their cultural choices and left them generally unable to form meaningful political alliances. The strategies households devised to get by and get ahead under the pressures exerted by the accumulative state also influenced their ability to craft wider networks of social cooperation. Though networks remained important in the villagers' consciousness, they were harder to form and mobilize and increasingly problematic, given the widespread competition, distrust, and dishonesty that network relations now encouraged. Each household strategy demanded the mobilization of network ties but each household also saw those ties as useful for limited and immediately utilitarian ends. As people thus engaged each other for their own immediate ends, their orientations, outlooks, and identities came to be related to those ends.

[7]

Meanings of Life in
the Socialist Village

> We are working for the formation of a truly humane human
> being . . . a communist human being. We are witnessing the cre-
> ation of the most propitious conditions for each person to manifest
> himself fully in all domains of social life, each with his or her
> capacities and unique characteristics, in the common spirit of the
> entire society, with love for righteousness and truth, courage and
> honesty, simplicity and commitment to work together with one's
> fellows for the common good, for the good of all society.
>
> Nicolae Ceaușescu, 1982

> If we had Solidarity [the trade union] here in Romania, every
> Romanian would have their own.
>
> Popular joke, 1984

The political ambiguity of Olt Land village life and the struggle
between household and state for control of labor were reinforced and
shaped by local identities and conceptions of state, self, and others. As
anthropologists understand it, identity is a complex phenomenon
comprising diverse strands of meaning and experience that people
weave into a coherent yet changeful sense of themselves, of others,
and of their societies. Individuals create identity by contrasting their
experiences with those of other people, by interpreting the political
and economic conditions in which they live, and by arriving at their
own understanding of history. This creative process is shaped by the
way power is used to control the production and nature of meaning
and value in society (cf. Roseberry 1989, Williams 1980). The groups
most able to control meaning, and hence to influence identity forma-

tion, are most able to have their purposes and interests defined as those of society at large (Kahn 1985, Turton 1984).

In socialist society the state's control of the elements and processes of identity formation influenced both its ability to control local communities and villagers' relationships with one another. Forty-odd years of life in the accumulative state and exposure to its educational institutions, media campaigns, ceremonies, symbols, architecture, and workplace organization no doubt had their effects. Despite the complete separation of public and private identities posited for socialist societies (Milosz 1981, Verdery 1987, Wedel 1986), many state principles were thoroughly integrated in the local mind-set.

Still, state control of meaning was not perfect. The persistence of households as viable social and productive entities ensured their continued influence over the meanings ascribed to local life. The diverse social, political, and economic experiences of individuals and households in the socialist state further ensured a continuum of identities. And the constant strategizing of network exchange provided additional experience to influence conceptions of life. Thus Olt Landers' senses of themselves, as compromised as they were at times, cannot be seen as any kind of false consciousness. Olt Landers actively modified the state's values through their consciousness of labor, their household and network relations, and their ritual practices. Even as they took key tenets of the socialist state, such as Romanian nationalism, as their own, they denied the legitimacy of other state values. Their own senses of themselves were sometimes in accord with socialist principles, sometimes in opposition to them, and sometimes uncertain about them. These often contradictory values shaped both their political domination by the socialist state and their resistance to it.

Nation, Region, and God in Olt Land Identity

Few elements of the Olt Land identity were as seductive as Romanian nationalism, for "the conditions of [Romanian] life were such as to make the idea . . . compelling" (Gellner 1983:126). Playing Romania's national groups off against each other was one of Ceaușescu's strategies for maintaining his power. Some observers have suggested, in fact, that Romanians' acceptance of those hyperbolized notions of their uniqueness long postponed his downfall (Sampson 1983a, Shafir 1985).

Belief in the destiny of the Romanian people, the importance of Romania's past, and the difference between Romanians and other Tranlyvanian ethnic groups came easily to the Olt Landers.

The Olt Land's history and social ecology contributed greatly to the power of Romanian nationalism. Its population had a strong sense of the region's role in the formation of a Romanian national identity and Olt Landers who figured in the Romanian national movement of the nineteenth century were regularly celebrated. The ethnographic museum in Cîrţişoara, visited regularly by schoolchildren from all parts of the region, offered powerful testimony to the Romanian national idea. Among its most cherished exhibits were memorabilia of Badea Cîrţan, a self-educated shepherd who traveled on foot to Rome to view Trajan's Column, which depicts the Roman conquest of Dacia and, by implication, the origin of the Romanian people. To reinforce and justify Romania's claim to Transylvania, Olt Land teachers organized hikes across the Carpathians to show the ease with which Romanians on the two sides of the mountains maintained contact when the region was under Hungary's control. A playwright friend wrote mainly on the lives of Romanian heroes because, he said, "these are the most important themes for Romanians to understand." I was impressed by the way episodes in Romania's history and tales of its heroes were woven into the normal course of household life. My questions about family or regional history regularly prompted elders to regale their grandchildren with images of Mihai Viteazu—Michael the Brave—who unified Transylvania, Moldavia, and Wallachia in 1593; the depredations of the Austro-Hungarian border police, about which they had heard from their parents; and Nicolae Grancea, an Olt Land hero of the 1877 Romanian War of Independence.

Nationalism was also encouraged by the visibility of non-Romanian nationalities and the quality of their daily contacts with the Romanian majority. Unfortunately, no accurate census of the region's minorities was available. Still, several Olt Land villages, such as Cîrţişoara and Şercaia, just to the east of Făgăraş, had fairly large populations of Saxon Germans. In Făgăraş in the late 1960s over 16 percent of the total population of 25,000 were minorities (8.1 percent Magyar and 8.2 percent Saxon), though they accounted for only about 8 percent of the Chemical Combine's work force (Herseni 1972:280, 249). The Olt Land also has long had a large concentration of Gypsies, who settled in the region early and have played a large role in its long-distance trade and animal husbandry (Nicolae Gheorghe, personal communication).

Nearly every Olt Land commune has at least one Gypsy neighborhood; Hîrseni commune had an entire Gypsy hamlet, Mălăniș. Yet Romania's socialist government consistently refused to recognize the reality of its Gypsy population.

Daily contact between Romanians and Magyars was occasionally highly charged. Their relations were shaped by the cultural memory of Magyar domination and fears of Magyar revanchism in Transylvania. Together they made Olt Landers often receptive to anti-Magyar propaganda and rumor (any factory explosion or industrial accident was said to be the work of Hungarian saboteurs). To Olt Landers the Magyars' ineptness at speaking Romanian or their refusal to learn it at all was particularly grating. This prejudice actually assisted my field-work: my efforts to master Romanian immediately set me apart from the alien Magyars, who "live in our country and never even bother to learn our language."

Criticism of Magyars and liberal use of ethnic epithets such as *Bozgor* (Bohunk) and *Cuțitar* (Knife-wielder) were normal parts of daily life, even among the presumably enlightened. One day a Hîrseni functionary who prided himself on his lack of prejudice (he was one of the few, he claimed, who tried to prevent the burning of the Gypsy house in the incident mentioned in Chapter 4) hired two Magyars to split wood. One was a respected work-team leader at the Făgăraș Chemical Combine. After the job was done and the workers had left, he praised them as hard working and "just like us"—not like the rest of the Hungarians, who were not to be trusted. But then, without a pause, he said, "Even these Bohunks can't be trusted. They smile nice to you, but it's only for the money. If they had half a chance, they'd slit your throat."

As an out-group, scapegoat, and focus of regional paternalism, Gypsies, too, served the cause of Romanian nationalism. Gypsies filled important niches in the Olt Land's economy. They worked in its factories, were increasingly employed on its labor-starved collective farms (especially in animal husbandry brigades), and made a number of commodities necessary for local life, from wooden spoons and scythe handles to bricks, roof tiles, and brass boilers for brandy distilleries. Still, their obvious differences in language, dress, habits, residence, and relationships made it easy for Olt Landers to disparage them and use them as foils for their own sense of themselves. Gypsies were beyond hatred and suspicion. Romanians mainly pitied and condescended to Gypsies, whose way of life was in such contrast to their own, who refused their children education, lived in dilapidated shacks, and constantly begged for handouts at funerals, weddings, and major holidays. My friends in Făgăraş and in Olt Land villages, from collective farmers to local intellectuals, took me mildly to task for my interest in Gypsies and my visits to their homes, though their concern was more for my sanity and health than for my safety.

Even the Saxons were subjected to increased criticism by the 1980s. Olt Land Romanians had long respected the Saxons for their business acumen, industriousness, and cleanliness, but large-scale emigration of Saxons to the West (Custred 1990, McArthur 1976, Verdery 1984) prompted them to reevaluate these people. Emigration was both equated with disloyalty to Romania and increasingly envied in the economic crisis of the 1980s. Olt Landers' envy was exacerbated when Saxon emigrants returned on visits laden with blue jeans, electronic marvels, cigarettes, and other highly prized goods.

Nationalism fed into an intense concern for Romanian political independence, which became especially evident in the local response to the so-called Sonnenfeldt Doctrine in 1976. Helmut Sonnenfeldt was an assistant to Henry Kissinger, then U.S. secretary of state under Gerald Ford. In a speech to U.S. ambassadors in December 1975 (Binder 1976:1), Sonnenfeldt suggested that to ensure the stability and peaceful intentions of the USSR, the United States should support a "more natural and organic" relationship between the USSR and the Eastern European states. This statement was widely interpreted in Eastern Europe as American acceptance of Soviet hegemony over those states, if not an actual invitation to the Soviets to annex them.

News of Sonnenfeldt's statement quickly spread throughout Romania. To Olt Landers it simply meant that "the Russians are coming," and launched three months of panic buying and hoarding of food. People seemed to be able to think of little else. I was regularly stopped on village streets by people of every description—old women, teenagers, young mothers, heads of households—all demanding an explanation of Sonnenfeldt's remarks. At a wedding in Făgăraş the guests clamored for political commentary from me rather than attending to bride, groom, and godparents. After a few drinks, two young men boldly announced that they intended to marry within the month because they wanted to experience marriage before enlisting in the army. This was an astonishing plan, for it inverted the traditional practice of marriage after one's army stint. They looked forward, they said, to fighting the Russians.

[177]

By the mid-1980s, Olt Land nationalist sentiment was in a process of transformation. Some officials and teachers held to the state line that Ceauşescu's campaign to amortize the national debt was really an attempt to maintain Romania's independence. Most Olt Landers, however, thought otherwise. For many of my informants, pride in Romania's achievements had receded, leaving behind only a sense of betrayal and growing uncertainty about other ethnic groups. Attitudes toward Nicolae Ceauşescu changed from respect to outright hatred. Now people had as many epithets for him, his wife, and his government as for the Hungarians. They even blamed themselves for the crisis: "We Romanians are fools," they said, and even, incredibly, "It would be better if the Russians came."

Viewing the National Day Parade in Hîrseni: A Decade of Change

These changes were particularly brought home to me by the contrast between two National Day ceremonies, over a decade apart, which I witnessed in a mobile household ostensibly committed to the socialist program. This Hîrseni family came from a long line of workers, had three members in the Communist Party, and even participated (grudgingly) in CAP labor. In August 1976, Dml. P. enthusiastically called his wife, child, and parents to the TV, urging them to hurry and to hush as the announcer identified the various groups present at the ceremony commemorating the end of fascist rule after World War II. Mention of some foreign ambassadors prompted Dml. P. to comment that Ceauşescu had achieved world respect for Romania. His elderly mother talked about Ceauşescu's hair in poetic terms and said it reminded her of the hairstyles worn by important Romanians in the past. Dma. P. and her daughter commented favorably on the crowds and the children presenting flowers to the Ceauşescus.

By 1984 the mood had changed. Dml. P., in the midst of our discussion, abruptly said, "C'mon, let's watch the fool," and turned on the TV. Other family members were about, but he did not call them to watch. My host silently shook his head as the president arrived to the strains of the national anthem. P.'s first comment came as a battalion of tanks passed in review: he had heard that "the parade was rehearsed for over three months—think of the gasoline it wasted." As helicopters flew past, the TV narrator gushed that they were "all made in Romania and indicate our capabilities as a people." P. snorted, "All the parts were probably imported." Moments later Dma. P. passed the doorway, towel in hand, on her way to the kitchen. Without stopping she chuckled and said, "My goodness, what are you watching?" On TV a phalanx of banners indicating planned production were carried by workers from Bucharest factories. P. laughed but said nothing. However, a float bearing Nadia Comăneci, the gold-medal gymnast of 1976, and the current Romanian Olympic team, fresh from triumphs at the Los Angeles games, prompted a derisive comment: "At least a hundred people will eat off her victories."[1] The last parade group was a column of men in white shirts and black trousers, the *oameni de ordine* (men of order)—the state security police. As they sang "E scris pe tricolor unirea" (Our flag symbolizes unity), P. shook his head and snapped off the TV. "This is what we work for—to pay these people to stay fat and have power in their fists."

Olt Land Religion: A Question of Community

Religion also embellished nationalism and thus served the state's interests in the Olt Land, though in more ambiguous fashion than nationalist discourse itself. On the surface, religious identities provided potential rallying points for antistate resistance. Thus in the decade before the 1989 revolution church attendance rose sharply, conflict between Orthodox and Uniates declined, and membership in Protestant anticollectivist denominations also expanded (Funderburk 1987). Nonetheless, such ideological transformations never acquired overtly political overtones in Olt Land villages. On the contrary, they ultimately deemphasized group sentiment, promoted individualism, and vitiated joint action.

Such effects are particularly, though paradoxically, apparent in the waning significance of the Orthodox-Uniate split. By the 1980s most Olt Landers had set their religious differences aside and no longer gave much thought to the schism that had divided the two faiths. In Copăcel village, once completely Uniate, a few older women still refused to attend Orthodox services, but most former Uniates, when

1. Nadia Comăneci attended the Los Angeles games but did not compete. The Romanian women again won most of the medals for gymnastics but none captured the public's interest as Nadia had done in 1976.

asked about the differences between the two faiths, typically laughed, mentioned a few liturgical practices, and said that such differences were significant only to priests. Furthermore, knowledge of sectarian differences was no longer transmitted to the young. In Hîrseni I could find no young worker or student who could explain why the village had two churches, used on alternate Sundays.[2]

Still, even though religion no longer divided the villagers, the blending of the two faiths probably worked more to facilitate than to challenge the state's hegemony. Thus Uniatism's decline brought more people into the official state Orthodox church, whose clergy were often compromised by Communist power and whose organization and liturgy were used to further the state's purposes. Priests were formally state employees, supervised by the Ministry of Cults, and were reassigned if they became too vocal or popular in their parish.[3] Many Sunday and holiday sermons focused more on the state's concerns than on spiritual matters. Official Easter messages called for intensified work on the collective farms to fulfill the five-year plan, defense of the homeland, support for Ceaușescu's policies, and prayers for his health.

As the increase in church attendance was in direct opposition to state policy and practice, local officials attempted to limit it by organizing "voluntary labor" on community improvement projects on Sundays and religious holidays. At Easter in Hîrseni the CAP sponsored work details of local activists and publicly feted them afterward with a huge meal of pork, chicken, potatoes, vegetables, pastries, and copious brandy. Community-wide assemblies and official cultural events were normally held on Sundays, a fact duly noted and criticized by the villagers. All the same, church attendance rose over the course of my fieldwork. Though Sunday and holiday masses in the mid-1970s were well attended (especially by women), few young unmarried men were seen there and the churches were filled only at Easter. In 1979, however, young men were regularly seen at church, and by the summer of 1984 the church was crowded for Sunday mass.

2. The decline in emphasis on Uniate identity in the Olt Land contrasts with the situation elsewhere in Transylvania (Shafir 1985), where Uniate activists organized for formal recognition, restoration of church property, and religious freedom. This ostensibly religious movement also spoke to issues of political and economic freedom. One of the foremost dissidents in Ceaușescu's Romania was the Uniate priest Gheorghe Calciu, who was imprisoned in 1979 and forcibly exiled in 1984. He settled in the United States.

3. The attempted forced removal of the Reformed minister Laszlo Tökes from his parish in Timișoara in December 1989 was the catalyst that sparked the Romanian revolution.

As church attendance rose, so did social divisiveness. Believers and clergy were constantly at odds, usually over money. In Hîrseni the village priest was criticized by all except those who had been members of the interwar sect Oastea Domnului (the Army of the Lord). They were disgusted by his demands for ever more money for his prayers and funeral services, but he complained that people expected too much from him. A priest in a village in the western region concurred: "People are more demanding here than elsewhere. They want service from you, and if you give it to them, they will gladly pay you. But if you don't, they quickly become your enemy and nothing will bring them around." According to priests and lay informants alike, conflicts over the auctioning and disposition of pews had also become more frequent, and in Hîrseni I witnessed a shouting and shoving match between two old men over control of the local church council and its budget. Money, competition, and socialist instrumentality were evident even in the prayers of the faithful. According to two Olt Land priests, villagers used to ask priests to pray for their good health, that they might find a good spouse, or that children might be born to them. In the decade before the 1989 revolution, however, prayers were sought for the success of children at school, for the cows one watched on the CAP to make their milk quota, and for allotment of a good use plot by the collective farm.

The growth of evangelical Protestantism and Seventh-Day Adventism (Radio Free Europe 1984, Shafir 1985:153) also pointed to increasing individualism. The Protestants' emphasis on a personal relationship with Jesus and individual responsibility for change in one's life implied rejection of both state policies and the Orthodox community (Annis 1987 presents an analogous case). Protestantism in the Olt Land dated to World War I, when some of the region's soldiers converted during their military service. Through the interwar years, however, no Protestant denomination made major inroads among the Orthodox and Uniate faithful. In the socialist years, however, with their economic difficulties, social decline, and compromised Orthodoxy, evangelical Protestantism found more fertile ground there.

Olt Land Protestants were individualists. The three Protestant households I knew in Hîrseni were all mobile in orientation. Only one person was devout, and the villagers regularly chided another for his fondness for a good glass of brandy. The few Adventists I knew, in contrast, were extreme millenarianists and fervent antistatists. In 1979 there were about twelve families of Adventists in Făgăraş. Most made their livings as private craftworkers of one sort or another in order to have as little to do with state authority as possible.

In sum, whatever their creed, Olt Land believers allowed themselves few possibilities for the kind of communal politics practiced by Roman Catholics in Poland. With the exception of the fervent Adventists, most believers in the Olt Land were suspicious of the clergy, intensely concerned with their earthly salvation, and nonpolitical. Though their beliefs did not expressly support the state, neither did they question it. And those who did come close to challenging the accumulative state foundered over questions of status and wealth.

Labor and the Second Economy
in Olt Land Identity

Olt Landers commonly expressed their identity in their attitudes toward work, technology, and prestige. Like nationalism and religious belief, such attitudes were ambivalent in regard to regional politics. Though they reflected understanding of their common political predicament, they simultaneously encouraged compromise with the socialist hierarchy. Though some Olt Landers vigorously criticized the socialist system and its labor and educational systems, their concepts of themselves and of others were nonetheless shaped by the socialist division of labor, the system of training on which it was based, and the second economy that it encouraged.

Be Prepared: Prestige and Position as Personal Goals

Olt Landers' concepts of goodness and propriety revolved first around the concept of *pregătire* (preparedness), denoted by occupational qualification and achievement in labor. The hallmarks of a prepared person were education, skill and mastery of a craft, and opportunities for advancement. To a young electrician and part-time television repairer, *pregătire* meant "to learn well at school and know everything you can about your work. Prepared people are *pricepuţi* [perceptive, capable, quick studies]. They are not so clever with books but they know how to get by at work."

Before socialism, *pregătire* referred exclusively to formal education. Since few people aspired to much education, however, *pregătire* was an infrequent goal. Instead one's identity was bound up with the reputation of one's household, specifically the degree to which it reflected a proper middle-peasant life. With socialism, the education system was transformed to enable all to specialize, from collective farmers to storekeepers. And as education became the criterion for entry into all occupations, educational credentials became the mark of a prepared person.

All but the most marginal villagers aspired to *pregătire*, though not all agreed on its meaning. The majority of aggrandizing and integrated Olt Landers rarely expressed occupational preferences for their children; they were concerned only that their children be well prepared for a good job. Occasionally people spoke of being *pregătit* for collective farm or factory work, but for the aggrandizers and the integrated a good job was nonagricultural and nonmanual: bookkeepers and production engineers of every stripe had good jobs. Mobile householders, however, equated *pregătire* with university training and a professional career. Preparation was also important in one's choice of a spouse and tended to supersede "being from a good household" as the primary criterion for a marriage partner.

The emphasis on education, upward mobility, and success at work which *pregătire* implied conformed closely to Romanian socialist values. It promoted labor and, like the socialist state in general, supported the idea of hierarchy. Though all prepared people were laudable, the prepared of some occupations were more so. In accord with the socialist division of labor, mental work was evaluated more highly than manual labor. Furthermore, party officials and activists saw their dominance as resulting from their own preparation, which they explained by the practice of *rotația cadrelor* (cadre circulation) and the training it offered in diverse administrative and production functions. Preparation was also a common theme as cadres exhorted collective farmers and the assembled members of consumer cooperatives and other organizations to fulfill their plans or mobilize their energies in one campaign or another. Olt Landers, though, found the idea of cadre *pregătire* ridiculous. "In the past," a Cîrțișoara machinist chuckled, "leaders had *pregătire* and workers and peasants didn't. Now it's the opposite."

Preparation and Socialist Education

Since education was a chief criterion for position in the socialist division of labor, all Olt Land households were concerned about it.

Attitudes toward education varied widely, however, with contradictory results for state control of meaning and identity. Like public education the world over, schooling in the Olt Land overtly supported the hegemonic concerns of the state. Entering the Radu Negru Theoretical High School in Făgăraş or the Hîrseni and Cîrţişoara primary school, one was struck by the overwhelming images of labor. The walls of the central foyer at the Hîrseni school were covered with a massive collage of posters, pictures, graphs, and charts depicting heavy industry beneath a border of red posters bearing the words of Ceauşescu in white calligraphy. Each classroom displayed posters extolling industry, party history, and heroes, dominated by Ceauşescu's portrait and slogans exhorting students to persevere, build socialism, defend the fatherland. Collectivism was reflected by the uniforms worn by all children from nursery through high school and by the group activities, greetings, and recitations that filled the day.

Romanian law required ten years of education, much of it focused on practical experience. During the agricultural campaign, for example, each village primary school was allotted one hectare of land for pupils to tend. As the Educational Reform Law of 1973 required two-thirds of all postelementary education to consist of technical and vocational training, the number of places in theoretical high schools, which prepared students to enter a university, was severely curtailed.[4] Educational selection was therefore especially critical after eighth grade (cf. Ratner 1980). The bottom 10 percent of students remained for ninth and tenth grades in village schools and then took low-skill jobs in factories or on collective farms. Other students continued in vocational high schools or in a sixteen-month program at a professional school, often a factory auxiliary that trained students for jobs they were contractually obligated to perform for the next three to five years. Făgăraş had three high schools, each with its own place in a pecking order that was of concern mainly to the aggrandizers and the mobiles. The Radu Negru Theoretical High School was the most prestigious; next came the Industrial High School, and last the Agroindustrial High School. Aggrandizing and mobile households strove to get their children into the industrial or theoretical high school; integrated and marginal households rarely expressed a preference.

Few people were happy with the schools, but the complaints varied in accordance with the household's socioeconomic strategy. Members

4. After the 1989 revolution, high school teachers in Făgăraş claimed that this law was promulgated solely by Elena Ceauşescu, who was suspicious of intellectuals because she felt inferior to them.

of integrated households, committed to agriculture and village life, said the schools paid too much attention to academics, too little to agriculture, and took children from home when they were needed. They were particularly incensed about the school's expectation that children would assist the CAP instead of their families with the potato planting and harvest. One man, watching a school soccer game, said, "They wouldn't need to play if they worked in the fields more often." Members of mobile households, in contrast, worried about the poor quality of village schools and hired tutors for their children or sent them to relatives in the city for better schooling.

Olt Landers also failed to see eye to eye on schoolteachers. The teacher had always commanded respect in the village, and still did in the socialist period. Members of mobile households, in fact, often held teachers up as role models for their children. When teachers were expected to be political activists and guardians of socialist morality, however, others found them bothersome and morally high-handed. In fact, a few teachers occasionally intervened with local families to encourage better school attendance or health care. Such intervention was all the more offensive to many villagers when the teacher did not live in the commune. Of thirty-two teachers in Hîrseni's four villages in 1979, fourteen, including the school director, lived elsewhere, most of them in Făgăraş, and two were soon to move there. Six who lived locally were originally from outside the region, and only one of them had lived in the commune longer than five years.[5]

Even as parents complained about teachers, teachers complained about parents. A Hîrseni history teacher, originally from the village but now resident in Făgăraş, said, "It's very difficult to talk to many families about their children. People are only interested in their own affairs and their own pockets. Students from the village schools are poorly prepared and don't want to go on with their education. Girls especially don't try for the harder jobs that call for more preparation, so they end up in commerce or as operatives at the chemical factory."

Political Identity: Persisting Noninvolvement

The availability of education encouraged thoughts of social mobility, but a career in the Communist Party was rarely an appropriate way to

5. This situation, in fact, characterized rural schools throughout Romania (Ratner 1980, Sampson 1984:252).

achieve it. Party politics was viewed with much the same skepticism as supervisory work in the factory or on the farm. Political responsibility was so burdensome that people avoided it if they could and limited it if they could not. Even party members, including some commune mayors, saw it as something they were forced to assume. Party meetings, after all, were mandatory and tedious, and they accomplished nothing. Knowing my interest in political meetings, two Hîrseni women deputies jokingly asked me to take their places and report back to them.

Rejection of politics was reflected in definitions of goodness, which semantically divided *oameni cumsecade* (proper people) into two subcategories, those with functions (that is, formal political responsibilities) and those without. The functionaries gained or lost propriety by the way they behaved toward others. They were expected to "speak correctly [or nicely] to others," to "treat others honestly." A good person without functions—and most of my informants put themselves in this category—was defined as one who "has no business with anyone," who "doesn't create scandals," who "is peaceful and quiet—a person of the house."

Despite their derision of formal politics, Olt Landers respected some local officials and, until the bleakest days of the economic crisis, even lauded some Communist ideals, though often in clichéd terms, to highlight the state's failings. According to a nonparty metal cutter, a true Communist must be "more moral, harder working, and more honest than others, and there are only one or two people like that in the whole commune" (and they, I might add, were not party members). Respected local officials were also pitied. They were respected for protecting their communities from the state's ravages by lackadaisical enforcement of tax and collection procedures, and pitied because they were forced to do the bidding of an all-powerful party that left them with no capacity for independent action.

Local political leaders sometimes took out their frustration on their communities, and their abuse of power only furthered political apathy. In one case, some Copăcel men were severely treated for going over the heads of the Hîrseni People's Council to county executives in an effort to get something done about their aged, crumbling meeting hall. The men wanted to have it demolished and another built with local money and labor, but the commune leaders approved only the refurbishing of the old hall. When the commune leaders learned that the villagers had taken their case to county officials, they castigated them at a public forum, threatened them with demotion and loss of bonuses at their work, and denied them funds even to refurbish the hall. A few other Copăcelers said the fellows were fools. An older collectivist reasoned that "it's better to talk to the church bell" than to try to change things.

Mastering the Material World

Along with the quest for *pregătire*, bargaining on the job and in the second economy prompted a desire to control or master other people, possessions, and positions. Those who achieved such mastery were said to be *domni* (lords). *Domnie* has various meanings. Before socialist ethics required the use of *tovărăş* and *tovărăşă* (comrade), men and women from outside the village were addressed as *domnul* and *doamnă*. Other villagers were *ţărani* (countrymen), *ai noştri* (our kind), or, if they were older, *badi* (uncle) and *nene* (aunt). *Domn* also had ideological and political meaning. *Dumnezeu* (God) is derived from it, as are the formal and semiformal second persons singular, *dumnevoastră* and *dumneata*. *Domnii noştrii* (our lords) were the politicians and potentates who dominated village life from afar.

In the socialist era the meaning of the concept changed to reflect the incessant striving for status and prestige. Thus to be a *domn* was to work as little as possible, and the little work a *domn* did do had to be *curat* (clean; that is, not manual and preferably not agricultural). Some informants saw *domni* as "people who have any kind of function) (that is, a white-collar job or a profession), though party cadres and factory and farm administrators were often excluded from this category. *Domni* were also known by their visibility. One informant said that *domni* "have things that no one else has, have anything they need," and another that one became a godparent to be seen at the wedding and thus to be a *domn*. A young worker said, "A *domn* has whatever he wants. He has money. He doesn't have to work so much. He knows how to have a good time . . . he dresses well, eats well. When I buy my automobile and I drive through the village, people will see me and know I'm a *domn*."

Despite socialist disapproval and elder informants' claim that "*domni* aren't found in villages, only in cities," people in all social groups aspired to be *domni*, though the meanings they attached to the term varied. For men it referred mainly to control and consumption, but to be a *doamnă* implied style, gentility, and above all minimal labor outside the home: "A *doamnă* is a housewife and needn't work at a factory or on a collective farm"; she is "a woman who has seen things"; she is "well dressed, with pretty hair"; she is "a fine woman."[6] To aggrandizers, the visibility of *domnie* validated the superiority of their position, while integrated households saw *domnie* as permitting them a bit of ease, along with material comfort. Many people referred to the concept when they spoke of retirement and unfulfilled dreams of fishing and meat grilled over an open fire. Even marginals and Gypsies responded to *domnie*'s call. A young Gypsy man who had recently landed a job in a CAP's animal barn told me proudly, "Now I'm not only a Gypsy, I'm a *domn!*" Only some members of mobile households and professional transitionals saw *domnie* as frivolous.

As a household's material distinction reflected its *domnie*, the quest for *domnie* encouraged speculation in the second economy and accumulation of scarce commodities. Yet "to have what others don't" demanded expenses and labors out of proportion to the results. Jerry-rigged central heating, multimedia house facades (paint, plaster, mirror, brick, tin), marble foyers, and tiled bathrooms were all highly desired. Since the materials for these status symbols were often in short supply, would-be *domni* had to be alert to opportunities to acquire them through calculated gift giving, and to be watchful of others' acquisitions. Some commodities were objects of intense struggle. Even before rationing people competed to purchase white bread at village bakeries because it was more *domnesc* (classier) than *semi* (bread made of mixed bleached and unbleached flour), which in turn was more *domnesc* than *mămăligă* (corn-meal mush). Coffee was *domnesc*, as were American cigarettes and foreign beer and liquor, especially in the original containers (Kideckel 1985:440).[7] As *domni* dressed fashionably, it was important to wear a business suit or sport coat during working hours.

Domnie encouraged particular presentations of self. Olt Landers

6. A woman who lived for a time in Sibiu, then divorced and returned to Cîrţişoara with more urban tastes and manners, was referred to both directly and in general conversation as Mama Doamnă, a term that combined the local honorific Mama with the modern status referent.

7. Throughout Romania foreign cigarettes (especially Kents) were a second currency, used more for display and exchange than for consumption. Some acquaintances replaced the cigarettes in a Kent pack with a Romanian brand, then displayed the Kent pack when they smoked in public. I heard that some people filled empty Kent packs with sawdust before exchanging them for other commodities or services.

and other Transylvanian Romanians have long been known for their taciturnity (a Moldavian friend called them "wall-builders" in reference to both their houses and their personalities), but even this characteristic was eroding in the late years of socialism. Some people bragged of achievements to impress others and improve their chances of acquiring *domnesc* objects, while others, to be "seen," gave frequent *bakşiş* (bribes for services). *Bakşiş* was offered even when it was not solicited because "people would think you were nothing if you didn't give them something. It makes you feel like you're somebody."

Though people embellished their own responsibility and status, such airs still embarrassed and amused them. A member of a mobile Hîrseni household likened Ceauşescu, with his grandiose plans and projects, to "the *domn* who parades through the village in a suit coat while his courtyard is deep in manure." And a Cîrţişoara housewife, exasperated by the economic manipulation associated with wedding preparations, said, "People here are jealous and they're liars. We run after each other like chicks in a courtyard and we all want to be something we're not. The worker tells you he's an assistant engineer, the assistant engineer tells you he's an engineer, and the engineer tells you he's head of the factory. Everybody wants to be a *domn*."

Competition for status and resources in pursuit of *domnie* discouraged the cooperation that the Olt Landers sought in their second-economy pursuits. These economic concerns led people to rank each other along a continuum of trust and cooperation. At one end were *oameni de treabă* (forthright or businesslike people), whom one could count on, who were fair, hardworking, and helpful. In the middle of the continuum were *şmecheri* (tricky, manipulative sharpies), who couldn't be trusted but were only mildly threatening. At the far end of the continuum were *afacerişti* or *bişniţari* (speculators), who used others for their own ends and constantly sought to profit at others' expense.[8] *Şmecheri* and *bişniţari* did what everyone else did, but more often, more visibly, and with greater success. To be so classified, however, was to lose others' trust and, by implication, their cooperation as well.

Domină (dominate) has the same root as *domnie*, yet *domnie* was generally not attributed to party or state officials while they served in

---

8. The term *bişniţă* is borrowed from the English "business," and has all the negative connotations of exchange for profit.

their official capacities. These dominant ones were addressed as *tovărăş* (comrade) and referred to in private as *conducători* (leaders), *tovărăşi* (comrades), *ăldesusi* (those above), or *oameni de răspundere* (responsible people). People also used joking distinctions for party and state cadres. Thus leaders were regularly *hoţi* (thieves), *ţigani* (Gypsies), or, in conversation with me, "our Nixon," "our Ford," or whoever the American president was at the moment. By refusing to call their officials *domni* they denied them the status to which they themselves aspired.

The Prepared Person and the Master as Contradictory Identities

Though both *domnie* and *pregătire* evoked the Olt Landers' drive *să fie cineva* (to be somebody), at first glance they appear contradictory. Whereas *domni* avoided work, *pregătire* required one to be as capable as possible in his or her field. Whereas *domni* lied about their social status, prepared people were admired for their real knowledge and their assistance to others with the myriad problems of production. Whereas *domni* desired high-status foreign goods for display, prepared persons valued objects of use in their work. Such contradictions were clearly demonstrated when I offered gifts to friends and informants: the people who requested practical items were as numerous as those who wanted *domnesc* ones. Workers asked for tape measures, levels, arc welding equipment, wrenches. Teachers wanted books, maps, and scientific charts. The People's Council secretary asked for carbon paper and ball-point pens. And librarians and scholars wanted typewriters—a politically dangerous request because all typewriters had to be registered with the police.

An analogous contradiction can be seen in Olt Landers' attitudes toward technology. Though people were attracted to and understood modern technology, they were also deeply suspicious of it. Pointing to the smokestacks of the Făgăraş or Victoria Chemical Combine, people called them *aurul nostru, aurul Făgăraşului* (our gold, Făgăraş gold). Depending on the context, however, "gold" referred either to the factory's contributions to a household's income and standard of living or to the sulfurous smoke that destroyed people's health. Similarly, people blessed electrification but condemned the nervous disorders they attributed to emissions from the power lines that crisscrossed the region. They knew agricultural yields had improved since collectivization, and mechanization eased their lives, but still they criticized the practices of the tractor station as destructive of the land.

As disparate as they were, all of these contradictions were actually quite logical, as they expressed the struggle between state and household over the meaning of labor. Regional history, education, participation in socialist industry, even state ideology prepared the Olt Landers to take pride in their work and to find great meaning in it. They spoke lovingly of the techniques of metal grinding, bookkeeping, auto mechanics, and occasionally even agriculture. Yet though they loved their work, its social and political context made them abhor their labor. That is, though they prized work itself, the hierarchy of factory and farm and the struggle for resources made them reject that system in the sense of a set of social relations. In this context, then, the concern for preparation, lies about status, and hunger for the goods that validated it made perfect sense.

Thus the joke that serves as this chapter's epigraph. Much like the contradictions of *pregătire* and *domnie*, work and labor, it implied the possibility of a unified politics by acknowledging the severe labor regime under which people lived. Simultaneously, however, it implied that social atomization made political change unlikely. Though it posited a clear understanding of the state's political economy, it renounced political action and organization in the common interest (cf. Hobshawm 1084, Wright 1979:103- 4) in favor of individual compromise and stagnation.

The Changing Nature of Social Celebration

The ambiguities of Olt Land identity were also reflected and shaped by changes in ritual. As Clifford Geertz (1973:93–94) has made clear, ritual serves as a model both of society and for appropriate social behavior. To understand how it serves these functions, however, one must observe a society's entire ritual complex rather than any one ritual event alone. The changes in the range, nature, and relative intensity of household and individual-centered rites of passage, state secular ritual, and community-wide ritual in the socialist Olt Land clearly reflected the struggle between household and state hierarchy and the repudiation of central accumulation. But even as ritual repudiated socialism, it instructed individuals to compromise with the system and worked against political unity.

State Secular Ritual

State secular rituals especially modeled the opposition between state and household in their indelible portrayal of the us/them distinction prevalent in socialist labor. In their overbearing use of hierarchical, nationalist, and industrial symbols, state rituals were distressingly similar to ceremonials throughout socialist Eastern Europe (Binns 1979, 1980; Lane 1980; Silverman 1983). The fact that these rituals were produced and organized by state ideologues and that local people's participation in them was involuntary impoverished their symbolism and prompted the Olt Landers to reject them almost in toto.

This situation was evident in celebrations of socialist Romania's two major holidays, May Day and National Day. Though both were critical for national and socialist identities, they were all but invisible in Olt Land villages. Posters and slogans designed to whip up enthusiasm for the celebrations were displayed at the school, CAP, and People's Council from a month to a week in advance; but I never saw a single villager examine them even cursorily. Nearly everyone knew the significance of August 23, but a good number of middle-aged and older men and women had no idea what May Day symbolized. Though they received these days off, every worker said they would prefer to celebrate Christmas and Easter as official holidays. Olt Landers also drew a blank about other national labor holidays. No one remembered celebrating Chemical Workers' Day, Oil Workers' Day, or the Day of the Newly Hired, the September ceremony for people beginning their formal work life. Only a few older people remembered ceremonies at collective farms to celebrate Harvest Day, and then only in the mid-1960s, when the farms were new.

Olt Landers also made light of the national folklore contest, Cîntarea României (Song of Romania). All institutions were required to take part, and many people used their forced participation as an occasion for symbolic resistance. High school teachers and students in Făgăraş often begged off by feigning injury or claiming lack of talent for singing and dancing. Other institutions edited politically acceptable plays and skits into veiled criticism of the Ceauşescus and state policy. Still others acted, sang, and danced as clumsily as possible in the hope of being eliminated.

To be sure, other state rituals were viewed more favorably. School Pioneer Days and Culture Days, organized by local Councils for Political Education and Socialist Culture (a wing of the people's councils) were considered entertainment and were not so overtly political, though they often modeled proper work habits, socialist values, and hierarchy. Consider two Culture Days at Hîrseni commune. One program featured papers on the commune's history—the founding of the consumer cooperative, the history of regional place names (with emphasis on their non-Magyar origins), and an essay titled "The Role of Copăcel Amateur Folklore Groups in Retaining and Transmitting Social and Educational Values."9 The other was a performance of folksong, dance, and drama organized outside the framework of Song of Romania. The skits' socialist-realist themes were especially interesting. The prize-winning skit was set in a bar. Three swarthy, hirsute workers (clearly Gypsies) are drunk and boisterous, and we are given to understand that they were drunk on the job. A proper-looking young man lectures them on diligence at work and its relation to patriotism. He then physically boots them from the bar, to the laughter of the audience.

In contrast to Culture Day exercises, a general assembly of a collective farm or a consumer cooperative was fraught with inter- and intraclass tensions and was a raw exercise in symbol manipulation by state authorities (Kideckel 1982). To play on local sympathies, the stage was draped with rugs of local manufacture and design, and the embroideries hanging from the ceiling and the icon-like portraits of Ceauşescu on the walls gave the meeting hall the look of a church. Speeches by the local elite and visiting dignitaries were replete with household metaphors suggesting an identity of interest between them and the villagers. The split between them, however, was all too visible. The villagers sat on benches in the audience, the elite in chairs on the stage. The villagers arrived shortly after the time for which the meeting was called, the elite often two hours later. Only the elite knew the agenda of the meeting beforehand, and they read their reports, on which the citizens were supposed to vote, at breakneck speed. Villagers who attended received a chit worth half the cost of a brandy at a local bar. The elite were feted after the meeting with a multicourse meal served by team leaders and brigadiers. When the meal finally ended, amid a spate of pornographic jokes, everyone was fairly drunk.

9. Having returned to the commune two weeks before this program, I was also invited to speak about my research. My prepared remarks on the relationship between local households and the CAP were censored beforehand and turned into a general discussion of the concept of culture and the nature of anthropological fieldwork.

[193]

Such meetings indelibly choreographed the differences between "us" and "them" but still failed to forge solidarity among the villagers. Indeed, they often had the opposite effect. When CAP members took the floor to protest farm conditions, they invariably criticized each other as well, and the rejoinders the criticisms drew were sharp with anger. These meetings emphasized social distinctions, for only full-time farm members had the right to speak; people who worked part-time in agriculture were effectively silenced. The meetings were invariably long, and when the women angrily urged an end to the bickering as they felt the pressure of domestic responsibilities awaiting them at home, the elite scolded them for putting their own interests ahead of those of the collective and thus justified their own control.

Waning Rituals of Social Solidarity

State-supported rituals thus encouraged rejection of a socialist identity even as they isolated and differentiated households and left no room to craft an active opposition politics. Even ceremonies ostensibly produced and controlled by the communities themselves—those concerning the *ceată* (young men's association), dances and discotheques, soccer matches, cinema nights—were so few and so narrow in content that they pointed up the waning of a community identity. According to informants throughout the region, dances and such groups as the *ceată* were harder to organize and attracted fewer people each year. This was the case even in Drăguş, known for its persisting community identity. One Drăguş informant blamed the young and their devotion to sports, partying, and city life for the lack of commitment. In Hîrseni people spoke of the demands of industrial labor and community-wide jealousy as responsible for the waning of ritual.

Village dances had become rare, too. Until the socialist breakthrough, village dances—paid for by the young men, who then charged a small entrance fee—were held every few months. Young people attended dances in all the nearby villages, and many people recalled that they had met and courted their spouses at village dances. By the mid-1970s and 1980s only a Christmas dance and the Mare Bal (Great Dance, the Saturday after Easter) were held in Hîrseni. Both were well-attended but low-key affairs that broke up well before midnight. The lack of spirit at one Christmas dance was a particular disappointment to the village barkeeps, whose sales of food and liquor fell far short of the plan set for them by the consumer cooperative. Even soccer, the passion of young village men, failed to promote community identity. Older people complained that the players' time could be better used in work at home. In Hîrseni village, too, the youthful fans of the successful team were disappointed and disaffected when they discovered that their team had sold their hard-earned place in a regional championship tournament for 3,000 lei in order to buy new uniforms.

Olt Land Rites of Passage

The stylistic elaboration and expanded importance of rites of passage during the socialist epoch were in sharp contrast to the conflicting messages of state ritual and the decline of community celebration. Always prominent in the life of the region, rites of passage underwent great changes in socialism's last decades. First, ritual practice intensified. Baptismal and wedding gifts became more numerous and more extravagant. Weddings and funerals became larger, and the foods served at them became more elaborate. Grave markers became larger and more ornate. Second, rites of passage came to play new roles. As they called for increasing numbers and varieties of scarce or prestigious items, such rituals required intensified activity in the second economy (see also Kligman 1988:269), forced households into prolonged association with state institutions, and thus encouraged behavioral compliance. Third, the changes in rites of passage reinforced other changes in Olt Land life. They modeled the increased instrumentality of social relations, differentiation of village households, and the importance of *domnie* and *pregătire* in the socialist community.

The Olt Land Wedding in Form and Practice   Under socialism the *nuntă* (wedding) became an exercise in conspicuous consumption and competition. In form it changed only slightly. The civil ceremony that the state required had little meaning for Olt Landers; only the poorest of households made do with it, and very few of them. The civil wedding was held at the People's Council offices about a week before the church wedding. The mayor donned his official sash and led the couple in their vows of fealty to the state as well as to each other. Sometimes a few friends or the couple's parents attended. Most couples brought pastry and brandy to serve to their friends, the mayor, and employees of the People's Council, but this was no more than a gesture. The marriage was official and the couple could now legally live together, but I know of only one couple who admitted they did so.

The church wedding was the real thing, even for party members. Preparation for the ceremony and feast often began years in advance. Gold jewelry, a bridal gown, and occasionally reservations at a desirable restaurant were sought early. Then the bride's family turned their attention to dowry items such as appliances and furniture (cf. Kligman 1988:328–29).

Preparations for the wedding feast began three to four days in advance in the courtyards of the bride, the groom, and the godparents, though the busiest household was the one where the couple was to reside. In what seems to be a remarkable expression of social solidarity and cooperation, relatives, friends, and neighbors assembled, wood and bottled gas stoves were borrowed from neighbors and hooked up in the courtyards, women organized themselves into task groups to prepare the various dishes, and men hauled wood, crates of seltzer, furniture, and the like. Depending on the size of the wedding, from twenty to forty-five people worked at the three locations, and other villagers came by with small gifts of food—a few eggs, some flour, a bottle of cooking oil—and messages of good luck for the couple.

The wedding celebration lasted one day—no one could stay away from work longer—but what it lacked in duration it made up for in lavishness. Around 10 A.M. of the wedding day, guests assembled at the home of the bride, groom, or godparents, depending on who had issued the invitation. The number of guests varied considerably. Aggrandizing households regularly invited 700 or so, of whom 500 to 600 would attend. Most households invited about 300 people, expecting 150 to attend. The groom and his men friends drank and danced at his house for an hour and then his whole party, led by the unmarried men and a Gypsy band, walked to the godparents' house for more drinking and dancing. After another hour the entire party, now led by the groom, his godparents, and candle-bearing maidens of honor, proceeded to the bride's house, where their entry was blocked by her male relatives. After mock negotiations over the bride-price and chants about the groom's virility, the parties of the groom and godparents broke into the bride's home, in a way that suggested sexual aggression, for more feasting. Early in the afternoon all the celebrants, many quite drunk by now, were led to the church by the bride, groom, and godparents. Most remained outside, dancing and drinking.[10] The church service was brief, and the closest relatives of the bride and groom did not attend. They continued their work on the preparations for the wedding feast, which was the true testament to a family's worth.

The wedding feast lasted throughout the night and into the morning. Up to ten courses of food and four kinds of alcoholic drinks (and other beverages) were served as people danced and wandered in and out. The highlight of the evening was the bestowing of gifts on the couple. The godparent or his representative held a hat or bucket and, beginning at the head table, collected cash, held it up, loudly announced the amount, placed it in the hat, joked about the donor or the size of the gift, and then moved on to the next guest. The godparents began the proceedings by giving the largest cash gift of the evening. Then each subsequent gift declined in value as the social distance between the wedding couple and the donor increased. I was approached near the end and gave one of the smallest gifts. Finally, the day after the wedding the members of the wedding party who had prepared and served the feast were served in turn by the new couple in the courtyard of the house where they were to live.

Meanings of the Olt Land Wedding All weddings uphold marriage as an institutional ideal. They initiate men and women into new social statuses and ally families through their offspring. In the socialist years, however, Olt Land weddings also furthered social differentiation as celebrating households manufactured social standing by the amount of money they spent, the gifts they gave, the status of the godparents, and the general grandeur of the affair.

Table 16 shows the variety of expenses at the wedding of the son of the collective farm president and the daughter of the founder and former head bookkeeper of the commune consumer cooperative, who were to live in the groom's household after the wedding. Large weddings were justified by the status that accrued to households that entertained lavishly and by the loss of status they would suffer if they skimped on the affair. A Hîrseni household head whose daughter was to marry into a politically well-connected family said, "A big wedding is prettier and more luxurious. It shows other people that we are

10. In testimony to the waning significance of the Orthodox-Uniate schism, all church weddings in Hîrseni were held at the larger south (formerly Orthodox) church.

Table 16. Outlays of bride's and groom's households for a lavish wedding,
Hîrseni village, 1979 (lei)

Groom's household	
Orchestra (6 musicians, 2 days)	8,000
Artificial boutonnieres and corsages	1,200
Flowers for godmother and maids of honor	800
Brandy (250 liters) and wine (500 liters)	18,000
Beer and mineral water (2,000 half-liter bottles of each)	10,000
Pork, beef, veal cutlets (400 kg.)	12,000
Salami, other sausages (100 kg.)	4,000
Olives, cheeses, appetizers	5,000
Rental of table settings	2,000
Rental of village culture hall	1,000
Rental of buses to transport guests	1,000
Kitchen help	1,000
Formal photographs	2,000
Clothing and gifts to groom	10,000
Miscellaneous expenses (telephone, postage, pastry, etc.)	4,000
All groom's expenses	80,000
Bride's household	
160 liters brandy, 120 cakes, 70 breads, 500 pastries;	
gifts to bride, groom, groom's parents, other in-laws	10,000
Wedding gift*	18,000
Bride's trousseau†	20,000
All bride's expenses	48,000

*Cash, new furniture.
†Includes sheets, pillows and cases, bedspreads.

domni. It would be shameful to be able to have a first-class wedding and not do it. Our household would be the butt of jokes."

New features—beer and seltzer, an orchestra of more than four musicians—were constantly being added to weddings in the competition for renown. Weddings held in status-laden urban restaurants were considered especially luxurious, though families of middling rank celebrated weddings only in their courtyard or the village culture hall, and even aggrandizers seldom moved their wedding feasts out of the village. Still, some state resort complexes, such as Poiana Braşov, in the mountains above Braşov city, were especially prized for lavish weddings. Poiana's Şura Daciilor (Dacian Barn) restaurant, which provided a near-complete wedding package of food and drink, was an extraordinarily prestigious location. Access to such places and to chartered transportation for wedding guests required the kind of planning, maneuver, and negotiation that only an elite household could manage.

Various enclaves in the Olt Land had their own unique customs and expenses. Around Cîrțișoara and in the village of Racovița, a suburb of Sibiu, nearly all wedding parties, whatever the status of the celebrants, were outfitted in national costume, and households competed over their quality, embroidery detail, and cost. At the end of the 1970s a first-rate costume cost 3,000 to 4,000 lei, more if it were made by a talented seamstress. Around Cîrțișoara some households paid up to ten *călărași* (young men on horseback) to ride in the wedding procession. This was a double expense because the *călărași*, who would have been invited to the wedding in any case, were excused from giving gifts. One Cîrțișoara woman, the wife of a high commune official, said, "A wedding today is a great craziness, and the only reason for it is to show others how fine a family you are."

As the money spent on weddings rose, so did the amount of the gifts. In 1974, 1,000 to 3,000 lei was expected from the *naș*, 500 from siblings and close relatives, and 50 to 100 from less intimately connected guests. By 1979 these figures had more than doubled: now 5,000 lei was expected from godparents, 1,000 or more from close family members, and 200 from others, no matter what the status of the celebrants. At a very high-status wedding a couple could receive up to 150,000 lei in cash and another 10,000 in other gifts (exclusive of those given by the parents). At the black-market rate prevailing at the time, 36 lei to the dollar, the couple thus had nearly $4,200, but this sum could still fall short of the amount the parents had spent for the wedding.

Competition at weddings extended to the guest list and the acceptances. In the past, etiquette required a household to send two or more members to any wedding to which they were invited, and only extreme ill health or financial difficulties allowed one to send regrets. Recently, however, attendance at a wedding had come to depend on the celebrants' status. Given the inflation in wedding gifts, households generally sent only one member to most of the weddings to which they were invited. Two or more members attended only if the couple were from important households or if the bride, groom, or a godparent was a very close friend or relative. Attendance was optional if one of the spouses was from outside the region or if a villager married an urban resident, especially if the couple intended to live in the city.

A socioeconomic calculus also appeared to motivate the cooperation of relatives in the wedding. In fact, weddings were one of the few remaining areas of regional life where kin reciprocity was predictable.

[199]

One might have difficulty arranging a reciprocal labor party or even a simple exchange of favors, but the friends and relatives who labored at weddings seemed to do so willingly. Some cooperating kin came from as far away as Bucharest and stayed in the village for the week or so required to prepare for the feast. Gail Kligman (1988:262–64) suggests that this behavior acted as a cultural anchor in a world of change, mobility, and migration. Work at weddings, however, had definite instrumental functions as well. The visibility of the wedding in village life provided cooperating kin with the reflected glory of membership in a prominent family. It also established an obligation to be reciprocated, symbolized by the service of bride and groom on the day after the wedding. Work on the wedding feast enlarged the social and economic opportunities of all: the larger the wedding, the larger the network; the larger the network, the greater the options.

Changing Funerary Behavior

Funerals were less elaborate than weddings but their expansion, the frequency of *pomane* (offerings for the dead), and the increase in other expenses connected with them suggest that they, too, were way stations on the road to status. Like weddings, they expressed household and family solidarity. During the funeral close kin arrayed themselves around the open coffin in accordance with their relation to the deceased: the closer in life, the closer in death. Close women relatives keened over the coffin and lamented: "Our household will be empty without you"; "Why have you left your household alone?" The household's *naşi* raised a plate of nuts three times heavenward to assist the soul's passage. At the end of the service, before the open coffin was carried to the cemetery, the cortege bowed at the household gate in recognition of its loss. As the mourners left the cemetery they received *pomane* in the form of *popuri* (ceremonial bread), a candle, and a shot of brandy at the gate, and a member of the deceased's household whispered an invitation to close friends and relatives to attend a simple funeral meal. *Pomane* were then offered again after six weeks, six months, and one year, and optionally after mass each year on the Sunday closest to the anniversary of death.

In the late years of socialism several changes appeared in the Olt Land funeral. As recently as the late 1970s only close friends, relatives, and neighbors were invited to the funeral meal, which consisted of a thin vegetable soup and a bowl of rice, milk, and cinnamon; glasses of *rachiu* were raised in a toast: "May God forgive her [or him]." In the 1980s, however, all mourners at the cemetery were invited back to the meal, which now included meat and potatoes. Some Hîrseni funerals were so large and the guests so numerous that the meal was served at the meeting hall instead of the home. The meal served after the funeral of a local tractor driver in August 1984 was attended by about 200 people and cost about 15,000 lei, including 5,000 lei for an 80-kilogram pig and 2,000 for two lambs. In a telling comment his sister-in-law said, "We have to do all this. It's so bad now, there has to be more luxury."

Status concerns were also evident in the frequency of *pomane* and the elaboration of graves and markers. Wealthier households scheduled *pomane* not only at the traditional times but after a dream of the deceased or even at random to manufacture good luck. Rationing made *popurí* and *rachiu* expensive luxuries, but *pomane* became more frequent than ever. The greater the attention that had to be paid to exchange relations in the second economy, the more frequent the *pomane*. Most households other than the marginal ones began to replace simple wooden crosses on family graves with elaborate ones of welded metal with fanciful decorative elements, pictures of the deceased, and cement grave borders. Some households even invested the money, time, labor (occasionally of a master craftsman at 200 to 300 lei a day), and connections to turn their household grave site into a cement-encased vault.[11]

Ritual certainly functions to provide stability in changing lives, but the struggle to maintain a sense of self in the accumulative state demanded more from it. Though traditional elements survived, the Olt Landers transformed their ceremonies in an effort to come to terms with and control the changes brought by socialism. By elaborating household-based rites of passage, limiting collective expressions of community identity, and rejecting state rituals and symbols, Olt Landers both recognized and challenged the state's domination. Simul-

---

11. Sam Beck (personal communication) suggests that the elaboration of *pomane* and grave markers represented an emerging "cult of the dead." I agree with this characterization, but I am uncertain of its full meaning. It may have represented both recognition of and resignation to the difficulty of life in the accumulative state.

taneously they rewrote their codes of social life and identity and shaped their political lives in the world before the revolution.

Political Implications of Olt Land Identity

Olt Land identity was thus politically contradictory. Concepts of nation and person and their ritual expressions certainly imply acquiescence in centralized accumulation, but acquiescence was not tantamount to surrender. Even as it encouraged proper behavior in the socialist system, Olt Land identity denied the worth of this system and encouraged resistance to it. This contradiction modeled political possibilities and framed the relations of villagers to one another and to the state.

As Olt Land identity and ritual modeled hierarchy, they generally encouraged its acceptance. Identity demanded position, possessions, and knowledge, access to which depended on formal qualifications and political ties. The effort to gain these prizes thus encouraged compromise with the dominant, which in turn stifled local cooperation. Though the quest for *domnie* and elaboration of ritual were rejections of the state's ideology, they effectively limited challenge to it by encouraging individuals to seek satisfaction in display instead of unified action. Similarly, preparation not only qualified one for a position in the state economic system but also subjected individuals and households to the discipline, behavior, and ideology that the position entailed (cf. Therborn 1980:20).

Denial of *domnie* and *pregătire* to party officials also indicated rejection of the state but acquiescence in its dominance. This alternate scale of success thus encouraged peasant-workers to reject political responsibility even as it modeled the social and political hierarchy. In fact, the economic crisis of the 1980s not only failed to dim aspirations to *domnie, pregătire*, education, and ritual distinction but actually intensified the desire for them. Widespread shortages of basic and high-status commodities provided even greater opportunities and higher potential rewards for calculated display, and the desire for preparation was intensified by the state's restrictions on education and increasing demands for manual labor.

Thus display, possessions, mobility, preparation, and rejection of politics all contributed to social atomization in the years before the revolution. At the same time, they indicated the Olt Landers' strengths as they persisted in their struggle for dignity under increasingly difficult conditions. These were the motivations that spurred the revolution, when finally it came. Olt Landers marched, chanted, and challenged state security forces not only to express their despair but even more to demand recognition that "I am somebody!"

[8]

The Revolution and Beyond

Now we'll rid ourselves of reds
And remove their memory from our heads.

Postrevolutionary slogan on a Bucharest wall

Our living standard has fallen and we now are confronting many
grave problems—lack of trust between people, fights over the
division of land, the mass emigration of good teachers from the
villages to the cities, 300 percent inflation.

Petru M., Făgăraş construction engineer

The Ceauşescuite state is now gone and Romania is allegedly on the
road to reconstruction. Though the last years have witnessed many
changes—relatively free elections, privatization, decollectivization—
the country remains mired in a social, political, and economic morass.
Postrevolutionary optimism has given way to the view that Romania's
problems will not be resolved any time soon. Though one hopes
otherwise, this appraisal seems realistic. The fragmentation of Romanian society has been prolonged, if not intensified, by rumors of
renascent communism, vicious ethnic conflicts, and political violence of various sorts. This political climate puts Romania at an extreme disadvantage to other East-Central European states—Poland,
Hungary, and even the fragmentary Czech and Slovak states—as they
seek to unlock their own internal energies and compete for investment, assistance, and respect in the world community. Both the
reality and the rumors of revolution in Romania impede its people's
efforts to throw off the legacy of collectivism and transform their social
lives.

The December Revolution: National Events
and Uncertainties

The Romanian revolution began on Friday, December 15, 1989, in the western city of Timişoara, when a multiethnic group of protesters gathered to prevent security police from removing the popular Hungarian Calvinist Reformed minister Laszlo Tökes from his church to provincial exile.[1] The protest grew as word of it spread, and by the next day it had assumed the proportions of an insurrection as marchers chanted and looted stores. In Bucharest Ceauşescu was enraged that the riots had not been put down immediately, and on December 17 he ordered authorities in Timişoara to shoot all protesters. That matter taken care of, he left for a scheduled three-day state visit to Iran. The army hesitated to comply with the dictator's orders, but as large-scale rioting continued, the police stepped in and fired on the crowd. So began three days of disorder and death. Many people, even mothers with babies in their arms, rushed the police, shouting that it was better to die than to go on living as they were. And die they did, though how many is still uncertain. Estimates ranged from thousands during the revolution to fewer than a dozen afterward.

Romanian social networks being what they are, news of Timişoara spread rapidly by veiled telephone calls, commuting workers, and students who returned home after Timişoara University was closed. The rumored deaths of unarmed protesters galvanized the nation, and Bucharest was electric with tension on December 20, when Ceauşescu returned from Iran. He was oblivious of the gathering storm. Playing on old, usually reliable nationalist hatreds, he claimed in a televised speech that the protesters were hooligans and agents of foreign powers intent on destroying the country. Then, in an act of such political stupidity that it was still a source of rumor a year after the revolt, he decided to demonstrate his control by calling for a rally in front of the Palace Square headquarters of the party's Central Committee the following day. The crowds came, and as Ceauşescu ha-

1. The following account was pieced together from a variety of sources. The best summaries of the events of the revolution are found in Cullen 1990 and Macpherson 1990. Codrescu 1991 offers an assessment of the revolution refracted through memories of his youth in Romania. I also consulted a variety of articles in the daily *New York Times* and collected accounts of the revolution tape-recorded both in Bucharest and in Făgăraş. Kideckel 1989b gives a brief prognostication.

rangued them from a balcony, students at the back began to boo, whistle, and unfurl antiregime banners. Unaccustomed to protest, the dictator was befuddled, and his nonresponsive stammers were beamed throughout the nation.

This demonstration of fallibility emboldened the protesters. Chanting and rock throwing continued in Bucharest through the night. Again the troops fired. By morning the whole city knew that many had been killed; one friend said that "the fire trucks tried to wash away the blood, but couldn't. There was too much." Knowledge of the slaughter brought out tens of thousands early on Friday, December 22. Again Ceauşescu attempted to sway the hostile crowds. This time masses of people shouted and flung debris, and his talk was fumbling and barely audible. He was quickly pulled into his office by his wife as crowds surged toward party headquarters from every direction.

More army units were sent to stop their progress, but still they came. Marching on Bucharest's main boulevards, the growing ranks of protesters shouted to the people watching from apartment and shop windows, "Come with us!" and "To the palace!" One young woman, an architect and by her own account a timid person, was so emboldened that when her column was confronted by a tank unit, she rushed up to the commanding officer, kissed him squarely on the lips, and urged him to turn his tank around and head for Palace Square. "Don't you understand what's happening here?" she said. "Don't you want to be involved in history?" The tanks, now dripping with embracing protesters and soldiers, turned toward the palace. When they appeared there minutes later, irrefutable evidence that the army had gone over to the protesters, the Ceauşescus and some of their high command boarded a helicopter on the roof and fled, only to be captured later that day. Nicolae and Elena Ceauşescu were held in constantly moving armored vehicles for two more days and then tried and executed on Christmas.[2]

Intense fighting raged in Bucharest for days after the Ceauşescus'

2. Some Romanians consider Revolution Day to be December 22, the day the Ceauşescus fled, but that date has yet to be formalized as a state holiday because of the debate about the character of the revolution. Many people opposed to the current government consider the revolutionary actions taken by ordinary Romanians from December 17 to 21 as more indicative of true commitment to oust the communist regime, and believe that those who joined the Revolution on December 22 and later, as many members of the Salvation Front did, were really only accepting a fait accompli and attempting to protect their political power. Nevertheless, one of the more insightful critical journals of political and social commentary established after the revolution took its name, 22, from that date.

flight, and everyone I interviewed in the city told me that people on the street were sniped at from buildings through the day and night. Damage to the city center was extreme.[3] Responsibility for the fighting, death, and destruction has never been determined with certainty, and despite investigations, events remain murky. Rumors of plot and counterplot attest to the mistrust bred by the accumulative state. Though security forces were everywhere, seemingly moved at will through Bucharest, and had access to ample supplies of weapons and ammunition, the postrevolutionary government officially blamed the army for the indiscriminate firing and made only halfhearted moves to hold the Securitate accountable. The soldiers were culpable, the reasoning went, because they never trained with live ammunition, they were used for farmwork and construction, and so they stampeded when the crowds got out of hand. Romanians are largely skeptical of this explanation, and they have registered their suspicion of Securitate and state in graffiti all over Bucharest: "Cine a tras?" (Who really did the shooting?). Most fighting ceased after the execution of the Ceauşescus, and between Christmas and New Year's the Securitate was dissolved. According to many Romanians, however, the new leaders, in reality Communists, helped the security police escape to be held in reserve for future action.

Almost from the first days of the revolution, questions were raised about the revolutionary government, how it took power, and its commitment to democracy and a free economy. Since the revolution, state power in Romania has been held by the National Salvation Front (FSN), which, according to its own account, was formed in haste during the revolution by about 150 people of diverse social groups who happened to be at the Bucharest television station when it was captured. According to one student, "I was standing in an entrance [of the TV station] and someone came downstairs and said the Council [which soon became the Front] needed a student. Someone else pointed to me and said I was a student. That's how I became a member of the Council" (Cullen 1990:106–7).

Almost as soon as the FSN took power, rumors began that the revolution had been stolen by Communist loyalists who had been planning a coup d'état all along, but advanced their timetable when unrest broke out in Timişoara and Bucharest. These rumors were

---

3. Among the buildings severely damaged or destroyed were the turn-of-the-century Athénée Palace (a luxury hotel) and the central library of the University of Bucharest, where more than 500,000 volumes were lost to fire.

fueled by other suspicious developments. Though the FSN ostensibly began as a revolutionary coalition, over time former high Communist Party officials took control and nonparty elements were pushed out or quit in disgust. Though FSN leaders originally claimed only provisional status, they soon declared the Front to be a political party and fielded candidates for the presidential and parliamentary elections in the spring of 1990. And how, people asked, did so many party activists happen to gravitate to the TV station during the revolution, and why were only those at the station rewarded with power? One informant, who occupied the Central Committee offices during the revolution, said he began to believe that the revolution had been stolen as he watched TV before the New Year. "We were marginalized when the most important figures went to the TV station. Those who went to the TV station knew well the role of mass media. They made their own revolution at the TV station; they made themselves heroes" (Kideckel n.d.).

Other incidents also suggested a resurrected Communist Party. In January 1990 a huge popular demonstration at FSN headquarters demanded dissolution of the RCP and death for convicted high officials of the Ceauşescu regime. Though the Front agreed to these demands, it rescinded the agreement the next day. Other anti-FSN demonstrations in January were countered by huge pro-FSN rallies, first by hundreds of workers from the December 13 Industrial Complex on the outskirts of Bucharest, then by thousands of Jiu Valley miners. In interviews later the demonstrators said they had been spontaneously expressing sympathy for the FSN. To observers, however, the FSN rallies bore all the hallmarks of Communist agitprop techniques, including violence against those opposed to state policy.

The opposition did not give up easily. When the FSN leaders—President Ion Iliescu, Vice President Gelu Voican Voiculescu, and Prime Minister Petre Roman—declared the Front a political party with electoral intent in February, protests led to the inclusion of other parties in a provisional government. So-called provisional councils of national unity were formed, with counterparts at each level of political administration. The FSN still held the major positions in this structure, however, and to guarantee its victory in the May 1990 elections it began to undercut its opposition by policy pronouncements and allegedly by manipulation of the election.

Calling up the specter of mass unemployment, the FSN staked out a position to the left of a social democratic party and advocated a

Supporters of the Peasant Party rally against the National Salvation Front in Bucharest, April 1990

phased in market economy, state control of heavy industry, and maintenance of a state agricultural sector. At the same time it accused its major opponents, the National Liberal Party and the National Peasant Party–Christian Democrat (PNŢ-CD), of trying to sell the country to foreign interests by their policies of rapid and complete privatization.[4] Specific FSN industrial policies included immediate increases in workers' wages and pensions, an end to the withholding of 10 percent of wages, implementation of the five-day workweek, and an increase in the number of three-day holidays. FSN agricultural policy was more ambiguous, especially with respect to privatization. Though the Front did not immediately encourage large-scale privatization of agriculture, all CAP members were offered rights to a half-hectare use plot, regardless of the sizes of their gardens and courtyards, and the government looked the other way as some CAPs dissolved themselves and returned land to their members. The FSN encouraged all CAPs to

---

4. Besides these major "historical parties," eighty-odd others were formed in the wake of the revolution, some organized on an ethnic basis (there were about five Gypsy parties and two Hungarian parties), a few to advocate stands on ecological issues. Many parties were rumored to be splinters of the FSN, organized to confuse the opposition even further.

distribute some animal stock to member households, nullified CAP and individual contracts with the state for delivery of agricultural and animal products, and freed the CAPs to establish their own contractual relations with the machine tractor stations. It also raised farmworkers' pensions.

Romanian workers and peasants supported these policies, but other FSN campaign activities suggested that they were sops to ensure its electoral victory and subsequent reinstitution of communism. The FSN extensively manipulated the mass media. All kinds of publications circulated after the revolution, but presses, ink, and newsprint were still controlled by the government, ostensibly to ensure their fair distribution. The two main FSN papers, *Azi* (Today) and *Dimineaţă* (Morning), and the FSN-leaning *Adevărul* (Truth) were published regularly and distributed on schedule to the farthest reaches of Romania. Opposition papers, however, appeared irregularly and were haphazardly circulated. On occasion loyal FSN pressmen refused to print what they considered antigovernment propaganda, and people circulating opposition papers were beaten and their papers destroyed. Iliescu's presidential campaign received favorable coverage on state television but his rival candidates, Radu Câmpeanu and Ion Raţiu, were largely ignored. Issues were avoided in favor of personal politics, and Iliescu himself was shown as fatherly, competent, and a long-time opponent of Ceauşescu.[5]

Ethnic conflict also continued to fuel the boiling political pot. In February 1990 Transylvanian Magyars, who had been chafing under Ceauşescu's nationalities policy, especially restriction of education in the Hungarian language, began to force Romanian children out of formerly Hungarian schools. Rumors abounded that Hungarian physicians refused to treat Romanian patients and that Romanian physicians turned away Hungarians. Romanian-Hungarian riots broke out in the Transylvanian city of Tîrgu Mureş in March, and elsewhere in the country there were sporadic actions against Gypsies, who were quick to take advantage of the freer economic climate and who were blamed for any and all economic problems. Spicing the stew, a number of political parties and cultural movements organized along ethnic lines advocated a wide variety of exclusivist policies. Prominent among

5. Suspicions about Iliescu's integrity were expressed in the slogan "Iliescu ne zimbeşte şi cu drag ne păcăleşte" (Iliescu smiles at us and with love he dupes us).

them was Vatră Românească (Romanian Hearth), which was especially strong in Transylvania.

With the opposition fragmented and unable to mount an effective campaign, Iliescu and the FSN won the national election in May 1990 with about 85 percent of the presidential vote and 75 percent of the parliamentary seats (Socor 1990:25). Rather than settle the issue of political transition, the election invigorated anti-Front protesters. During the last month of the campaign they barricaded a main intersection, established a "Communist-free" zone in Bucharest's University Square, and spent the days in political debate and cultural communion (Beck 1990). During this protest, which extended from April 22 through the election until June 13, the government and protest leaders engaged in fruitless negotiations over a range of issues, from the creation of an independent television station to bringing former Communists to trial.

Each week brought the two sides closer to confrontation. In the sociopolitical vertigo that was postrevolutionary Romania, University Square became a tent city of the disaffected. The organized opposition was joined there by the homeless, street vendors, the emotionally unstable, and individuals on hunger strikes for redress of various personal grievances. Together they acted out their anger in front of the international press at the Intercontinental Hotel, just down the street from the U.S. Embassy. The government, for its part, became increasingly intransigent as its authority waned. It ordered the regular police force to clear protesters from University Square, but the police had lost all legitimacy and respect and were reluctant to act. Feeling cornered and unused to democratic procedure, the FSN government finally struck back at the protesters with fury. At a meeting on June 11, President Iliescu, Prime Minister Roman, and others decided to call out groups that supported them, principally the miners, to clear University Square.

Before they could act, however, a group of protesters left the square and assaulted the main TV station, police headquarters, and other Bucharest sites. Then the miners were unleashed. Their two-day bloodletting in University Square and throughout Bucharest was clearly planned; they not only beat protesters indiscriminately but attacked specific opposition figures, such as the student leader Marian Munteanu, and besieged the home of Ion Rațiu, the National Peasant Party leader.

[211]

Later the parliamentary opposition termed this act a "trampling of the norms that characterize states based on law" (Cunescu et al. 1991:3a). The miners' brutality and Iliescu's praise of their actions again raised suspicions about Romania's leadership and the political direction of the post-Ceauşescu state. At the very least it signaled that society would remain in disarray and torn by competing forces for some time to come. Unfortunately, recent events have done much to support those conclusions.

Much has changed since the miners invaded Bucharest. The Front first consolidated its power at local and county levels by legislating the government's right to name county administrators (Ionescu 1990). Demonstrations against this policy continued in the provinces, however, and the Front's position was further eroded in the 1992 local elections when the electorate of many larger cities chose leaders from opposition parties. Still, the Front maintained its strength in most rural areas and small towns. Large steps toward full-fledged privatization have also been taken, to the accompaniment of steep increases in prices and unemployment. A land law passed in February 1991 legalized private landownership but also supported a state and cooperative agricultural sector, and did little to untangle the jumble of land claims and counterclaims. Still, by late 1991 approximately 80 percent of Romania's farmlands had reverted to private ownership, and commerce, too, was opened up to private capital. Of the commercial firms in operation in late 1991, 7,572 were listed as owned by the state, 338 as owned jointly by the state and private parties, and 75,917 as privately controlled (Dumitrescu 1992:1). Most major industries remained in the state's hands, but even here a process of downsizing had begun; unprofitable sections were closing and large numbers of workers were losing their jobs. Together the political and economic uncertainties contributed to a restive social situation. Strikes quickly became common, and everywhere nationalist sentiment was on the rise, if tempered by the building Yugoslav horror next door. Clearly, though much has changed since Ceauşescu's downfall, much remains the same.

Revolution in the Olt Land

The revolution took a less violent course in the Olt Land. According to informants in Făgăraş, theirs was a "romantic" or "peaceful" revolution. Ever aware that gunplay around the city could cause the 10,000-cubic-meter ammonia tank at the Chemical Combine to explode, both protesters and authorities kept their actions in check. Still, there were some tense moments. People in Făgăraş were among the first in Romania to hear of the events in Timişoara. A number of Făgăraş residents were students in Timişoara, and army units and officers based in Făgăraş were sent to Timişoara to quell the rioting and then, after the army changed sides, to Sibiu to attack security forces there under the command of Nicu Ceauşescu, the dictator's son and heir apparent.

As people learned of Timişoara, a few Făgăraş dissidents planned demonstrations, though they had not yet learned of the events in Bucharest. A large demonstration was held in Făgăraş on the evening of December 21. One Combine engineer, demoted to manual labor for refusing to attend party meetings, had a friend at the factory photocopy hundreds of small announcements, then distributed them in factories and neighborhoods to inform the city of the meeting. Though the meeting was intended only to commemorate the Timişoara dead, it attracted about 2,000 people and quickly took on both a religious and an antistate character. The organizers gave out 500 candles, and Orthodox priests joined the marchers as they sang hymns in a candlelight procession that reminded many observers of Easter sunrise services.

Though most Olt Landers either demonstrated peacefully or avoided the protest altogether, some people were geared for violence if it became necessary. A conservator at the Cetate Museum obtained gasoline at work and prepared a few dozen Molotov cocktails, which he and a friend carried in their briefcases. Military units held their fire, however, and the Molotov cocktails stayed in the briefcases. One armored vehicle twice attempted to split the column of marchers, but in each instance the procession divided, went around the vehicle, and re-formed. After its second failure, the vehicle withdrew.

Another demonstration began on the morning of December 22. Informed of the events in Bucharest and sensing revolution, the protesters in the center of town marched toward the IUC and Chemical Combine, urging the workers to join them. IUC supervisors allowed many to leave, but security officers barricaded some doors and posted signs threatening anyone who joined the protest. The protesters tore down the barricades and IUC workers joined the procession en masse as it moved toward the Combine. There they encountered no trouble

[213]

because, some people said, its director was a Ceauşescu ally and feared for his life if he tried to hold his workers back.

Returning to the center of town, the crowd assembled in front of city hall/party headquarters and demanded an end to the Ceauşescuite state. After an hour of speeches the crowd broke into the building, went upstairs to the RCP secretary's office, tore the socialist state's symbol from the center of the flag, threw out volumes of Ceauşescu's speeches to the street, and proclaimed victory. An Orthodox priest offered mass from the balcony of the RCP office and the crowd fell to their knees in unison. A few police who remained standing at the fringes of the crowd were forced to their knees as well. That was the end of Ceauşescu's power in the Olt Land.

The revolution was even quieter in the villages than in the city, and the majority of villagers with whom I spoke claimed they avoided involvement with the Christmas events. Villagers first heard of the revolution either on radio, at their factories, or in messages from relatives in Făgăraş on the twenty-first. Most commuting villagers left Făgăraş that day to avoid the evening demonstration, hurried home to share their knowledge with their families, and then spent the few days until Christmas glued to the television and, less frequently, Radio Free Europe.

Despite the predictable reluctance to assume responsibility, some villagers did participate in the revolution. Those who came to work on December 22 did so to take part in the demonstration planned for that day. One friend told me that he hitchhiked to the Combine, ran into the IUC procession along the way, and quickly joined it. In his excitement he screamed so energetically for the Combine workers to join the protest that his false teeth fell out of his mouth. Another IUC worker, who had a reputation for stinginess and often brought milk from his cow to sell to co-workers, carried as many liter bottles as he could to give away to the protesters. Telephone operators kept the villages abreast of events and even transmitted requests from Braşov revolutionaries for food. Some young men from villages between Făgăraş and the mountains barricaded intersections to check the identities of passing motorists. Some people, though, said they only wanted to build reputations as revolutionaries without exposing themselves to real danger.

The joy of revolution was short-lived, for the nation's postrevolutionary political confusion was soon felt in the Olt Land. The Olt Landers' practicality initially served the region well, and a Făgăraş city government was quickly formed by representatives elected from various workplaces. After protests against the FSN rocked Romania, a provisional unity council was formed in Făgăraş by the seven major political parties represented in the region. At a meeting where I spoke with five of the seven party leaders about the region's future, I sensed a degree of good feeling among these men. They differed on many key issues, however, and it was difficult to keep the discussion orderly, as every question sparked loud debate, humorous insults, and accusations that the FSN was illegally claiming relief funds from foreign countries for its own use and tailoring its policies to suit public opinion. Since these leaders all worried about being submerged economically and politically by Braşov and Sibiu in the postrevolutionary state, one issue on which all agreed was independent county status for the Olt Land. They also agreed on the need for housing to accommodate an expected influx of people and for expansion of private enterprise in the region. To this end a commission was formed to analyze commercial space in Făgăraş, force out inefficient state enterprises, and develop means to license private workshops, vendors, and the like. None of these activities had formal state support or any legal basis.

The revolution in the countryside was most noticeable in the commune centers, where most of the institutions of state power—people's councils, schools, collective farms—were located. There most transfers of power were accomplished peaceably. Groups of unarmed citizens simply told the People's Council officials to leave their keys, seal their files, and go home. I heard of no physical threats, beatings, or intimidation of local officials. After the old officials left, many villages elected committees of respected individuals to run their affairs, though in others some officials of the socialist state retained their power. In Hîrseni commune a few people took advantage of the power vacuum to advance their own ambitions. A factory engineer acting on no authority but his own dismissed the mayor and took his place. After the fact he was appointed by the FSN to be its local representative. At first the engineer won supporters by making promises he had no authority to keep, but after the Unity Council was formed, the villagers largely ignored him.

The Olt Landers were as befuddled about the national election as everyone else. In April 1990 it was clear that Iliescu and the FSN were popular, though the reasons varied. The Front's policies, especially its advocacy of state support for large industries, were well received, and the national media barrage made Iliescu attractive to many people. Others supported him out of inertia and exhaustion. Overall, however, the FSN enjoyed less support in the Olt Land than elsewhere in the country, because many Olt Landers were suspicious of its privatization policy. A friend reported after the election that the vote in Făgăraş was 38 percent for the FSN, 14.8 percent for the Social Democrats (nationwide they polled only 0.5 percent), 7.5 percent for the National Peasants, 11 percent for the Liberal Party, and a surprising 7.5 percent for the Ecological Party. The remaining votes were split among weaker contenders.

The Aftermath in the Olt Land

As in Romania as a whole, the revolution and its aftermath had mixed results in the Olt Land. At first it improved people's daily lives and brightened their outlook; it even galvanized a few to participate more extensively in community decision making. Ultimately, however, the persistent uncertainties intensified the competitive and divisive forces that had so long been at work in Olt Land society. Every sphere of life, from labor to identity to household strategy, has been directly affected by the revolution and the possibilities and problems left in its wake. Scrutiny of these changes suggests that a politically open, economically productive civil society will be difficult to craft (cf. Kligman 1990:414–15) as the suspicions, depredations, and prevailing social relations of the socialist years reverberate through Olt Land life (cf. Marrant 1991, Verdery & Kligman 1990).

Transformation of Industry and Labor Hierarchies

Some of the quickest and most intensive changes the revolution provoked were in workplace organization and operation. Early in 1991 nearly every work group in nearly every kind of enterprise held an election to decide whether to retain or dismiss its administrators. Those who were considered to be in league with state authorities, such as the director of the Combine and a few members of his staff, were dismissed; the IUC director, who had a more paternalistic relationship with his workers, was retained. A number of master technicians, especially those who strictly enforced factory regulations, were also voted out, but I heard of no work-team leader who was dismissed at either the Chemical Combine or the IUC.

The explosion of workplace democracy also had less salutary consequences and encouraged enmity in labor relations. The workplace elections prompted a knee-jerk, class-based response in some instances and petty score-settling in others. The director of a Făgăraş economics institute, part of the regional consumer cooperative, was voted out of office by a majority consisting largely of low-level service staff—doorkeepers, office cleaners, painters, and the like—who also voted pay raises for themselves but not for the professional staff. And according to the IUC director, the workers voted out one *maistru* solely because he kept the pace of production brisk, even though they always fulfilled their plans and he distributed bonuses equitably. The director had to intervene personally to persuade the workers to retain this man.

Over the coming years the Olt Land's industry will be transformed, and workers realistically fear that the process will be wrenching. According to workers and administrators alike, few of the region's factories have access to the most modern production technologies, which were denied them in the last decade of debt repayment. If they are to acquire this technology now, they will have to continue to produce goods for export. Thus the goal of production has changed but, for the present at least, the results for workers will be the same or worse. Some unprofitable sections of factories are being shut down and workers transferred or let go entirely. Those who remain will have both to increase their productivity and to restrict their consumption. Olt Landers recognize the problem and are disposed to tackle it. Pretensions to *domnie* aside, labor is still appreciated for its own sake, and people will do their part if compensation and labor relations are equitable. In fact, absenteeism was never a big problem in the Olt Land, though it plagued many other zones in postrevolutionary Romania. Many senior Olt Land workers even tried to return to work as early as the Christmas of 1989!

One problem area for Olt Land workers is the development of strong, independent labor unions. There has been some union activity in the factories, but like so much else in the country, unionization has been stymied by lack of knowledge. No one knows how to structure an independent union, what policies to advocate, or even who properly ought to belong. All discussions about the formation of independent unions, whether at factories or at high schools, have similar sticking points. Should a union be factory-based, for instance, as in the socialist state, or should it represent workers across an entire industry? Most opinion seems to favor the old socialist model. As one worker told me, evoking the kind of bargaining that pervaded socialist work relations, then the workers would "be assured of better relations" with the union hierarchy. Workers have even debated whether administrators should be allowed in the unions. The high school teachers, most of whom seem to favor a broader union structure, recognize the contradiction in such an arrangement, but some IUC workers are strongly in favor of it.

The Future of Agriculture

The situation is as confused in agriculture as in industry. Despite the passage of a state land law, both the fate of the region's collectives and the future of its private agriculture were at first uncertain, and this uncertainty provoked considerable local debate and conflict. By late 1991, however, such uncertainty had dissipated, most Olt Land collectives were dissolved, and agriculture was placed fully in the hands of a reemerging middle peasantry comprising households that farmed from 5 to 10 hectares. Still, though the land-tenure situation has been somewhat sorted out, the decollectivization process was as socially wrenching as collectivization had been in the first place. In addition, though Olt Land agriculture is now fully privatized, many difficulties remain for the families that work the newly acquired land. Some people have the needed knowledge and energy but lack the necessary technology, while the aged and infirm and those whose households have been reduced in size lack even the necessary labor to make a go of private agriculture.

How did the process of collectivization promote discord? Much of the problem initially centered on working out the relationship, if any, of collective farming with private agriculture and the extent to which the state supported both forms. Though many villagers disparaged the collective farms, many others at first supported them, and these differences began to create tension as soon as the dust of revolution had settled.[6]

6. Kideckel 1990 and 1992a provide more detailed discussions of the politics of decollectivization.

A large part of the problem was provoked by the government's indecision in regard to private agriculture. It severely punished some attempts to disband collective farms (Ionescu 1990), yet it did nothing when other CAPs were disestablished and divested of resources. In liberalizing the access of collective farm members to CAP land it took the middle way. Each farm member (and each nonmember who fulfilled the CAP work minimum) received the right to farm a use plot of one-half hectare; and to the government's credit, plots were allotted without regard to the amount of other land available to a household. This was a considerable improvement over the old 15-are plots, with land subtracted for excess courtyard and garden plots, but some Olt Landers were still critical of the policy because they had expected privatization of all CAP lands. In response to the government's privatization policy a joke went the rounds: "Now they're giving land to the peasant—and if the peasant isn't home, they leave it at his doorstep." Furthermore, even the expanded use plots were still the property of the collective farm and could be rescinded or diminished at will.

Catalyzed by governmental indecision, the tension between privatization and recollectivization burst into open conflict in Hîrseni commune. At an assembly held at the end of January 1990 a large majority of villagers voted to allow households to claim as much land from the CAP as they could work and to dismiss the CAP president, who doubled as RCP secretary and had held office since 1979. The CAP supporters heatedly contested the outcome. A group of CAP officials managed to have the results of the first meeting nullified on the grounds that workers from nonmember households had taken part in the vote, and a second meeting was called. There opinion was hopelessly divided. According to the Hîrseni farm's chief agronomist, most households in Copăcel village chose to go private and reclaim some amount of land (from four to ten hectares) from the farm; about half of the households in Mărgineni and Sebeş elected to stay in the CAP, half to go private; and over 90 percent of voters from Hîrseni village voted to stay in the CAP.

The diversity of these responses seems to be related to both the postrevolutionary political climate and the socioeconomic strategies adopted by the various households. In the first instance, the government's agricultural policies left the villagers uncertain of its intentions. As some people said, privatization made no sense if the land could be taken back at a moment's notice, and no one could tell them how much the state would charge them for land if they were allowed to buy

[219]

it back. The figures being rumored for rent fluctuated from 7,500 to 14,000 lei per hectare per year (paid in kind to the state) for an indeterminate period.

Insofar as household socioeconomic strategy was concerned, many of the people who elected to leave the collective were members of integrated households that had been deeply involved in agriculture to begin with and thus had access to sufficient technology and draft animals to support their decision. The Marcius, for example, were among the first to privatize, and Octavian's son Viorel, now head of the household, was even thinking of giving up his job at the IUC to work full-time in agriculture when I spoke with him in April 1990. A few aggrandizing households also sought to leave the collective. The president of the local consumer cooperative, whose late father was past president of the CAP but who had little or no farm experience himself, nonetheless decided to claim ten hectares of CAP land. Asked how he planned to work the land, he said, "We'll find a way." His response suggested to me that he might be counting on his social network and cash reserves to manipulate the requirement that owners must work private holdings themselves.

Daunting problems faced the villagers who opted for private agriculture, and the decision was not easy to make, despite the emotional push toward it. The strategy was on shaky legal and financial ground, as the FSN government dawdled over a privatization law and set high tentative prices on land for purchase and lease. Most problematic of all was access to good land and appropriate technology. CAP supporters, after all, sought to retain as much good-quality land as possible, and this issue was further complicated by the great variability in the quality of soil from one village and field to the next.

As the farms gave up land in niggardly fashion, disgruntled privatizers were provoked into legal action against them. A half-dozen Sebeş households, for example, filed a claim specifying the amount and quality of land to be returned to them. As the diminished CAPs also hesitated to divest themselves of draft animals, only people with their own horses and water buffaloes, sufficient hay to keep them, and the necessary plows, harrows, and carts had much hope of success in private agriculture. Though tractor ownership was legalized, tractors were in short supply, prohibitively expensive, and of little use without cooperation from other households.

In an interesting twist on socialist realities, the lack of animal traction on the private farms forced an improvement in the always-tense relationship between tractor park and household. In the spring of 1990 the provisional government suspended forced deliveries of produce to the tractor parks, and tractor operators worked for both CAPs and private households on a straight cash basis. According to villagers, they charged reasonable fees and collected payment only after they had performed a guaranteed amount of work of a stipulated quality. Unfortunately, this improvement did not last. The state has raised the fees for tractor services, and as expenses have risen, opinion has returned to that of the socialist past (cf. Cămaşoiu & Sasu 1991). No doubt it will remain that way as state and private sector contend over prices and technology.

CAP supporters also based their decision on their household's socio-economic strategy. Many were from transitional households, while some were members of integrated households who worked in various salaried capacities on the farm (brigade and team leaders, quarter-masters, accountants). Privatizing informants criticized these people with the same kind of antibureaucratic rhetoric I heard during the Ceauşescu years. The people who supported the collective, they said, hoped to save their own sinecures and go on collecting their monthly salaries without too much actual agricultural labor. One informant who declined to take his land back, but who nonetheless supported private agriculture, laughingly said, "Those with the long nails should use them to harvest our potatoes."

The relative ease and economic security of CAP labor gave some villagers, especially those committed to factory work, second thoughts about private agriculture. Some people actually feared it. One couple in their early forties, both commuters whose parents owned about twenty hectares of arable land before World War II, were horrified when they heard a rumor that people were to be required to take back the land their households had registered in the CAP. They had no desire to work in agriculture, and to them the half hectare to which they were entitled was a burden. Many people who were close to retirement or recently pensioned and some younger unmarried people also saw private agriculture as not worth the effort. They had grown accustomed to the shared risk and shorter workdays of collective farming. Even if they rejected the farm, they preferred to work their plots to supplement their pensions or wages and depend on no one.

Finally, education and occupational choice also influenced the decision not to reclaim land. Some young people liked the idea of private agriculture but doubted that they knew enough to be successful at it. Because agriculture was so poorly treated in the Ceauşescu years, many villagers rejected it entirely. Even graduates of the Făgăraş Agroindustrial High School had tried to avoid the CAP at all costs. Consequently, few young Olt Landers have either the desire or the knowledge to work in agriculture.

Politics and Civil Society

An upsurge in political participation and the growth of a vibrant civil society among Olt Land villagers in the near future seem unlikely (Kideckel 1992b). The suspicion of politics and politicians that characterized life under Ceauşescu was certainly not nullified by the revolution, nor did the recent election do anything to dispel it. Consequently, though the downfall of the centralized accumulative state left a political vacuum, few Olt Landers are either attracted to or capable of filling positions of political responsibility in their villages. The state will still have the lion's share of influence and power in the region by default (see also Ost 1991).

Household socioeconomic strategy plays a role in this situation, too. The aggrandizers' ties to the Communist Party, on which their former influence depended, now disqualify them for political positions. Integrated households' time and energy are taken up by the demands of private agriculture, and some people who have chosen other strategies already view their incessant labor as greedy or slightly crazy. State-employed transitionals are fewer and are deprived of any kind of formal authority. And the social position of Gypsies has slipped even further in the postrevolutionary period as they have become the targets of accusations of economic speculation and unleashed ethnic passions (Radu 1990).

Mobile households will perhaps be most likely to accept some political responsibility. Their orientation to modernity, *pregătire*, and access to "European" cultural values could easily translate into political respect. For the moment, however, their commitment appears unlikely. Many are leaving their communities for the economic and educational opportunities available elsewhere. A friend in Făgăraş reported in 1991 that his mother-in-law, sister-in-law, and two nephews had left their village and moved in with him and his wife to make sure the two boys received a good education. The move was necessary, he said, because "the best teachers leave the villages for the cities and those who remain in the village are poorly prepared and of mediocre ability." After this initial surge out of the village, however, perhaps the educated people who remain will regain their political voices.

Privatization, at least at this moment, seems to have intensified the political divisiveness of local social networks, which continue to be significant means to cope with the demands of the informal economy, and so perpetuate bargaining and petty corruption (Popa 1991). Persistent shortages, the increased desire for luxury imports and opportunities to acquire them, erosion of the state commercial sector, and 300 percent inflation all contribute to familism and its implied political atomization. Even former *chiaburi* are reinserting themselves into the local political economy, to ill effect. According to informants, 87-year-old Ioan Cioră showed up in February 1990 to demand the return of the distillery he sold the Voievod family in the 1950s. The Voievods still had all the documents pertaining to the sale, however, so Cioră's attempt failed, but he vowed to return to press his case.

Though politics is still anathema to Olt Landers, villagers nonetheless relish their renewed participation in the "information age" and European culture. Thus television sets are always on in Olt Land homes.[7] In the late years of socialism television was largely ignored, as its two hours of daily programming consisted of the comings and goings of Nicolae Ceauşescu interspersed with a few other news reports and folk entertainment. Television gained legitimacy when the revolution was transmitted live from Bucharest. By the time the revolution was over, people said, they had become accustomed to leaving their TVs on. In the first months after the revolution they trusted TV news more than the Radio Free Europe broadcasts on which they had depended in the past. Postrevolutionary programming consisted of foreign films, dramatic serials, religious services, expanded news reports, and government bulletins explaining various policies, such as the decision to refuse a visa to former king Michael before the election.

The popularity of television, however, made it useful to the Iliescu government for the manipulation of public opinion. Every night during Holy Week in 1990, for instance, Romanians were treated to an all but continuous showing of *King of Kings*, which Olt Landers accepted

---

7. In fact, people now claim that they spend more time watching Romanian TV than they do listening to the Voice of America and Radio Free Europe.

as a clear demonstration of the government's support of religion. The Sunday after Easter, April 22, most people in the country also tuned in to a complete videotape of the capture, trial, and execution of Nicolae and Elena Ceauşescu. This broadcast, too, legitimized the FSN government by showing some of its leaders in prominent roles in the revolutionary events. And as we have seen, Iliescu and the FSN used television extensively as a tool in their bid for election. Their broadcasts swayed many a local vote, even though some Olt Landers are wise to the ways of modern media. The joke during the election campaign was that "Ceauşescu consumed our days [with labor] and Iliescu devours our nights [with television]."

Olt Landers, like other Romanians, also took to the revived Romanian press with enthusiasm, and the diversity of publications truly galvanized social and political debate at all levels of society and provided a glimmer of political hope. In Bucharest and Braşov people waited in long lines to buy daily papers from private vendors, and even in Făgăraş and the surrounding villages many people regularly bought at least three daily newspapers and a few weekly magazines. When I visited Vasile L. in April 1990, he showed me the new cow, plow, mower, and harrow he had bought in anticipation of receiving four hectares of land, and then spent an hour regaling me with what he had read in recent issues of 22, *Lumea Azi* (The world today, "an independent foreign policy weekly"), *Baricada* (Barricade, an "independent weekly of opinion and culture"), and the first issue of the capitalist *Profitul* (Profit). Gheorghe said he spent about 300 lei a month on newspapers and magazines, and four other Hîrseni families told me they did, too. How long this relative freedom of the press will continue, however, is open to question. The election set in motion unofficial restrictions on the opposition press, and its problems with circulation in the countryside persist today (Sam Beck, personal communication).

Education, perhaps more than other institutions, offers some possibility of political change, but its ability to speed democratization is ultimately problematic. Teachers I spoke with after the revolution bubbled with enthusiasm about the possibilities opening to them and their students, but their optimism was short-lived. State authorities introduced changes in the curriculum soon after the revolution, but the changes were designed primarily to distance the government from Ceauşescu. Other curricular changes being planned seemed more promising. At the Radu Negru High School in Făgăraş in April 1990 the teachers were planning new courses on religion, sociology, and world history, and the Industrial High School was planning to change its instruction to deemphasize training for jobs in large-scale agriculture and food-processing industries in favor of small-scale commercial and service enterprises, such as butcher shops, restaurants, and truck gardens.

Despite curriculum reform, many impediments lay in the way of democratization of the educational process. The teachers and school administrators with whom I spoke had little concern for pedagogical methods or participatory educational practices, and they did not recognize the benefit of active parent and community involvement in the schools. In fact, as state investment in the schools was rapidly declining, education seemed well on the way to becoming a luxury. The law requiring ten years of education, established in the 1970s, was rescinded soon after the revolution, to the unanimous approval of the Făgăraş teachers. Now the less serious students would drop out, they said, and the schools would be able to concentrate on the more deserving ones.

Democratic politics will also be impeded by nationalism, now reinforced by renewed religiosity and regional identity. Olt Landers fervently deny that they are nationalists. In April all the people I spoke with readily and sincerely condemned the participants (Romanian and Hungarian alike) in the ethnic riots in the town of Tîrgu Mureş in March. Further discussion, however, brought out their continued resentment against the Magyar Transylvanians, who, they say, provoked the riots and revealed their true separatist aims when they removed Romanian students from Hungarian schools in Cluj in January and February. And they *still* don't speak the Romanian language! Special opprobrium is reserved for Laszlo Tökes, who, they said, publicly advocated autonomy for Transylvania's Hungarians on a speaking tour in the United States in March 1990. Even the Radu Negru High School teachers, who universally favored curriculum reform, saw no need to change the pre–World War II history curriculum, which emphasizes the Romanian people's cultural uniqueness and the suffering endured by Transylvanian Romanians when their province was dominated by other nations. Though Olt Landers reject autonomy for Transylvania's Hungarians, they favor it for Romanians in formerly Soviet Moldova, even as they laud Iliescu for keeping Romania out of the Moldovan crisis.

Nationalism is supported by a renewed regionalism. The campaign

to separate Făgăraş from Braşov and Sibiu, though ostensibly motivated by economic concerns, is implicitly nationalist in outlook and
justified by reference to the region's historical autonomy. The Olt
Landers' support for the Vatră Românească movement also links regionalism with nationalism. Vatră Românească, whose more extreme
members bear a rough resemblance to the interwar fascist Iron
Guard, has a strong following in Braşov, where one of its chief newspapers, *Libertate cu Dreptate* (Liberty with justice), is published, and
cells have also been organized in Făgăraş factories. In April 1990 the
Vatră group in Făgăraş was headed by the director of the Cetate
Museum and tourist complex. According to the museum's assistant
director, who doubled as vice chair of the Vatră, they have about one
hundred adherents and probably two to three thousand local sympa-
thizers. Certainly these figures are speculative, but the widespread
concern about Romanians' rights in Transylvania and Moldova do lend
support to the Vatră program, even though there have been no chau-
vinistic outbursts in the region like those in Cluj and Tîrgu Mureş
after the revolution.

A final, and perhaps most difficult, barrier to an open political
culture is Olt Landers' attitude toward politics. Most people with
whom I talked—young and old, men and women, workers, peasants,
and clerks—said that one of the best things about the revolution was
that it allowed them to be left alone to live their lives as they saw fit.
Some workers, in fact, were elated to be relieved of the obligation to
belong to any party. Membership in the Communist Party was, after
all, a burden; it infringed on their time, energy, and personal autonomy. Now that party affiliation is voluntary, Olt Landers are gleefully
exercising their right "to have no business with anyone," as they say.
Some Olt Landers, mainly intellectuals under fifty, were more willing
to participate in politics but were uncertain what doing so would mean
for them and their families. They assumed that membership in a party
bound one to follow all its policies, as in the RCP. Others were concerned about how their friends and neighbors might react if they
joined a party. The head of the Făgăraş branch of the National Peasant
Party complained about his party's lack of members, but he was aghast
when I suggested door-to-door American-style political canvassing to
recruit new ones. If he tried that, he said, most of the people he
approached would give him a good thrashing. Local political skepticism was summed up by a former mayor of Hîrseni commune: "I am

an FSN-ist. I think like a Republican. I am for the Liberals. I don't believe in any of them. And if I vote, I'll vote with Ţiriac."[8]

The Olt Land Case: Implications for Eastern Europe and Anthropology

The transformation of East-Central Europe is well on its way, but the question remains: To what? Many Westerners believe that the vibrant personal network relations developed during the socialist years will give rise to a new "civil society" (Ash 1989). The more self-congratulatory partisans even suggest the final triumph of capitalism (Fukuyama 1989).[9] Such sunny prognostications show little recognition of either the dynamics and continuities of cultural and social institutions in Eastern Europe (Halpern & Kideckel 1983) or the often contradictory complexities of human choice and action. As Gerald Creed (1991) implies by his notion of the "socialist subconscious" and Katherine Verdery (personal communication) suggests by her idea of the "phantom limb," the relations of socialist society and the passions of revolution are certain to rumble and throb through East European life for years. If we are to have any hope of understanding Eastern Europe's likely future course, we must come to terms with the processes that have brought it to where it is now.

Any understanding of socialist Eastern Europe and its successor states must be built from the ground up. What Joel Halpern (personal communication) has called the "pig's-eye view of reality" (see also Cole 1980) enables us to recognize and document the various ways in which groups of people construct their lives and face the challenges of the political systems in which they live. Though the economic morality of their practices may be less than heroic and their lives may in fact be downright self-centered, this is the stuff by which society rises and falls; this is what must occupy center stage in our political drama. Such Western observers as Francis Fukuyama, like the socialist demagogues before them, deny both individual autonomy and a role in history to the peasants, workers, clerks, and functionaries of the socialist party-state.

8. Ion Ţiriac is a Romanian-born international tennis impresario who offered his native country a few million dollars toward development of a free market.

9. Kideckel 1989a offers an extensive critique of the "end of history" argument.

In considering Olt Land practice, however, I have come to question the salutary role of the family, household, and network in shaping resistance to the state and creating an alternate social reality for the people under state control. In this late-twentieth-century world of mass social institutions, such social relations are often looked at fondly, with a sense of nostalgia, respect, and political promise. And certainly in the Olt Land, households and social networks contributed to (and were almost the only sources of) the resistance of the dominated. As we have seen, however, a state's political and economic arrangements can manage to waylay and twist the political possibilities of local social relations. Thus whatever resistance persisted within the Olt Land's social networks was often indirect and produced many behaviors and attitudes that give pause. Increased attention to family and household at the expense of wider social relations, manipulation of those social relations in labor and the second economy, and bragging and dissimulation in social discourse all speak of the pain of life and the difficulty of direct resistance to the centralized accumulative state.

Olt Landers and all Romanians deserve respect for the quiet struggle they waged against the Ceaușescuite system, rejecting participation on the collective farms, manipulating the system in the national folklore contest, "running from responsibility," and giving flip responses to party cadres during collectivization. But mainly they relied on household skills and relations to find ways around barriers thrown up by the socialist system, thus atomizing their struggle and shaping a solitude within an intense social field.

Unfortunately, I fear that such social and political isolation is bound to persist as Olt Landers sort out their options and identities in their world turned upside down. But the fact that they resisted in ways large and small, under the intense pressures that only a centralized state can exert, is a lesson that ought not to escape either a critical anthropology concerned with human possibilities or the region's new masters as they grapple with the problems left where the party-state once stood. To play on the tendency to individualize one's problems or on the divisiveness of hypernationalism would be the simplest and most cynical approach that Eastern Europe's new leaders could take. If they do take that path, they guarantee their own failure and eventual defeat. Solitude and collective action, after all, are contradictions that people in quest of respect and predictability cannot long abide.

References

Primary Sources

Darea de seamă (Annual report), CAP Bujorul Carpaţilor, 1964–1975 (minutes of meetings, commission activities, plans, election results, etc.).
Darea de seamă statistică (Statistical reports), CAP Bujorul Carpaţilor, 1964–1975; GAC Racoviţa, 1951–1955.
Evidenţa zilelor (Work credit evidence), CAP Bujorul Carpaţilor, Hîrseni and Copăcel villages, 1962–1975.
Harta cadastrală (Cadastral map), Hîrseni village, 1936.
Registru agricolă (Agricultural register) for Cîrţişoara village, 1951–1963; Hîrseni commune, 1951–1976, Viştea commune, Drăguş village, 1951–1980; Racoviţa village, 1943, 1951 1955.
Schiţă sistematizare (Systemization plan), Hîrseni commune, 1980–1985; Viştea commune, 1981–1985.
Starea civilă (Civil statistics), extracts from Cîrţişoara village, 1861–1967; Hîrseni village and commune, 1895–1979.
Studiu agricol (Agricultural study), Hîrseni commune, 1971.

Secondary Sources

Anderson, Evan E.
    1983   "Central Planning and Production Instabilities in Eastern Europe." *Slavic Review* 42(1):221–29.
Annis, Sheldon
    1987   *God and Production in a Guatemalan Town.* Austin: University of Texas Press.
Ash, Timothy Garton
    1989   *The Uses of Adversity: Essays on the Fate of Central Europe.* New York: Random House.

[229]

References

Bahro, Rudolph
1978 *The Alternative in Eastern Europe*. London: NLB.
Banfield, Edward
1958 *The Moral Basis of a Backward Society*. Glencoe, Ill.: Free Press.
Bărbat, Alexandru
1938 *Desvoltarea şi structura economică a Ţării Oltului cu un plan de organizare*. Cluj: Tipografia Naţională.
1941 *Studiul economic al satului Drăguş-Făgăraş*. Bucharest: Imprimeria Naţională.
Barnes, J. A.
1972 *Social Networks*. Addison-Wesley Module in Anthropology. Reading, Mass.: Addison-Wesley.
Bazac, Ana
1981 "Cu privire la conceptul de autoconducera muncitorească." In *Democraţia socialistă şi autoconducerea muncitorească în România*, ed. Ioan Ceterchi et al., pp. 56–74. Bucharest: Editura Politică.
Beck, Sam
1976 "The Emergence of the Peasant Worker in a Transylvanian Mountain Community." *Dialectical Anthropology* 1(4):365–75.
1979 "Transylvania: The Political Economy of a Frontier." Ph.D. dissertation, University of Massachusetts at Amherst.
1986 "Tsigani Gypsies in Socialist Romania: Ethnicity, Class, and Public Policy." *Giessener Hefte für Tsiganologie* 3(1–4):109–27.
1987 "Privat-Bauern in Rumänien: Die sozialistische Umgestaltung in den 1970er Jahren." *Osteuropa* 37(1):851–61.
1990 "The Romanian Opposition's Symbolic Use of Space in June, 1990." Working Papers on Transitions from State Socialism, no. 90.9. Center for International Studies, Cornell University.
Bell, Peter
1979 "Social Change and Social Perception in a Rural Hungarian Village." Ph.D. dissertation, University of California at San Diego.
1983 *Peasants in Socialist Transition: Life in a Collectivized Hungarian Village*. Berkeley: University of California Press.
Bender, D. R.
1967 "A Refinement of the Concept of Household: Families, Co-residence, and Domestic Functions." *American Anthropologist* 69:493–504.
Benedict, Ruth
1953 "History as It Appears to Rumanians." In *The Study of Culture at a Distance*, ed. Margaret Mead and Rhoda Metraux, pp. 405–15. Chicago: University of Chicago Press.
Binder, David
1976 "Copy of Department of State Summary of Helmut Sonnenfeldt's Remarks to Group of US Ambassadors Is Made Available to the New York Times." *New York Times*, April 6, p. 1.
Binns, C. A. P.
1979 "The Changing Face of Power: Revolution and Accommodation in the

Development of the Soviet Ceremonial System," pt. 1. *Man* 14(4):585–606.

1980 "The Changing Face of Power: Revolution and Accommodation in the Development of the Soviet Ceremonial System," pt. 2. *Man* 15(1):170–187.

Bourdieu, Pierre
1977 *Outline of a Theory of Practice.* Cambridge: Cambridge University Press.

Braham, Randolph L.
1963 *Education in the Rumanian People's Republic.* Washington, D.C.: U.S. Government Printing Office.

Brezinski, Horst, and Paul Petrescu
1986 "The Second Economy in Romania –A Dynamic Sector." Working Paper of the Economics Department, n.s. no. 6. University of Paderborn, Germany.

Burawoy, Michael
1985 *The Politics of Production.* London: Verso.

Butură, Valer
1978 *Etnografia poporului român.* Bucharest: Editura Dacia.

Cămaşoiu, I., and E. Sasu
1991 "Statul ne-a cumpărat grîul cu 1,90 lei kg. şi ne vinde tărîţă cu 2,50 lei kg." *România Liberă,* January 17, p. 3a.

Campeanu, Paul
1988 *The Origins of Stalinism: From Leninist Revolution to Stalinist Society.* Armonk, N.Y.: M. E. Sharpe.

Cândea, Virgil
1977 *An Outline of Romanian History.* Bucharest: Meridiane.

Caramelea, Vasile V.
1944 *Composesoratele de foşti iobăgi din Ţara Oltului.* Craiova: Ramuri.

Ceauşescu, Nicolae
1971 "Expunere cu privire la îmbunătăţireă organizării, planificării şi conducerii agriculturii." In *România pe Drumul Construirii Societăţii Socialiste Multilateral Dezvoltate,* 5:246–50. Bucharest: Editura Politică.

1983 *România pe drumul construirii societăţii socialiste multilateral dezvoltate.* Vol. 24. Bucharest: Editura Politică.

Cernăianu, Liviu
1983 "Republica Răspunderii Creatoare." *Cîntarea României* 4(12):1.

Cernea, Mihail
1974 *Sociologia cooperativei agricole.* Bucharest: Editura Academiei.

1975 "The Large-Scale Formal Organization and the Family Primary Group." *Journal of Marriage and the Family* 37(4):927–36.

1978 "Macrosocial Change, Feminization of Agriculture, and Peasant Women's Threefold Economic Role." *Sociologia Ruralis* 18(2–3):107–24.

Ceterchi, Ion
1975 *Socialist Democracy: Principles and Political Action in Romania.* Bucharest: Meridiane.

1979 "The Exercise of Self-management in the Political System of Socialist Romania." In *The Political System of the Socialist Republic of Romania*, ed. I. Ceterchi, O. Trasnea, and C. Vlad. Bucharest: Editura Ştiinţifică şi Enciclopedică.

Cheetham, Tom, and Roger Whitaker
1974 *The Peasant-Worker of Eastern Europe: Report of a Seminar Held at Boston University Conference Center.* Boston: Inter-University Consortium on East-Central and Southeast European Studies.

Chirot, Daniel
1976 *Social Change in a Peripheral Society: The Creation of a Balkan Colony.* New York: Academic Press.
1978 "Social Change in Communist Romania." *Social Forces* 57(2):457–99.

Codrescu, Andrei
1991 *A Hole in the Flag: A Romanian Exile's Story of Return and Revolution.* New York: William Morrow.

Cojocaru, Constantin
1990 "Restructurareă proprietăţii." *Adevărul*, February 14, pp. 1, 3.

Cole, John W.
1976 "Familial Dynamics in a Romanian Worker Village." *Dialectical Anthropology* 1(3):251–66.
1980 "In a Pig's Eye: Political Economy and Daily Life in Southeastern Europe." *IREX Occasional Papers* 1(3):3–24.
1981 "Family, Farm, and Factory: Rural Workers in Contemporary Romania." In *Romania in the 1980's*, ed. Daniel N. Nelson, pp. 71–116. Boulder, Colo.: Westview.
1985 "Problems of Socialism in Eastern Europe." *Dialectical Anthropology* 9(2):233–56.

Cole, John W., and Judith A. Nydon
1990 "Class, Gender, and Fertility: Contradictions of Social Life in Contemporary Romania." *East European Quarterly* 23(4):469–76.

Comitetului Central al Partidului Comunist Român
1984a "Hotărirea Comitetului Politic Executiv al C.C. al P.C.R. cu privire la creştera răspunderii organelor şi organizaţiilor de partid, organelor de stat şi cadrelor medico-sanitare în înfaptuireă politicii demografice şi asigurareă unui spor coresponzator al populaţiei." *Scînteia*, March 3, p. 3.
1984b "Aplicarea fermă, neabatută a politicii demografice pentru vitalitatea tinereţeă şi vigoarea naţiunii!" *Scînteia*, March 6, pp. 1, 3.
1984c "Familia cu mulţi copii: O lege a vieţii şi împlinirii umane, o nobilă îndatorie patriotică." *Scînteia*, March 9, pp. 1–2.

Consiliul de Stat
1972 *Labor Code of the Socialist Republic of Romania (Legea nr. 10 din 23 noiembrie 1972).* Bucharest: Secţia Redacţională a Buletinului Oficial.
1975 *Constituţia Republicii Socialiste România.* Bucharest: Seviciul Buletinului Oficial.

Constantinescu, Olga
  1973   *Critica teoriei "România, ţara eminanmete agriculturii."* Bucharest: Editura Academiei.
Cotaru, Romulus
  1938   "Etica drăguşenilor: Criteriile morală şi filosofia practică în satul Drăguş." *Sociologie Românească* 3(7–9):310–38.
Creed, Gerald W.
  1991   "Civil Society and the Spirit of Capitalism: A Bulgarian Critique." Paper presented at the 93rd Annual Meeting of the American Anthopological Association, Chicago.
Cullen, Robert
  1990   "Report from Romania." *New Yorker*, April 2, pp. 94–112.
Cunescu, Sergiu, et al.
  1991   "O dramă naţională din nou în actualitate." *România Liberă*, January 30, pp. 3a–6a.
Custred, Glynn
  1990   "Voluntary Associations and Ethnic Survival among the Saxons of Transylvania." *Anthropology of East Europe Review* 9(2):30–36.
de Fleis, René
  1984   "Socialism in One Family." *Survey* 28(4):165–74.
de Janvry, Alain
  1981   *The Agrarian Question and Reformism in Latin America.* Baltimore: Johns Hopkins University Press.
Direcţia Centrală de Statistică a Republicii Socialiste România
  1973   *Anuarul statistic al Republicii Socialiste România.*
  1983   *Anuarul statistic al Republicii Socialiste România.*
Djilas, Milovan
  1955   *The New Class: An Analysis of the Communist System.* New York: Praeger.
Dumitrescu, Vasile
  1992   "Economia României în anul 1991." *Revista romană de statistică* 2:1–8.
Ellman, Michael
  1979   *Socialist Planning.* Cambridge: Cambridge University Press.
Enuţa, N.
  1952   "Chiabur: Duşman de moarte al gospodăriei colective." *Ştiinţă şi Cultură* 8:12–13.
Fehér, Ferenc, Agnes Heller, and György Márkus
  1983   *Dictatorship over Needs: An Analysis of Soviet Societies.* New York: Basil Blackwell.
Fél, Edit, and Tamas Hofer
  1969   *Proper Peasants: Traditional Life in an Hungarian Village.* Viking Fund Publications in Anthropology, no. 46. New York: Wenner-Gren Foundation for Anthropological Research.
Fernandez-Kelly, Patricia
  1983   *For We Are Sold, I and My People: Women and Industry in Mexico's Frontier.* Albany: State University of New York Press.

[233]

References

Filip, Gheorghe, Ovidiu Bădină, and Dorin Radulescu
   1972 "Migrațiuni, mobilitate, navetism." In *Tineret industrial: Acțiune și integrare socială,* ed. Ovidiu Bădină, pp. 77–90. Bucharest: Editura Academiei.
Fischer, Mary Ellen
   1989 *Nicolae Ceaușescu: A Study in Political Leadership.* Boulder, Colo.: Lynne Rienner.
Fortes, Meyer
   1958 "Introduction." In *The Developmental Cycle in Domestic Groups,* ed. J. R. Goody, pp. 1–14. Cambridge: Cambridge University Press.
Freedman, Maurice
   1958 *Lineage Organization in South China.* London: Athlone.
Freeman, Susan Tax
   1970 *Neighbors: The Social Contract in a Castillian Hamlet.* Chicago: University of Chicago Press.
Fukuyama, Francis
   1989 "The End of History?" *National Interest* 16 (Summer): 3–18.
Fulea, Maria, and Maria Cobianu
   1972 *Organizarea muncii în cooperativele agricole de producție.* Bucharest: Editura Academiei.
Funderburk, David
   1987 *Pinstripes and Reds: An American Ambassador Caught between the State Department and the Romanian Communists, 1981–85.* Washington, D.C.: Selous Foundation Press.
Gabanyi, Anneli Ute
   1987 "Ceaușescu Rejects Soviet Style Reform, Enforces Austerity Policy." *Radio Free Europe Research Reports,* February 6, pp. 3–6.
Gati, Charles
   1990 *The Bloc That Failed: Soviet–East European Relations in Transition.* Bloomington: Indiana University Press.
Geertz, Clifford
   1973 (1966) "*Religion as a Cultural System.*" In *The Interpretation of Cultures,* pp. 87–125. New York: Basic Books.
Gellner, Ernest
   1983 *Nations and Nationalism.* Ithaca, N.Y.: Cornell University Press.
Georgescu, Florin
   1984 *Muncă—Temei al condiției umane.* Bucharest: Editura Politică.
Gheorghiu-Dej, Gheorghe
   1962 *Cuvîntare rostită la încheierea consfatuirii pe țara a țăranilor colectiviști,* pp. 671–714. Bucharest: Editura Politică.
Gilberg, Trond
   1975 *Modernization in Romania since World War II.* New York: Praeger.
Giurescu, Constantin C., and Dinu C. Giurescu
   1971 *Istoria românilor din cele mai vechi timpuri pînă astăzi.* Bucharest: Albatros.

Giurescu, Dinu C.
1989   *The Razing of Romania's Past.* New York: World Monuments Fund.
Goody, Jack R.
1976   *Production and Reproduction: A Comparative Study of the Domestic Domain.* Cambridge: Cambridge University Press.
Granick, David
1975   *Enterprise Guidance in Eastern Europe: A Comparison of Four Socialist Economies.* Princeton: Princeton University Press.
Gwertzmann, Bernard, and Michael T. Kaufman, eds.
1990   *The Collapse of Communism.* New York: Times Books.
Halpern, Joel M., and David Anderson.
1970   "The Zadruga, a Century of Change." *Anthropologica* n.s. 12(1):83–97.
Halpern, Joel M., and Barbara Kerewsky-Halpern
1972   *A Serbian Village in Historical Perspective.* New York. Holt, Rinehart & Winston.
Halpern, Joel M , and David A. Kideckel
1983   "Anthropology of Eastern Europe." *Annual Review of Anthropology* 12:377–402.
Hammel, Eugene A.
1968   *Alternative Social Structures and Ritual Relations in the Balkans.* Englewood Cliffs, N.J.: Prentice Hall.
1972   "The Zadruga as Process." In *Household and Family in Past Time,* ed. Peter Laslett and Richard Wall, pp. 335–74. Cambridge: Cambridge University Press.
Hann, C. M.
1980   *Tázlár; A Village in Hungary.* Cambridge: Cambridge University Press.
1985   *A Village without Solidarity.* New Haven: Yale University Press.
1990   "Second Economy and Civil Society." In *Market Economy and Civil Society in Hungary,* ed. C. M. Hann, pp. 21–44. London: Frank Cass.
Haraszti, Miklós
1977   *A Worker in a Worker's State.* New York: Universe Books.
Helin, Ronald A.
1967   "The Volatile Administrative Map of Romania." *Annals of the American Association of Geographers* 57:481–502.
Herseni, Traian
1977   *Forme străvechi de cultura poporană românească: Studiu de paleoetnografie a cetelor de feciori din Țara Oltului.* Cluj-Napoca: Dacia.
Herseni, Traian, et al., eds.
1972   *Combinatul chimic Făgăraş: 50 de ani de existenţă.* Sibiu: Întreprindera Poligrafică.
Hirszowicz, Maria
1980   *The Bureaucratic Leviathan: A Study in the Sociology of Communism.* New York: New York University Press.

References

Hitchens, Keith
1969   *The Rumanian National Movement in Transylvania, 1780–1849.* Cambridge: Harvard University Press.
1979   "Religion and Rumanian National Consciousness in 18th Century Transylvania." *Slavonic and East European Review* 57:214–39.
Hobsbawm, E. J.
1984   (1971) "Notes on Class Consciousness." In *Workers*, pp. 15–32. New York: Pantheon.
Hobsbawm, E. J., and Terence Ranger, eds.
1983   *The Invention of Tradition.* Cambridge: Cambridge University Press.
Hoffman, George
1972   *Regional Development Strategy in Southeast Europe: A Comparative Analysis of Albania, Bulgaria, Greece, Romania, and Yugoslavia.* New York: Praeger.
Hoffman, Oscar, et al.
1984   *Clasa muncitoare din România în condiţiile revoluţiei tehnico-ştiinţifice.* Bucharest: Editura Academiei.
Holmes, Douglas
1983   "A Peasant-Worker Model in a Northern Italian Context." *American Ethnologist* 10:734–48.
1989   *Cultural Disenchantments: Worker Peasantries in Northeast Italy.* Princeton: Princeton University Press.
Humphrey, Caroline
1983   *Karl Marx Collective: Economy, Society, and Religion in a Siberian Collective Farm.* Cambridge: Cambridge University Press.
Ianoş, I.
1981   "Puncte de vedere privind analiza geografică regională a teritoriului a României." *Studii si cercetari* 28:103–11.
Ionescu, Constantin
1973   *Omul, societatea, socialismul.* Bucharest: Editura Academiei.
Ionescu, Dan
1990   "Government Moves to Recentralize Local Administration." *Report on Eastern Europe* 1(36):19–24.
Ionescu, Ghita
1964   *Communism in Romania, 1944–1962.* London: Oxford University Press.
Ionica, Ion
1943   *Dealu Mohului: Ceremonia agrară a cununii în Ţara Oltului.* Bucharest: Bucovina.
Irimie, Cornel
1948   "Relaţiile sociale din Ţara Oltului: Contribuţiă la problema genezei şi structurii unităţiilor sociale regionale." Ph.D. dissertation, University of Bucharest.
Jackson, Marvin
1983   "Romania's Debt Crisis: Its Causes and Consequences." In *East European Economies in the 1980's*, 3:489–542. For Joint Economic Commit-

tee of the U.S. Congress. Washington, D.C.: U.S. Government Printing Office.

Jowitt, Kenneth
1971   *Revolutionary Breakthroughs and National Development: The Case of Romania, 1944–1965.* Berkeley: University of California Press.
1978   *The Leninist Response to National Dependency.* Institute of International Studies, Research Series no. 37. Berkeley: Institute of International Studies.

Jowitt, Kenneth, ed.
1978   *Social Change in Romania, 1860–1940: A Debate on Development in a European Nation.* Berkeley: Institute of International Studies.

Kahn, Joel S.
1985   "Peasant Ideologies in the Third World." *Annual Review of Anthropology* 14:49–75.

Kideckel, David A.
1976   "The Social Organization of Production on a Romanian Cooperative Farm." *Dialectical Anthropology* 1(2):267–76.
1977   "The Dialectic of Rural Development: Cooperative Farm Goals and Family Strategies in a Romanian Commune." *Journal of Rural Cooperation* 5(1):43–62.
1979   "Agricultural Cooperativism and Social Process in a Romanian Commune." Ph.D. dissertation, University of Massachusetts at Amherst.
1982   "The Socialist Transformation of Agriculture in a Romanian Commune, 1945–1962." *American Ethnologist* 9(2):320–40.
1983   "Secular Ritual and Social Change: A Romanian Case." *Anthropological Quarterly* 56(2):69–75.
1985   "Drinking Up: Alcohol, Class, and Social Change in Rural Romania." *East European Quarterly* 18(4):431–46.
1988   "Economic Images and Social Change in the Romanian Socialist Transformation." *Dialectical Anthropology* 12(4):399–411.
1989a   "Anthropology in the Common European Home: Notes on the End of the Cold War (Maybe)." Paper delivered at annual meeting of American Anthropological Association, Washington, D.C.
1989b   "The Romanian Revolution Isn't Over." *Hartford Courant,* December 31, pp. D1, 4.
1990   "The Politics of Decollectivization in Romania after Ceauşescu." Working Papers on Transitions from State Socialism, no. 90.9. Center for International Studies, Cornell University.
1992a   "Once Again, the Land: Decollectivization and Social Conflict in Rural Romania." In *The Curtain Rises: Rethinking Culture, Ideology, and the State in Eastern Europe,* ed. David Anderson and Hermine De Soto, pp. 88–105. Atlantic Highlands, N.J.: Humanities Press.
1992b   "Peasants and Authority in the New Romania." In *Romania after Tyranny,* ed. Daniel N. Nelson, pp. 69–83. Boulder, Colo.: Westview.
n.d.   "Housefire in the Global Village: The Role of Television in the Romanian

References

Revolution." In *From Communism to Democracy: Lessons from Romania*, ed. Arthur Helweg. Forthcoming.
Kideckel, David A., and Steven L. Sampson
1984   "Fieldwork in Romania: Political, Practical, and Ethical Aspects." In *Anthropological Research in Romania*, ed. John W. Cole, pp. 85–102. University of Massachusetts Research Reports in Anthropology, no. 24. Amherst: University of Massachusetts.
King, Robert R.
1980   *History of the Romanian Communist Party.* Stanford, Calif.: Hoover Institution Press.
Kligman, Gail
1983   "Poetry as Politics in a Transylvanian Village." *Anthropological Quarterly* 56(2):83–89.
1988   *The Wedding of the Dead: Ritual, Poetics, and Popular Culture in Transylvania.* Berkeley: University of California Press.
1990   "Reclaiming the Public: A Reflection on Creating Civil Society in Romania." *East European Politics and Societies* 4(3):393–427.
Konrád, George, and Ivan Szelényi
1979   *The Intellectuals on the Road to Class Power: A Sociological Study of the Role of the Intelligentsia in Socialism.* New York: Harcourt Brace Jovanovich.
Kovacs, Iosif
1973   *Desfiinţarea relaţiilor feudale în Transilvaniei.* Bucharest: Dacia.
Lane, Cristel
1980   *The Rites of Rulers: Ritual in Industrial Society—The Soviet Case.* Cambridge: Cambridge University Press.
Literat, Valeriu, and Moise Ionaşcu
1943   *Oraşul şi Ţara Făgăraşului, Cetatea Făgăraşului.* Făgăraş: Haţiegan.
Lockwood, William G.
1973   "The Peasant-Worker in Yugoslavia." *Studies in European Society* 1:91–110.
McArthur, Marilyn
1976   "The Saxon Germans: Political Fate of an Ethnic Identity." *Dialectical Anthropology* 1(2):349–64.
MacCartney, C. A.
1937   *Hungary and Her Successors: The Treaty of Trianon and Its Consequences.* London: Oxford University Press.
Macpherson, William
1990   "In Romania." *Granta* 33(Summer):9–58.
Manuila, Sabin
1931   *Recensământul general al populaţiei româniei.* Vol. 2: *Neam, limbă maternă, şi religia.* Bucharest: Direcţia de Statistica.
Marcus, George, and Michael Fischer
1986   *Anthropology as Cultural Critique: An Experimental Moment in the Human Sciences.* Chicago: University of Chicago Press.

[238]

Marrant, Joel
  1991   "Has Nothing Changed? Perceptions of Post-Ceauşescu Romania." *Anthropology of East Europe Review* 10(1):34–37.
Marx, Karl, and Friedrich Engels
  1963   (1850) *The Manifesto of the Communist Party.* London: George Allen & Unwin.
Medick, Hans
  1976   "The Proto-Industrial Family Economy: The Structural Function of the Household during the Transition from Peasant Society to Industrial Capitalism." *Social History* 3:291–315.
Meteş, Ştefan
  1921   *Vieaţa agrară, economică a românilor din Ardeal şi Ungaria: Document contemporane.* Vol. 1: *1508–1820.* Bucharest: România Nouă.
  1930   *Viaţa bisericească a românilor din Ţara Oltului.* Sibiu: Editura Asociaţiunii.
  1935   *Situaţia economică a românilor din Ţara Făgăraşului.* Vol. 1. Cluj: Arhivul Statului din Cluj
Miłosz, Czeslaw
  1981   (1953) *The Captive Mind.* New York: Vintage.
Ministry of Justice of the People's Republic of Romania
  1956   *Legislaţia gospodăriilor agricole colective şi a întovărăşirilor agricole.* Bucharest.
Mitrany, David
  1930   *The Land and Peasant in Romania: The War and Agrarian Reform (1917–21).* London: Oxford University Press.
  1951   *Marx against the Peasant: A Study in Social Dogmatism.* Chapel Hill: University of North Carolina Press.
Montias, John M.
  1967   *Economic Development in Communist Rumania.* Cambridge: M.I.T. Press.
Móricz, Nicholas
  1934   *The Fate of the Transylvanian Soil: A Brief Account of the Rumanian Land Reform of 1921.* Budapest: Society of Transylvanian Emigrants.
Nash, June
  1979   *We Eat the Mines and the Mines Eat Us: Dependency and Exploitation in Bolivian Tin Mines.* New York: Columbia University Press.
National Conference of Peasant Collectivists
  1962   *Consfătuirii pe ţara a ţăranilor colectivişti.* Bucharest: Editura Politică.
Nelson, Daniel
  1981   "Romania: Participatory Dynamics in 'Developed Socialism.'" In *Blue Collar Workers in Eastern Europe,* ed. Jan F. Triska and Charles Gati, pp. 236–52. London: George Allen & Unwin.
Netting, Robert McC., Richard Wilk, and Eric J. Arnould, eds.
  1984   *Households: Comparative and Historical Studies of the Domestic Group.* Berkeley: University of California Press.

References

Nydon, Judy
  1984 "Public Policy and Private Fertility Behavior: The Case of Pro-Natalist Policy in Socialist Romania." Ph.D. dissertation, University of Massachusetts at Amherst.
Ortner, Sherry
  1982 "Theory in Anthropology since the Sixties." *Comparative Studies in Society and History* 26:126–66.
Ost, David
  1991 "Interest and Politics in Post-Communist Society: Problems in the Transition in Eastern Europe." *Anthropology of East Europe Review* 10(1):5–11.
Pacepa, Ion M.
  1987 *Red Horizons: Chronicles of a Communist Spy Chief.* Washington, D.C.: Regnery Gateway.
Pahl, R. E.
  1984 *Divisions of Labour.* Oxford: Basil Blackwell.
Pasternak, Burton, Melvin Ember, and Carol Ember
  1976 "On the Conditions Favoring Extended Family Households." *Journal of Anthropological Research* 32:109–23.
Pop, Iosif
  1990 "Împărţirea pamîntului—dereaptă, după lege!" *Adevărul,* February 10, pp. 1–2.
Popa, Alexandru
  1922 Editorial. *Ţara Oltului,* February 24, 1922.
Popa, Dinu
  1991 "Din privatizare a rezultat în bişniţă." *România Liberă,* January 22, p. 3a.
Prodan, David, ed.
  1976 *Urbariile Ţării Făgăraşului.* Vol. 2: *1651–1680.* Bucharest: Editura Academiei.
Puşcariu, Ioan Cav. de
  1892 *Date istorice privitorie la familile nobile române.* Sibiu: Tiparul Tipografiei Archidiecesane.
  1907 *Fragmente istorice despre boerii din Ţara Făgăraşului.* Sibiu: Tiparul Tipografiei Archidiecesane.
Radio Free Europe
  1984 *Eastern Europe: Toward a Religious Revival.* Research Background Report no. 88. May 23.
Radu, Dan
  1990 "Pogromul din comuna Mihail Kogăliceanu." *Opinia Studenţească.* Vol. and issue nos. unknown.
Randall, Steven G.
  1976 "The Family Estate in an Upland Carpathian Village." *Dialectical Anthropology* 1(2):277–85.
  1983 "The Household Estate under Socialism: The Theory and Practice of

Socialist Transformation and the Political Economy of Upland Peasant Workers in Romania." Ph.D. dissertation, University of Massachusetts at Amherst.

Ratner, Mitchell S.
1980 "Educational and Occupational Selection in Contemporary Romania: A Social Anthropological Account." Ph.D. dissertation, American University.

Rebel, Hermann
1989 "Cultural Hegemony and Class Experience: A Critical Reading of Recent Ethnological-Historical Approaches," pts. 1 and 2. *American Ethnologist* 16(1–2):117–36, 350–65.

Rév, István
1987 "The Advantages of Being Atomized: How Hungarian Peasants Coped with Collectivization." *Dissent*, Summer, pp. 335–50.

Roberts, Henry L.
1951 *Rumania: Political Problems of an Agrarian State*. New Haven: Yale University Press.

Romanian Research Group
1977 "On Transylvanian Ethnicity: Reply to Sozan." *Current Anthropology* 20(1):135–40.

Ronnås, Per
1986 "The Role of the Second Economy as a Source of Supplementary Income to Rural Communities in Romania: A Case Study." Typoscript.

Roseberry, William
1989 *Anthropologies and Histories. Essays in Culture, History, and Political Economy*. New Brunswick, N.J.: Rutgers University Press.

Ruscnescu, Mihail
1979 "Procesul cooperativizării agriculturii în România, 1949–62." *Revista de Istoria* 32:429–48.

Rusu-Şirianu, Ioan
1904 *Românii din statul ungarn*. N.p.

Sabel, Charles F., and David Stark
1982 "Planning, Politics, and Shop-Floor Power: Hidden Forms of Bargaining in Soviet-Imposed State Socialist Societies." *Politics and Society* 2(4):439–75.

Sampson, Steven L.
1976 "Feldioara: The City Comes to the Peasant." *Dialectical Anthropology* 1(3):321–48.
1983a "Is Romania the Next Poland?" *Critique*, no. 16, pp. 139–45.
1983b "Rich Peasants and Poor Collectives: An Anthropological Approach to Romania's Second Economy." *Bidrag til Ostatsforskning* 11(1):34–43.
1984 *National Integration through Socialist Planning: An Anthropological Study of a Romanian New Town*. East European Monographs, no. 148. New York: Columbia University Press.

References

1986a "Regime and Society in Romania: Ceauşescu's Social Contract." *International Journal of Rumanian Studies* 5:20–35.
1986b "The Informal Sector in Eastern Europe." *TELOS*, no. 66 (Winter), pp. 44–66.
1989 "Romania: House of Cards." *TELOS*, no. 79 (Spring), pp. 217–24.
1991 "Ethnic Tensions in Eastern Europe: Why Do Russians Die for Latvia?" *Anthropology of East Europe Review* 10(2):4–11.
Sampson, Steven, and David A. Kideckel
1989 "Anthropologists Going into the Cold: Research in the Age of Mutually Assured Destruction." In *The Anthropology of War and Peace*, ed. Paul Turner and David Pitt, pp. 160–73. Hadley, Mass.: Bergin & Garvey.
Sandu, Costache
1973 *Repartiţia producţiei globale a cooperativelor agricole de producţie.* Bucharest: Editura Politică.
Sanjek, Roger
1978 "A Network Method and Its Uses in Urban Ethnography." *Human Organization* 37(3):257–68.
1982 "The Organization of Households in Adabraka: Toward a Wider Comparative Perspective." *Comparative Studies in Society and History* 24(1):57–103.
Scott, James
1984 *Weapons of the Weak.* New Haven: Yale University Press.
Seddon, David
1976 "Aspects of Kinship and Family Structure among the Ulad Stut of Zaio Rural Commune, Nador Province, Morocco." In *Mediterranean Family Structures*, ed. J. G. Peristiany, pp. 173–94. Cambridge: Cambridge University Press.
Şerban, Ioan
1907 "Răscoala ţărănească în România." *Ţara Oltului* 1(12):1–2.
Seton-Watson, Hugh
1945 *Eastern Europe between the Wars, 1918–1941.* New York: Harper & Row.
1951 *The East European Revolution.* New York: Praeger.
Shafir, Michael
1985 *Romania: Politics, Economics, Society.* Boulder, Colo.: Lynne Rienner.
Shanin, Teodor
1971 "Cooperation and Collectivization: The Case of Eastern Europe." In *Two Blades of Grass: Rural Cooperatives in Agricultural Modernization*, ed. P. M. Worsley, pp. 263–74. Manchester: University of Manchester Press.
1972 *The Awkward Class: Political Sociology of Peasantry in a Developing Society: Russia, 1910–1925.* Oxford: Clarendon.
Silverman, Carol
1983 "The Politics of Folklore in Bulgaria." *Anthropological Quarterly* 56(2):55–61.

[242]

Simmonds-Duke, E. M.
  1987   "Was the Peasant Uprising a Rebellion? The Meanings of a Struggle over the Past." *East European Politics and Societies* 1(2):187–224.
Smith, Joan, Immanuel Wallerstein, and Hans-Dieter Evers, eds.
  1984   *Households and the World Economy.* Beverly Hills, Calif.: Sage.
Socor, Vladimir
  1976   "The Limits of National Independence in the Soviet Bloc: Rumania's Foreign Policy Reconsidered." *Orbis* 20(3):701–32.
  1990   "National Salvation Front Produces Electoral Landslide." *Report on Eastern Europe* 1(27):24–32.
Spigler, Iancu
  1973   *Economic Reform in Rumanian Industry.* Oxford: Oxford University Press.
Stahl, Henri H.
  1936   "Vecinătăţile din Drăguş." *Sociologie Românească* 1(1):18–31.
  1979   *Traditional Romanian Village Communities: The Transition from the Communal to the Capitalist Mode of Production in the Danube Region.* Cambridge: Cambridge University Press.
Szadeczky, L.
  1892   *Fogoras vara es uradalma torteneti emlekei.* Cluj.
Szelenyi, Ivan
  1988   *Socialist Entrepreneurs: Embourgeoisement in Rural Hungary.* Madison: University of Wisconsin Press.
Taussig, Michael T.
  1980   *The Devil and Commodity Fetishism in South America.* Chapel Hill: University of North Carolina Press.
Therborn, Goran
  1980   *The Ideology of Power and the Power of Ideology.* London: NLB.
Thompson, E. P.
  1966   (1963) *The Making of the English Working Class.* New York: Vintage.
Toranska, Teresa
  1986   *They.* New York: Harper & Row.
Tsantis, Andreas C., and Roy Pepper
  1979   *Romania: The Industrialization of an Agrarian Economy under Socialist Planning.* Washington, D.C.: World Bank.
Tudoran, Dorin
  1984   "De la condition de l'intellectuel roumain." 2 pts. *L'Alternative*, nos. 29 and 30 (September–October, November–December).
Turnock, David
  1986   *The Romanian Economy in the Twentieth Century.* Beckenham: Croon Helm.
Turton, Andrew
  1984   "Limits of Ideological Domination and the Formation of Social Consciousness." In *History and Peasant Consciousness in South East Asia,*

  ed. Andrew Turton and Shigeharu Tanabe, pp. 19–74. Senri Eth-
  nological Studies 13. Osaka: National Museum of Ethnology.
Verdery, Katherine
  1975 "We're All the Same Now: Prestige Ranking in a Collectivized Romanian
        Village." Paper presented at 74th Annual Meeting, American An-
        thropological Association, San Francisco.
  1983 *Transylvanian Villagers: Three Centuries of Political, Economic, and
        Ethnic Change.* Berkeley: University of California Press.
  1984 "The Unmaking of an Ethnic Collective: Transylvania's Germans."
        American Ethnologist 12(1):62–83.
  1987 "The Reordering of 'Public' and 'Private' in Socialist Societies." Paper
        presented at 89th Annual Meeting, American Anthropological Associa-
        tion, Chicago.
  1991 *National Ideology under Socialism: Identity and Cultural Politics in
        Ceauşescu's Romania.* Berkeley: University of California Press.
Verdery, Katherine, and Gail Kligman
  1990 "Romania after Ceauşescu: Post-Communist Communism?" Paper pre-
        sented at Conference on East Europe in Revolution, Yale University.
Wedel, Janine
  1986 *The Private Poland: An Anthropologist's Look at Everyday Life.* New
        York: Facts on File.
Wessman, James W.
  1981 *Anthropology and Marxism.* Cambridge, Mass.: Schenkmann.
Wilk, Richard, and Robert M. Netting
  1984 "Households: Changing Forms and Functions." In *Households: Com-
        parative and Historical Studies of the Domestic Group,* ed. Robert McC.
        Netting, Richard Wilk, and Eric J. Arnould, pp. 1–28. Berkeley: Univer-
        sity of California Press.
Williams, Raymond
  1980 *Problems in Materialism and Culture: Selected Essays.* London: NLB.
Willis, Paul
  1981 *Learning to Labor: How Working-Class Kids Get Working-Class Jobs.*
        New York: Columbia University Press.
Wolf, Eric R.
  1966 "Kinship, Friendship, and Patron-Client Relations in Complex Society."
        In *The Social Anthropology of Complex Societies,* ed. Michael Banton,
        pp. 1–22. ASA Monographs, no. 4. London: Tavistock.
  1969 *Peasant Wars of the Twentieth Century.* New York: Harper & Row.
  1982 *Europe and the People without History.* Berkeley: University of Califor-
        nia Press.
Worsley, Peter
  1981 "Marxism and Culture: The Missing Concept." *Dialectical Anthropology*
        6:103–21.
  1984 *The Three Worlds: Culture and World Development.* Chicago: Univer-
        sity of Chicago Press.

Wright, Erik Olin
  1979   *Class, Crisis, and the State.* London: NLB.
Yanagisako, Sylvia J.
  1979   "Family and Household: The Analysis of Domestic Groups." *Annual Review of Anthropology,* 8:161–206. Palo Alto: Annual Reviews.

Index

Anthropology of Contemporary Issues

A SERIES EDITED BY

ROGER SANJEK

Library of Congress Cataloging-in-Publication Data

Kideckel, David A., 1948–
    The solitude of collectivism : Romanian villagers to the revolution and
  beyond / David A. Kideckel.
        p.   cm. — (Anthropology of contemporary issues)
    Includes bibliographical references and index.
    ISBN 0-8014-2746-0 (alk. paper). — ISBN 0-8014-8025-6 (pbk.)
    1. Olt Region (Romania)—Social conditions.   2. Collectivism—Romania—Olt
  Region.   3. Socialism and society.   4. Post-communism—Romania—Olt Region.   5. Romania—Social conditions—1945–1989.   I. Title.   II. Series.
  HN650.048K53   1993
  306′.09498′2—dc20   92-31985